CW00822444

STORIES FROM THE SEVEN CONTINENTS

First edition: February 2023
ISBN: 9798376269022

Cover Image: Aurelie Choulet, photomontagist extraordinaire.

"Look beneath the surface. Things are usually very different from how they initially appeared, and ignorance, which didn't look beneath the surface, turns to disillusion when it penetrates to the interior. Falsehood always arrives first; it drags along fools with their endless vulgarity. Truth always arrives last, and late, limping along with Time."
Baltasar Gracián (8 January 1601 – 6 December 1658). Spanish Baroque prose writer and philosopher.

Acknowledgements

I didn't finish this in time for you, Dad. None of us knew that you would be taken so suddenly, so unexpectedly. I was thinking of your reaction when I was writing this book; I was imagining how you might laugh or shake your head; I was looking forward to talking with you about it.
And you were in my thoughts for the final phases, when I knew I would never hear your laugh again.
I'll miss you.

Deception

Outward and Inward Journeys

1914 · 1944

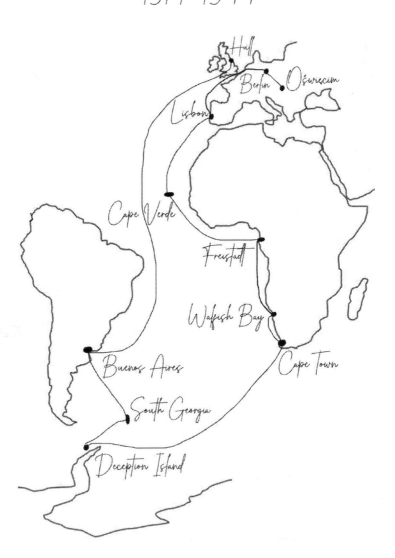

Deception Island

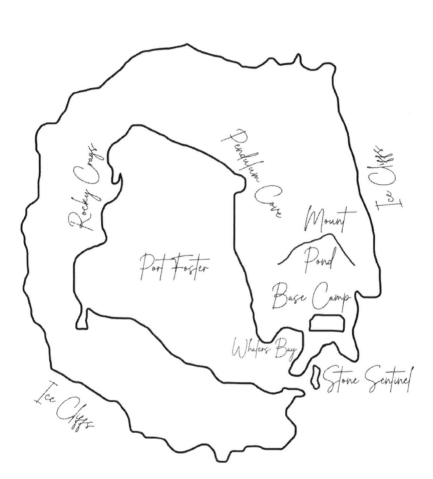

Antarctica

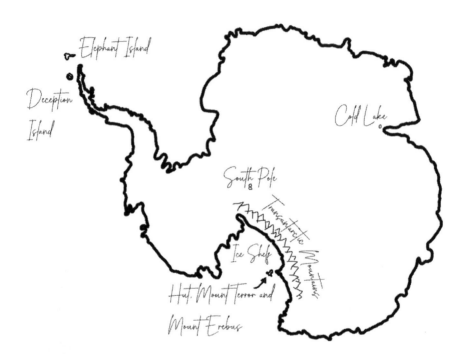

Elephant Island

Deception
Island

Cold Lake

South Pole

Transantarctic Mountains

Ice Shelf

Hut, Mount Terror and
Mount Erebus

I've got about eight thousand nautical

miles on an eight-thousand-ton, four-stroke-diesel engine German freighter ahead of me; I've got an old notebook that I found in my cabin; I've got a pen in my hand; and I've got a thirty-year story to tell. But before I begin: no, I'd never heard of Deception Island, either.

If you'd asked me anything about it, I probably would've said it was a fantasy place in some boy's-own adventure story, such as the Tom Swift books or those written by Captain W. E. Johns. Not that I've ever really been familiar with these works. The German sailors, happy that I could help them repair their freighter after a submerged column of rock tore a hole in the metal hull, have given me a couple of these books to read on the long journey home, and I've only just started them; staple reading for all good citizens, they said. I'm looking forward to the *Biggles* stories especially, and to finding out how a brave German intelligence officer worked with an English pilot to bring about the defeat of Great Britain. I'm not really into that kind of thing, but I'm aching for something new to read after so long, and, besides, who would've thought when my adventure started in 1914 that the Germans would end up saving the world? There's a lot I need to catch up on.

My father would've been pleased. He was German. He married my Polish mother in... I'm not sure when, but it must've been about 1890. They lived where my mother's family was from, in a small town in Galicia on the Sola River, called Oświęcim, about fifty kilometres from Cracow. I've never been there, but now I'm heading back to Europe, I think it's time I went.

Maybe I inherited my wanderlust from Papa, a boatbuilder who always dreamed of travelling the world in the vessels he helped to create. He told me that before I was born, an emigration fever had gripped Europe. The land of limitless opportunity, America, beckoned, and people were drawn to it as flies to a bright light. An ocean carrier called HAPAG opened a branch in Oświęcim to accommodate the huge influx of applications from Polish citizens. Their slogan said it all: *Mein Feld ist die Welt* – which roughly translated as 'the world is at our feet'. Mama was pregnant with me, and Papa wanted to give his young family everything the world had to offer; he decided to buy a ticket from the local HAPAG representatives.

All I know about what happened next is that in around 1895 a HAPAG agent conned my father out of his savings, then had him arrested and thrown in jail by some corrupt policeman, where he was beaten and only released after he agreed to pay the policeman what little money he had left. For a poor boatbuilder like my father, this was a financial catastrophe. When, just a few months later, Papa heard that rich businessmen were creating a boatbuilding boom on the picturesque lakes of Switzerland, it didn't take him long to convince my heavily pregnant mother that this was the move for them. It wasn't America, but it wasn't

Galicia either, and for Papa leaving that place counted for more than anything else because, after such a terrible setback, he had convinced himself that their future happiness definitely lay elsewhere.

I don't think Mama had much say in the matter. She was probably too tired to argue. I can imagine it must have been hard for her, having a husband with his head always somewhere else. I don't know how she felt, because I never knew her; she didn't survive childbirth. It's hard to feel an emotional bond with someone you've never met, and I can write about it without sentiment. Only when I think about the effect her death must have had on Papa does it make me upset, although he never really spoke about it.

However difficult it must have been, my practical father got on with life. He was a young man with an infant daughter, carving out a living by building and repairing boats in a wooden workshop on the banks of Lake Zürich, overlooked by the majestic Mount Rigi, the rugged Mount Pilatus, and the glacial Mount Titlis. I can certainly think of worse places to spend one's childhood.

My earliest memory, at least one I can definitely be sure is an actual memory and not just a scene created by my father's reminiscences, is of swimming in Lake Zürich. The lake is quite shallow in places, which helps when you're learning to swim. I became reasonably adept, and by the time I was ten years old, I was cold water swimming on my own, even when the outer edges of the lake began to freeze over. I used to hear people say that the best way to enter cold water is to plunge straight in. This is a mistake; the body must acclimatise. Walk in slowly, up to the shoulders, then start swimming vigorously. Of course, I couldn't have known it then, but all this stood me in good stead when I ended up on Deception Island.

It was also on Lake Zürich that I met *him*, in 1905. I'm not talking about some handsome boy or young man. No. That kind of thing doesn't interest me. He was certainly striking, in his own idiosyncratic way, but he was sixteen years older than me,

7

married, and far too clever to be a suitable match for me. I've been speaking to him these past thirty years, using the radio I found in a hut on Deception Island. Without that I guess I would have gone quite mad with loneliness. Anyway, his name is Albert Einstein, and the first thing I'll do when I get to Europe is visit him in Zürich.

It was during the Easter break that I saved Albert's life. I was only ten years old, and had taken a small skiff out on the lake one cold, early spring morning. It wasn't my boat, or even Papa's. He had finished mounting the oarlocks on the gunwales the day before and, as the boat wasn't going to be collected for a couple of days, he let me take it out for a row. He often let me do this sort of thing; it was our little secret.

Just imagine the thrill of the moment: dawn had not yet broken over the mountain horizon; a carpet of mist swirled noiselessly over the lake; my breath hung still on the air while I untied the mooring; and, as I pushed myself away from the jetty, I delighted in having the serene, silent lake all to myself. Or so I thought.

About five minutes into my stolen recreation, a loud splash from somewhere within the hazy vapour caught my attention. I might not have gone to investigate – a fisherman, someone dumping rubbish, even a fish leaping out of the water – anything could have explained the disturbance. But muffled spluttering told me that someone had fallen in. I rowed quickly towards the trouble.

A man was desperately trying to grab on to the side of his small yacht. I either knew or recognised many of the fishermen or pleasure-seekers on the lake, but I'd never seen this person before and I didn't know that he couldn't swim; moreover, I didn't know that given his shortcomings as a swimmer he was stupid enough to refuse to wear a life jacket.

"Are you all right, sir?" I called to him. He turned around and promptly disappeared under the water. I waited for a moment. A thrashing hand re-emerged. "Um... do you...?" He vanished again.

I'd never done anything like this before, saving someone from drowning; I'd never even learnt how to do it properly. But instinct

8

took over; I tore off my hat, scarf, coat and shoes, and dived in. I said before that sudden exposure to cold water isn't the best idea, and my body convulsed at the shock. However, I was not a novice at this, and I was over at his boat within an instant. Luckily, his flailing legs had somehow managed to keep him vaguely near the surface. I grabbed his hair, then found his hand, and helped him gain a firm grip of his yacht.

"Stay here," I said, then swam to my skiff, climbed in and rowed back to the man.

I'm not quite sure how it is possible to be so awkward, but he really made a meal of clambering into my boat, falling over a couple of times and nearly ending up back in the water before finally managing to step onto his yacht. I tied my boat to his and boarded his yacht, too. He had dancing, mischievous eyes, and I was not in the least bit scared. A smile formed under his black moustache.

"Thank you, little girl," he said.

"That's okay," I replied, wringing the bottom of my dripping pullover.

We stood looking at each other for a moment: he, grinning with satisfaction, while I looked at him with bemusement.

"Water's unusually warm for this time of year, don't you think?" he asked.

I didn't think so. "Maybe," I answered politely.

"It's happening all over, you know. The ice is melting and the seas are warming up."

"It'll be summer soon," I said.

"No, no. I don't mean that. It's…" He then seemed to notice I was soaking wet, and passed me a towel.

"Sorry you had to get so wet because of me. Could you do one last thing for me? Which direction is Kilchberg? I appear to have lost my way in all this fog." I recognised a few of the lights peeking at us through the gloom from the large lakeside villas. I pointed to Kilchberg, passed him his towel and made to return to my rowing boat. "No, no. Sit down. You must come with me and

9

dry off properly. I'll have someone take you and your boat back home afterwards."

"It's okay, I..."

"I insist. What do they call you?"

"Marianna."

"Marianna. What a beautiful name. Did you know it means 'star of the sea'? How very appropriate!" he chuckled. "I was hoping for some wind, but it looks like I'll have to row to the bank. That way, you say?"

We went to his apartment, where he looked after me as if I were the most precious thing that had ever been inside his home, giving me food, a hot drink, clothes from his neighbour which didn't fit, but were at least dry, and arranged for a driver to take me home; and so began my friendship with Albert.

I didn't see him that much; he didn't live in Zürich. However, he travelled to the city every now and then from Bern, where he lived, to visit friends, and in particular to see a friend called Fräulein Susanne Markwalder, with whom he liked to play music. Before his visits, he would always write and ask me to join him on the lake. I cherished those times with him, together on Lake Zürich. Several years were spent like this.

His brush with disaster during our initial meeting was no one-off. I'm not sure why Albert refused to wear a life-jacket, but his ability to stay afloat was about as good as the large rocks which he nearly crashed into on many occasions. He was also unusually poor at judging distance or speed, and very nearly collided with other vessels or bumped against pontoons or jetties. His boat was in such terrible repair, that leaks sprung everywhere and his mast often fell down so we had to be towed back. Imagine how embarrassing all of this was for a teenage girl; although I adored his company, I was mortified when anyone saw us flounder on one of his many mishaps.

Papa called Albert's boat a floating death-trap, and said "if Herr Einstein continues to sail so close to the wind, one day it will blow him right over and he'll never get up again." But Papa let me meet

10

up with Albert all the same. It was probably because I didn't really have any other friends. The girls I knew were just too, well, girly, and the boys just seemed keen to show off in one way or another, which bored me silly.

Albert, despite his carefree or even careless approach to safety, was an extraordinary man whose outward appearance and clumsiness belied an intensely sophisticated and dextrous mind. He did me good, and I learnt a lot from him. Not facts or anything that could help me in school; but observations about life.

"We will never understand everything up there," he said to me once, pointing up at the few visible stars in the dawning sky as the lake lapped gently against his yacht. "The best we can hope for is to make sense of our own place within such vastness. Like those stars, which always move to the same rhythm."

In such moments I felt the need to say something sensible. But the words often failed me.

"Hmm," I nodded sagely.

"Take this, for example." He produced a strange contraption from a wooden box. It looked like something a child might make if left alone with bits of metal and glue. "Do you know what it is?"

"No."

"It's called a sextant. It's one of the only machines I like to use. It doesn't pollute the world like most other human machines do, and only requires this here to power it," he said, tapping my head. "It allows us to read any heavenly body – the stars, the sun, the moon – and plot exactly where we are on our own planet. Look, I'll show you how it works."

After showing me how to take a sight with the sextant, Albert gave it to me, saying it was a birthday gift. My birthday was still several months away, but he said it didn't matter, that time was relative. I didn't understand what that meant, but practised with the sextant every time I was on the lake or on the mountainside, keen to show off my skills to Albert in much the same way as the boys who irritated me at school were keen to show off theirs.

Albert was a man people wanted to impress, and whatever the comment or occasion, he had a wise word to match it, but in a warm, encouraging way rather than with any hint of condescension. On another boat trip, when I was about thirteen, I asked him what he was scribbling in his notebook every time the wind stopped. He said it was something to do with relativity. I had heard him mention this before.

"Oh. What *is* that, then?"

"Put it this way: spending five hours with you here on this lake speeds by in what seems like a matter of minutes, but a few minutes with that wicked maths teacher you told me about will seem to you like five hours. That's relativity."

"Ah, I get it."

The next time I saw him was in the winter of 1909. The lake was frozen over, not as much as it normally was, nevertheless too frozen to consider sailing on. Albert had invited himself to our apartment to take early morning victuals, whatever they were. As Papa was preparing some hot soup, Albert told me that the condition of the lake, with its thinner ice, was due to all the fumes the industrialised countries were pumping into the atmosphere. I had no idea what he was talking about and let him ramble on until Papa came to my rescue by asking me to set the table.

Albert admired Papa intensely for his knowledge about boats and was very interested in Papa's personal background, too. They had some things in common: they were both born to rather secular Jewish parents; they were both German (Albert had considered becoming Swiss, he confessed, but had decided against it, as there were some notable German scientists emerging in his home country and he was keen to engage with them on matters of global importance); also, both Papa and Albert had emigrated; and both had married women from another country.

"I applaud you, Herr Dittrich, on how you have raised your daughter so beautifully, given everything you have been through."

12

I was fourteen by now, and I suppose I wanted to be part of this conversation, sound intelligent and, above all, appear grown-up.

"It's like this, Albert. One life goes, and another one comes. That's relativity," I stated proudly.

Papa scowled at me, and Albert's sparkling eyes darkened for a moment.

"No, Mari." (That's what he called me now). "That's not relativity. That's an example of how science cannot explain everything. Some circumstances can only be comprehended by indescribable emotion. There is nothing relative about losing loved ones." I felt scolded, and crept away to my room soon after.

Albert did not leave it there, however. He knocked on my door about thirty minutes later, and told me to come with him. He had determined that I must listen to some music. This was really not my thing. Give me a hammer to bang a nail, or some rope to tie something fast, and I'm happy; but drums and violins – no thank you. I'd much rather watch handymen at work than musicians at play. However, I felt compelled to acquiesce after my earlier blunder.

He told me he had recently bought an apartment in Moussonstraße, near the university where he now worked, and that he had arranged to meet his friend Fräulein Markwalder there. He had just had a new piano delivered and they were going to play some Mozart sonatas together.

"Susanne is bringing a girl with her." Albert gave me a sideways glance. "She's about your age, and her hands move across the piano as if the angels are waltzing through her fingertips. Just listen, and you will see what I mean when I say that some things need no explanation."

"I didn't know you played the piano," I remarked.

"Ah! You're thinking like a scientist. Very good. You've deduced that, because I have one in my home, I, too, must play the piano. Well, it is mainly for decoration, and for moments like the one I am going to treat you to. Come along now, they're probably already waiting. Do you know how to get Quaibrücke?"

"I thought you said you lived near the university."

"Well, yes, I do. But I only know my way home from the bridge."

I groaned; as on the water, Albert had such a hopeless sense of direction.

He was right that Fräulein Markwalder and the girl were already awaiting his arrival. Albert's wife, Mileva, ushered us into the living room. She told him to keep the noise down, as their five-year old boy had just fallen asleep after running himself ragged around the apartment. "And I'd like him to stay that way for a while!" she snipped, as if the boy's earlier exertions were Albert's fault.

"Of course, my dear," said Albert, kissing his wife on the cheek. "Young Hanserl must have his rest. Our harmonies won't travel beyond the walls of this room."

I didn't like Albert's living room. It was very ordered, and so unlike him. In the centre stood four red-cushioned chairs around a circular table, which was decorated by some yellow flowers in an orange and white vase. On the table there was also a jug of water and several glasses, all lined up neatly alongside one another like ducklets behind their mother. Along one wall ran a long, grey sofa; and on the opposite side was a tall bookcase, neat and tidy. Light flooded in from two tall windows, both framed by peach curtains that stretched from the ceiling to the floor. Fräulein Markwarder, whom I'd met several times before, nodded silently to Albert as we entered, and put a finger to her lips. She was standing over a girl with long, poker-straight brown hair who was sitting at the piano.

"Take a seat on the sofa, Mari," Albert whispered. He turned to Fräulein Markwarder. "We've got a guest today, Susanne. What are we going to play for her?"

"Hello Marianna. I'm pleased you're able to join is. Fetch yourself a drink and take a seat." She turned to Albert. "Carmen and I were just looking at some sheet music. What do you think of this one?" she asked, pointing to a page in a book on the piano.

"Sonata 18 for pianoforte and violin in G major, K 301. A wonderful selection!" enthused Albert.

I sighed. This was going to be very dull. I poured myself a glass of water and nestled into the comfortable sofa, wondering how long I would have to sit here.

Albert picked up a violin from the side of the piano, Fräulein Markwalder opened a case and retrieved hers. The trio played a couple of notes on their instruments, stopped, readjusted something or other, and nodded to one another. Then they began.

From the very first moment I was spellbound. I wish I had the words to describe the effect the music had on me. It sounded like a love song, with affectionate, sensitive notes like red petals floating down from the ceiling and filling the room; then the music became more lively, playful even, and the petals began to jump and dance. Soon the music resonated with virile passion, the petals exploded around me, erupting with volcanic fury through my body; then emptiness, as sad, soft melodies carried me across a strange wordless world and into a valley of sorrow, where all thought, all emotion, all experience transcended normal expression. Albert and Fräulein Markwarder were fine violinists, of that even my uneducated ear was certain. But I was not really listening to them. Carmen had my full attention. Albert was right; it was as if her delicate movements were guided by some divinity. This was my epiphany, and I knew I was in love with her.

I don't know how long they had been playing for – perhaps a quarter of an hour – but for me a lifetime of realisation passed during this sonata.

"Well, Mari, what did you think?" smiled Albert.

Carmen swivelled around and looked expectantly at me. I could not take my eyes off her.

"Um..." My cheeks burned with redness.

"Let's play some more," suggested Fräulein Markwarder. "Do you want to stay a bit..."

"Yes!" I interjected.

15

I have Albert to thank for proposing that Carmen and I should meet up again; I certainly would not have had the courage to do so. When their session was over, we, or rather he, arranged for us to meet the very next day.

If I had known that it would be only Carmen and I who would meet, I probably would have backed out. As it was, I was nervously looking forward to the meeting, reassured that any awkwardness on my part would be overcome by Albert's benign good humour. I was perhaps most worried about whether she would think I was stupid, so cautioned myself to stick to a topic I was familiar with: boats. At least that way I could largely hold my own with Albert's conversation.

But he wasn't even there. Carmen was waiting, as arranged, in front of the Grossmünster church. When I saw her I felt the music from the previous day begin to pulsate through my body again; my heart and mind were wandering all over the place, and I struggled to keep my legs from wobbling. She waved at me.

"Hello Marianna," she greeted.

"Hello. Where's Albert?" I scolded myself. It must have sounded like I was only interested in seeing him.

"At work, I guess. Do you want to walk along the riverbank? It's a bit cold to stand here."

"Okay."

I couldn't claim that the conversation was easy; we hardly knew one another. But it wasn't as stilted as I had imagined it might be. We talked about family, about Zürich, about Albert. I even managed to say one or two things about music, and she tried hard to ask pertinent questions about boats. In any case, the magic of the previous day had been so overwhelming that there was practically nothing she could say which would fail to enthral me, and by the end of our stroll up and down the riverbank, I not only admired her intensely for her talents, but felt a genuine attraction to her personality, too. It also helped that she was incredibly beautiful: silky, straight brown hair, with flashes of walnut, cinnamon and caramel; her gentle, chocolate eyes expressed both

16

kindness and intelligence; and her smile, subtlely playing on her lips with every word she spoke, warmed me from within. It would always be summer with her. I must have made a relatively good impression, too, as she invited me to her home. I think I managed to keep myself together, thanked her and said that I would like to.

A few days later her mother welcomed me into their apartment in the down-at-heel district of Aussersihl. It surprised me greatly that they lived here. I don't know whether it was due to her exceptional musical talent, her well-spoken manner, or simply because for me she was majestic in every way, but I had assumed Carmen lived in a large villa. She was an only child, yet even so the apartment was too small for the family. Her parents slept in the living room, along with a table, bookcase, sofa, piano, and an assortment of other things which I didn't really get the chance to see because the room was so completely cluttered. There was barely any space to move, but that didn't seem to bother Carmen's mother, who simply pushed a few objects to one side so that she could pull two chairs up to the piano. She was giving a lesson to a young boy, so we went into Carmen's room.

This room was hers alone, but it was tiny. We sat on her bed, and I nearly squashed a cat which I hadn't noticed before. It growled a little at my mistake, then stepped on to my lap, walked around in circles several times and went back to sleep. I stroked it absent-mindedly.

"When you said your mum was a music teacher, I thought she worked in a school," I said.

"She did, in Italy. That's where she's from. She moved here to be with my dad, but hasn't found a proper job yet."

"Oh." I looked around, searching for something to say. "What's the cat called?"

"Füchslein."

I laughed. It didn't seem an appropriate name for a cat. "Little fox! But she isn't even red."

"Well, she is a bit. Look." Carmen tickled Füchslein under the chin, and the cat purred happily.

"I suppose. I don't think I've ever stroked a cat before," I commented.

"Oh?"

The conversation didn't seem as easy as it had been last time. I searched for more things to say. "It's a nice piano. I mean the one your mum's using to teach." I coughed, then sneezed.

"It's a Feuerich. Mum got it cheap somewh... Are you all right?"

"Yes," I sniffed, rubbing my runny nose. "Have you got a handkerchief?"

Carmen sprang from the bed and went to the living room. When she returned, under a minute later, she yelped in shock. "Marianna! Your face! It's all red and puffy!"

I felt terrible, found it difficult to breathe, and could see for myself how itchy, angry hives were spreading up my arms. Carmen's mother, alerted by her daughter's cry, entered the room.

"What's happ... Mamma mia! Quick, get her outside! She's allergic to the cat!"

Carmen grabbed Füchslein and passed the cat to her mother while the animal protested loudly.

"No, not the cat! Get *her* outside!"

While the cat crossly settled itself down again on the bed, I rushed with Carmen down the stairs and into the open air, whereupon my condition began to improve rapidly.

It was incredibly embarrassing for me, and I declined Carmen's offer to walk me home. She, however, insisted vehemently, for which I was, in truth, very grateful. I felt like I had been pulled by a plough through a field of stinging nettles; although the worst of it was over, I was still weak and Carmen's presence was very restorative for me. This unfortunate episode only served to accelerate our friendship. She came to visit me the very next day, and I told her that I never knew I had this allergy, in fact, I hadn't even known that such allergies existed. We laughed a lot about the incident, and the awkward conversation between two people who barely knew one another was forever dispelled.

18

I told Albert about it, and he found the story mildly amusing, but didn't react with his usual concerned joviality. He seemed distracted, preoccupied, and I could not engage with him in our usual manner. At first I thought, with typical teenage self-indulgence, that he might be jealous of my friendship with Carmen. She and I did meet up most weekends and sometimes during the week. But Carmen reassured me that something else must be troubling Albert: perhaps he was worried about his job, his family, or global issues of which both Carmen and I had only limited understanding.

We knew that Mileva was expecting their second child, and whenever Albert and I did meet, he was certainly more withdrawn and hesitant to speak about the future. I suspected that he and Mileva were not a good match, and that he was unhappy in his marriage, but his topic of conversation was different, too. He began to talk more and more about the world changing, about humans destroying something so beautiful, so perfect, that no human mind would ever be able to fix it again should the system crumble. I didn't understand him most of the time.

The very last time I saw him was on 28th July, 1910. I remember the date so well because it was the day Albert's second child was born, Eduard. We were on Albert's boat, and he was talking about the rhythm of the wind and the waves, and how their simple harmony was so little understood by humankind.

"Is there anything that moves the soul so much as simply looking upon the lakes and the mountains, upon the fields and the forests, upon the earth, the sky and the sea?"

"Music," I hazarded. It was one of the few times I had actually responded to his musings.

"Ah, yes, Mari. There you are right. These are some of the most profound moments of human existence. The basic senses, that's what we need to return to."

"Yes, Albert. I think I understand what you mean. People need to be honest with themselves."

19

He looked at me with a kindness I had not seen for some time. His eyes softened and a smile danced on his lips. "You carry the scars of Odysseus," he said, ruffling my hair.

"Stop it, or you'll make my hair look like yours," I jokingly protested. Albert patted my hair down; I suddenly felt very childlike in his company.

"You know, Odysseus was versatile and perceptive, just like you. But as he did with his scar, you hide your hurt, your… grief, your… anguish," I sensed Albert was searching for the right word, but was either unable to find it, or say it, "because you think it shows your vulnerability. But I can see it as easily as Odysseus' enemies could see the scar running down his leg. It's not your weakness, Mari. It's part of you, your strength, your bravery. We don't get scars without a fight. Wear yours with pride."

My heart began to thump rapidly. Had he somehow perceived my feelings towards Carmen? Was he talking about that, or something else? I stared at him in mute confusion, wondering how I should respond. I decided to ask him, in a roundabout way, turning to look across the lake in case his sympathetic eyes should draw tears from mine.

"Do you mean when you like someone…" A dark shape distracted me. "Watch out for that boat!" I yelled.

A vessel had come streaking into our path with such speed that I assumed it had not seen us. Albert, with his eyes cast skyward, had definitely not noticed it. I'm not sure if Albert failed to hear me in his reverie, or if he decided that we all needed a shock of the senses to feel more human. In either case, I made a grab for the tiller to steer us away from the fast-approaching boat. However, I needn't have troubled myself, for just as abruptly as the danger had loomed, so did it disappear. The boatman had seen us all along. We were, in fact, the very people he had been looking for.

"Herr Doctor Einstein!" gasped the man breathlessly, as if he had swum all this way. "Your wife! Your baby! It's coming!"

Albert suddenly changed from a philosopher to an imbecile. He mumbled a few incomprehensible things, fell over, and bizarrely felt a sudden compulsion to brush his hair.

"You go in his boat. I'll bring this one in," I told him.

I suppose I should have realised that I wouldn't see Albert again. I don't think I was too far off the mark, after all, when I said in our apartment that as one life enters the world, another departs. In any case, an hour later, I moored his boat and walked home, thinking that if this were to be a day of declarations, perhaps I should tell Carmen I liked her. I didn't expect my father to make the day's next surprise announcement, and a very unsettling one at that.

"Sit down, Marianna. There's something I need to ask you."

The grave look on Papa's face worried me. I slid into a chair in the kitchen and waited for him to begin. He sat opposite me, and in the long moments it took for him to begin, in the very drawn-out period of time that Albert had explained to me could in fact be just the passing of mere seconds, I guessed it must be one of two things: either he was seriously ill, or he harboured suspicions about my feelings towards Carmen.

"I know you don't have many friends here…" he began. *It's Carmen*, I thought, "and I've been doing a lot of thinking over the last few months." *Definitely Carmen.* "The thing is, it was always my dream to go to the United States, but for one reason or another we ended up here." Now I wasn't so sure. *Where was this heading? Is he saying he wants to go to America?* "Your schooling finishes this summer, and you've got no real prospects around here." *He does! He wants to take us to America!* "I've been offered a job by a British businessman called William James Cook. He wrecked his yacht while on holiday here. I fixed it for him and he was very impressed with my work. He owns a ship building company in England, and he says they're going to be the biggest ship building company in the country in a few years. They're going places, and he wants me on board. I'd be out of my mind to turn down what he's offering me. But..." he paused for a moment, trying to read my face, "what do you think?"

I was never one for thinking quickly on my feet. I didn't really know what I thought; I had not seen this coming at all.

"Um, I don't know." It was honest, but not very helpful.

Papa nodded, and we both stared at the grain of the kitchen table, both wondering which direction this conversation would go.

"Well, if it helps you make up your mind..." He put a walnut-sized stone on the kitchen table.

"What's that?"

"A stone, well, er, a symbol. It's something your Mama said to me once."

I looked at him, perplexed. "I don't get it."

"When your Mama and I were going through a hard time, she put a stone on the table, just like that one there. She said to me to that no matter how difficult things got, we would get through it, like the stone always gets through everything. Stones are hard to break; whatever the weather, it just carries on being a stone. What I'm trying to say is, let's do this, let's see the lay of the land in England. We're stones, we'll be all right."

Why was he comparing me to a stupid stone? I really didn't understand his point at all. Whether I was confused by his speech or whether other factors were at play, I didn't know, but I let my frustrations out on Papa.

"Stones are boring! I don't want to go to England!" I stormed off to my room.

"I tell you what," he called after me, "have a think about it, and we'll talk tomorrow. You can ask me anything you like."

I didn't respond. I just started to cry. I wasn't even sure why. It took me half the night to understand my emotional state was down to the jumble of conflicting thoughts: I was happy for Papa, but bitter at the prospect of leaving Zürich; I was pleased for Albert, but saddened by the realisation that our relationship was altering; I was in love with Carmen, but aghast at the prospect of rejection. It was a troubling time for me.

I woke up early and without pausing to eat breakfast left the apartment before Papa rose. I wanted to see Carmen. She was bright and would know how to approach the issue with my father. I guessed she would still be sleeping, so had prepared a note which I slipped under their apartment door, asking her to meet me at the Grimmenturm in the old town. It didn't matter what time, I wrote; I would wait for her.

Horses, carts, labourers, gossipers and many people besides passed by as the morning rambled on. Time really had seemed to have come to a virtual standstill. Noon came and went, my heart in a battle with my stomach: one crying for Carmen's arrival, the other screaming for food. I persisted. Only when the light began to seep from the day, did I give up hope that Carmen would come. Maybe her mother had found the letter and not passed it on, I reasoned. Maybe Carmen had to be somewhere; maybe she had piano lessons. There were any number of possibilities to explain her failure to arrive. I returned home, hungry, thirsty, tired and disappointed. It was not an ideal mood to begin the conversation with Papa, who was waiting for me at the kitchen table.

When I reflect upon it, Papa had no chance. He had done all he could have done to make the situation as agreeable as possible: he had prepared a dinner of chicken and potatoes; he was willing to hear my point of view; he was even willing to compromise. But I wasn't. About five minutes after it had begun, I ran out of the house, crying and screaming that I didn't want to go England, and that he could go to hell as far as I was concerned. Poor Papa.

I ran all the way to Carmen's apartment and banged at the door. Her mother opened it, her face strained with what I guess must have been deep concern and abject fear at the banshee-like figure wailing unintelligibly before her.

"Is it the cat?" she asked. I shook my head violently. "I'll fetch Carmen," she said, after failing to get any sense from me.

23

As soon as I saw Carmen, I started to wail even more. She put her arm around me, guided me into the street and held me as we walked, in silence, until my sobbing quietened down. We found ourselves on a bench in the arboretum on the west bank of Lake Zürich. It was now quite dark, and the only few people around were couples strolling arm in arm, enjoying the warm summer's evening.

"Where were you all day! I was waiting for you!"

"Sorry. We've been in Vienna for a few days. I visited the University for Music and Performing Arts. I only saw your note this evening when we got home."

I wiped away my tears. "Oh. What were you doing there? Did you have a concert or something?"

Carmen looked at me sheepishly. "No, I haven't mentioned it before, because I didn't know if I would get a place. I went for an interview, kind of like an audition, for a scholarship. They really liked me and said I could start there in September."

"What, in Vienna?"

She nodded. I couldn't believe what was happening to my world. Everyone was changing everything.

"But I'll be back here a lot," she added quickly. "Vienna's not that far. We'll still see each other, and we'll definitely write," she promised.

I shook my head, probably less to contradict her last statement, than out of a refusal to accept the reality of the situation. "No, no." I whimpered. I flung my arms around her and buried my face in her neck. "This can't be. You can't go. You have to stay." My tears spilled over her floaty yellow dress.

She embraced me too. "It'll be all right. Please don't worry."

I pulled myself to face her and softly stroked her perfect, silken hair. "You don't understand, Carmen. I love you. I'm in love with you! I always have been!" I kissed her.

Heaven knows what she was thinking at that moment; certainly not the same as me. Now that I am older I can look back on it with a certain amount of dispassion, but at the time her reaction

24

wrenched my heart from its foundations and flung it into an abyss of despair.

"Marianna, no," she protested, pushing me away. "This isn't right." She looked about her, horrified that someone might have seen. "I've... I've got to go." She leapt from the bench and hurried away.

I did not chase after her; my confused, teenage mind struggled with such an intense barrage of emotions until it felt only fatigue. Somehow, I found my way home. Papa was beside himself with worry, but I brushed him aside, went into my room and hid myself under the blankets.

When I awoke the next day, the deep blue of sky told me that I had slept through most of the morning. Papa would be at work. He must have been in my room at some point, as there was a glass of water on my bedside table, which I eagerly gulped down. I felt exhausted, but more composed, and sat on my bed for an age, staring at the expanse of cloudless azure stretching way beyond the distant mountains. Eventually, I was done with thinking and was beginning to ache with hunger. It had been two whole days since I had last eaten.

Papa was not at work; he was at the kitchen table. He must have been considering all morning what he was going to say to me; he couldn't have chosen better.

"Marianna," he said. That was it. A word that told me I was his everything. I was all that he needed, all that he thought about, a word of fatherly protection and uncompromising love. I went to his chair, hugged him and quietly said, "Let's go to England."

Under leaden skies I stood at the stern

of *MS Schwabenland*, imagining the freighter was motionless and it was the bare rock of King George Island which was floating away from us. We steamed onwards, our progress northeast past the South Shetland Islands running smoothly, much more smoothly than when I passed these islands thirty years ago. Then, thick ice floes threatened to crush my boat and raging storms hurled angry waves upon me. It was a wonder I survived. Now, the sea was calm and the ice was all but gone.

I mentioned this to the captain, Kapitän Ritscher, who had come to speak with me. He was taking a keen interest in my story and quizzed me often about my background. He guffawed when I pointed to King George Island.

"You really have been away a long time, haven't you!" I forced a laugh; I didn't think it was very funny at all. "That island," he continued, "has been renamed. We've taken it from the British; we've taken everything from them. They called it King George Island because that was the name of their king when they found it. So *we've* called it by a name of a great German leader who died in the same year, in 1819."

"Oh. What's it called now, then?"

The captain puffed up his chest and answered proudly: "Chlodwig Carl Viktor Fürst zu Hohenlohe-Schillingsfürst, Prinz von Ratibor und von Corvey Island."

"Really? All of that?"

"Yes, rolls nicely off the tongue, don't you think?"

"I think I need to write it down."

What had happened since I'd been away? I couldn't quite believe two things: one, that the war which began thirty years ago was still continuing; and two, that Germany had defeated Great Britain. When I left England in 1914, war had just been declared, the British Empire was the master of the seas, and everyone expected to be home by Christmas. Well, nearly everyone; I never intended to come back.

I spent almost exactly four years in England and by the time I left, I was fairly fluent in the language. The start had been difficult, though, especially for Papa. The company who had employed him was called Cook, Welton and Gemmell, based in Hull. Never has a town been more appropriately named as Hull; a depressing pit that belongs exactly where its name suggests – under the sea.

On paper everything looked fine: Papa was earning more money; I was learning a trade in the maritime industry as an apprentice boatbuilder, a circumstance which my father had insisted on as a condition of his employment; we had rented a small house with a garden near the town centre, which was something we would never have been able to afford in Zürich; and the North Sea was just a stone's throw away, so there was plenty of opportunity for me to indulge in some bracing cold water swimming. But… we were in Hull, where the local mood was as flat as the landscape, the skies were permanently grey and everything around the dockyards seemed to be covered in the slime and smell of rotting fish. The only saving grace of the town, at least as far as I was concerned, was the fact that thousands of people from all over Europe passed through the port on their way to new lives in America and elsewhere. Although this only served to make me, and probably Papa, too, feel that we were missing out on something better. Oh, how I missed the mountains and clear water of my home country.

I also missed Carmen. I wrote to her five times in total, never mentioning my faux pas in the park; I remember each letter almost verbatim. I tried to keep the tone light and positive and asked her all sorts of questions about the university. But not once did I get a reply. Only through Albert did I get an occasional update. However, even he struggled to keep in contact; he was evidently becoming a famous scientist, and his energies were being stretched right across the globe.

When we lived in Switzerland, both Papa and I had largely lived on the margins of our community. Sure, I had school, Albert and, latterly, Carmen; Papa had spoken to his clients and suppliers. But, by and large, we had kept ourselves to ourselves. This was not possible in the fishing communities of England. When the trawler entered the harbour, when the fish were weighed and when the haggling was done, the fishermen would almost always head to the nearest pub. Alcoholism was rife, and it soon sucked Papa into a dangerous undercurrent of gambling and violence.

His new home became the smoke-filled Alexandra Inn on Humber Street, just a few minutes' walk from the docks. He only ever returned to his real home when I went to the inn to fetch him. To raucous cheers from a roomful of bearded, loud and stinking men, I would put his arm over my shoulder and, with his feet dragging along the ground like a couple of pointless flippers, somehow carry him through the streets, through the front door, up the stairs and into his bed. I hated having to go and get him: the leering, jeering men, the choking tobacco fumes, the yellow-stained walls and wooden floor sticky with spilled beer – it was not a place any sixteen-year-old girl should have to frequent; and one night, the inevitable happened.

I had managed to haul Papa several streets away from the Alexandra and we were almost home. He was particularly heavy this night; it felt like he had swallowed the whole beer barrel. I paused for breath, and before I could react, someone rushed up to me, put one strong arm around my waist and the other hand around my mouth, then dragged me into an alleyway, leaving Papa to slump on the street, completely oblivious to everything. Years of climbing mountains, of swimming, and a whole year of lifting heavy boating equipment all made me an underrated adversary, and I put up a good fight. But I was no match for this man, I couldn't prise his hand away from my mouth, and my strength rapidly weakened under his iron-like grip.

"Let her go!" snarled someone from the entrance to the alleyway.

My attacker only had time to push me aside before the newcomer was upon him. My saviour easily ducked under a wildly swung fist then promptly landed a perfect uppercut on the brute's jaw, knocking him out cold.

"Are you hurt?" he asked me, offering me a hand to help me up. I was in shock and could barely respond. I shook my head. "Come on, let me take you home. I won't hurt you. My name's John, John Vincent. But my friends call me Jack." He walked back up the alleyway and stopped next to my barely conscious father. He lifted Papa to his feet as if he were no more than bag of feathers, then beckoned for me to join him. "You lead, and I'll follow. Let's get you and your dad home."

Jack, as I decided I should call him, was a trawler fisherman but also, which had been far more useful to me, an enthusiastic boxer and wrestler. He was stocky, powerful, and no-one ever troubled me again when I had to collect Papa. Even the incessant jeering stopped. Jack was certainly not afraid to use his fists, even when he shouldn't have. He was fairly young compared to most fishermen, and if beards were a determining factor of age, clean-shaven Jack was surely the youngest. But he was still much older than me. Jack was, in fact, only a few years younger than Albert, which gave me much amusement, considering how vastly different they were.

Often when I saw him in the Alexandra, he was bullying or intimidating someone, usually over who was going to be served at the bar, or who had won how many cigarettes in their gambling games. Few stood up to him. I discovered that hardly anyone called him 'Jack', and it was clear that he wasn't well-liked. He had one friend, or at least someone who spoke to him voluntarily, a man named Willy Stephenson. Willy was such an instantaneously forgettable person that if he stood still in front of beige wallpaper, he probably wouldn't even be noticed. I'm not sure what Jack saw in him, but I assume it was a mutually beneficial acquaintance, for neither man commanded a great social following. I, however, had an enduring affection for Jack for what he had done for me that night. He seemed to have an affection for me, too, and I suspected he wanted something more. Although he hadn't long been married and had a child, I'd already seen and heard enough in the pub to know what men were like, and was careful not to encourage him.

In fact, there was no-one in this harbour town that I encouraged. Nor did I see the remotest sign that there was in Hull anybody like me. Romantically speaking, I was fairly marooned in this fishing community. So I committed myself to pouring all of my affections into looking after Papa and, when he didn't require my attention, my energies went into mastering my shipwright skills.

A few months after Jack had come to my rescue, it must have been about September 1911, I went to fetch Papa as usual. This time I was surprised to find him not half-comatose with his head on the beer-soaked table, but engaging in an animated conversation with a group of fishermen. Jack was with them.

"Marianna! Come and join us!" he beamed as I entered. Everyone knew me by now, and someone made space for me, probably after Jack had given them some sign to do so. "Listen to what this man from Ireland has to say."

The man from Ireland, his twinkling eyes barely visible through a mass of matted hair and beard, took a large swig from his tankard and set it confidently down on the table. He wiped the froth from his mouth and looked at each one of his attentive listeners. He was clearly enjoying his moment of importance.

"I've been working on a ship in Belfast. It's the largest ship in the world. Twenty-five thousand tons of steel, a marvellous feat of marine engineering, the pinnacle of naval architecture," he trilled in his bird-like accent.

"Tell us again what they're saying about it!" clamoured a man next to me.

"A vessel of this like has never been built before. It is the mistress of the seas, truly unsinkable," sang the Irishman.

"Tell us what it's called again!" insisted another.

"Ay, it's got a name befitting a bulk of this enormity. The *Titanic*."

"The *Titanic*!" cooed several men at once.

One of them didn't look that impressed. "What's that mean, then?" he asked. A slap around the back of his head answered his question; at least, he didn't ask again.

"And do you know what, Marianna?" added Papa excitedly, "It's going to America next year. We're going to be on that boat! We're going to the United States!"

Everyone cheered and raised their glasses, and I got showered in beer.

However hard he tried, the siren that kept calling Papa back to the pub hindered his attempts to save any money for the transatlantic journey he had promised us. A third-class ticket for immigrant passengers, such as we would be, was three pounds. Papa earned a shilling an hour, which meant it would have taken him six full working days to save up for one fare. Even if he had not squandered the money on drink and gambling, it would have been a tall order, considering the costs of rent, food, coal and everything else. And we needed two tickets.

However, by the middle of February 1912, and not without a little help from me, we had enough for one fare. The *Titanic*, however, was due to sail in just two months' time; there was no way we could save another three pounds in that time.

"It's okay, Papa," I said to him one morning. "You go. It's always been your dream. I'll get my boatbuilding licence and join you just as soon as I get the money together."

"No, Marianna. We'll go together."

"Papa, you've saved the money. The boat is leaving soon. I mean, it's the *Titanic*. Everyone's talking about it. It's an opportunity of a lifetime! This is what all the hardship over the last couple of years has been for," I implored.

"I'll see." He went to work.

After our conversation, I suspected Papa might do something stupid, so that evening I went to the Alexandra earlier than usual. He was there, he was drunk and he was gambling with half a dozen other men. He was playing Put and Take, a game involving a six-sided spinning-top, turned on a table. I'd seen the men play it before, with cigarettes. An unlucky spin required putting either one cigarette in the kitty, or two, or everything the gambler still had; or, if he had more luck, he could take one or two cigarettes, or all of them from the kitty. But Papa wasn't playing with cigarettes; he was playing with money. At stake was his very future. Seventy shimmering shillings were stacked up in seven neat piles of ten coins in front of him. They were playing with a maximum pot of three shillings per person each round. Papa had already won ten, and he was eager for more.

I took one look at the situation and begged for him to stop. Not even Jack could stop the men from telling me, in their own choice language, to get lost.

"Your dad's already had to put three shillings in several times, but he won it all back again next spin. Leave him, he's on a winning streak," Jack said.

"But what if he loses it all?" I cried.

"Bah, just watch."

I was powerless. I was powerless to see Papa win, then lose, then win again. The captive crowd incited the gamblers to up the ante: some lost everything and cursed their luck, others bought a round of drinks when they were doing well. Patrons and players alike were revelling in this high-spirited, high-stakes game. It was,

I have to say, mesmerising, and part of me did want the game to carry on.

But only ten minutes after my arrival, Papa had a mere twenty shillings left, and just one opponent; the others had left to nurse their financial injuries or were drinking away their winnings. Papa, however, convinced himself that he needed at least to recover the forty shillings he had lost. The two gamblers agreed to play without a limit. Papa spun first. *Put all*. Twenty shillings went into the pot. His opponent spun. *Put one*. Twenty-one shillings in the pot. Papa's turn. *Put one*. He had to pass. His opponent. *Take all*. It was over; Papa had lost everything. The onlookers roared with ecstasy; I was showered in beer again; Papa was showered in shame, and he left the pub to commiserating slaps on the back and words of consolation.

As Papa himself said all those years ago about Albert, if you sail too close to the wind, you'll eventually get blown over and won't be able to get back up again. And this, of course, is what happened to him.

It was Jack who offered to come to our rescue. His job, trawling, was one of the most dangerous jobs around. The sea was a very treacherous place and trawlermen did practically everything any other sailor would not consider doing. There were a number of ways in which these fishermen could meet their end or come to serious injury: opening the hatches in heaving seas; operating machines on rolling boats; collisions with other vessels; grounding the trawler on shifting sandbanks; drowning; the hazardous weather which they so often had to endure made any one of these more likely. But the financial rewards were great. If they could land a couple of really lucrative catches, Jack said, then Papa could easily get all of his money back.

Of course I was worried; Papa had never fished beyond the calm waters of Lake Zürich before. But he was so depressed after gambling away our savings that, although I didn't like it, I didn't oppose the idea, either. I still thought it was possible that he could, after all, get a place on the *Titanic* and all would be well again.

Jack was right, and within one month, just thirty days before the *Titanic* was to depart from Southampton harbour, America bound, Papa had not only recouped all of his losses, but had made a further thirteen shillings besides. I hadn't seen him so happy since coming to England. He had even cut down on his drinking as the strain of trawling made him simply too tired to drink and keep up with the sea-hardened sailors. The *Titanic* was within his sights, and I began to grow excited, too.

In the end, I wish that man from Ireland had never told us about the accursed ship. Everyone knows what happened to the *Titanic*: it set sail on the 10th April 1912, and by the small hours of the 15th April it was lying on the bottom of the North Atlantic Ocean. When I told Kapitän Ritscher this part of my story, he said that there are some advantages to the icebergs disappearing.

But Papa did not perish along with the fifteen hundred or so who lost their lives in those cold waters; he wasn't even on the ship. Papa was saved from the fate of the *Titanic* not by any remarkable stroke of good fortune but, through his bid for both of us to be on the doomed vessel, he himself succumbed to the perils of the sea during a storm which swept him overboard. By the time the *Titanic* settled on the seabed, my father's body had already been churning around somewhere in the North Sea for a couple of weeks. He and the *Titanic* dream were dead, and I was alone.

Elephant Island ahead. Or maybe its

name had changed, too. I thought I'd better check with Kapitän Ritscher. He has asked me for a few extra details, anyway — mainly about my father's and mother's background. He's really taking an interest in my story.

"Of course it's still called Elephant Island. English elephants look the same as German ones, don't they?" snorted Kapitän Ritscher.

"Are there such things as English elephants?" I asked. I was genuinely intrigued.

"No, not any more. Now they're all German," he chuckled.

"I didn't know there were German elephants, either."

"Oh, you have been away for too long. I'm joking with you. You have lost your German humour! Even if the sea level has risen since you were last here, the island still looks like an elephant's head, doesn't it?" he retorted.

"Does it? I thought it was called that because of all the elephant seals there. At least I saw a lot of them there," I replied. Years ago, after my short stay on the island we were now approaching, I had a found a map of Antarctica in my hut on Deception Island, but had never really noticed that the shape of this fifty-kilometre-long island in the outer reaches of the South Shetland Islands might resemble an elephant.

"Well, it's still called Elephant Island. So you were there, too?" he asked.

"Briefly. I left because a ship passed by and I tried to row out to it to get help for me and the Norwegian who was stranded there with me. He had hurt himself badly so had to stay back, otherwise he would have been dead weight and slowed me down. Anyway, the currents got hold of my boat and I couldn't get to the ship, or back to the island. I drifted east for days after that, before I ended up on Deception Island."

"Eh? That's not poss... Oh! I know!" Kapitän Ritscher could not stop his shoulders shaking with mirth. "You entered the water on the south side. You were quite lucky you did, because from most places on Elephant Island the west wind drift takes you right out into the open ocean."

"Yes! That's what the sailor said. He said it would help me catch up with the ship."

"Well," continued the captain, "you wouldn't have survived long in those seas. Even the current on the south side would normally take you there, but the winds must have been favourable, and you probably hit a sweet spot of the coastal counter current, running in the opposite direction. You didn't know it at the time, but I suspect that fluke saved your life."

"I guess that's what happened."

"Although I suppose," added the captain, scratching his chin thoughtfully, "you might have made it all the way to South Georgia as that other group... No, you would've definitely drowned. By the way, we're heading there now, only it's not called South Georgia anymore. That, again, was named after the British king, George III. A few years back the Royal Navy had a plan to strengthen their Antarctica bases on the island. They called it Operation Tabarin. There was an armed ship there and there were some shore guns, too. But we've destroyed the lot; we knew all about their secret plans. Nothing in Antarctica belongs to the British anymore."

"What's the island called now?"

"Come on Marianna, you know how we Germans work. You are half-German, yourself, after all! We stuck to the same system we used for King George Island."

"Don't tell me it's…"

"That's right!" he interrupted, "*South* Chlodwig Carl Viktor Fürst zu Hohenlohe-Schillingsfürst, Prinz von Ratibor und von Corvey Island."

"But it's further north than the other one," I commented.

"Blame the British."

I did have a lot I could blame the British for. I could blame them for offering Papa a job; I could blame them for creating Hull; I could blame them for leading my father into drinking and gambling; I could blame them for his death; but I couldn't blame them for a ridiculously named island in the South Atlantic Ocean. That one was down to the Germans.

Jack clearly felt guilty about the situation I found myself in after Papa's death, as he kept telling me about new jobs or ways I could travel to America. America hadn't been my idea at all, but somehow I felt a compulsion to fulfil the dream for which had claimed's Papa life. If only for a few months, I was determined to go.

Over the next year or so, this compulsion grew into an obsession. I was now a master boatbuilder and could easily fashion a seaworthy vessel out of several pieces of lumber, some nails, and some animal hair mixed with tar. The men would come to me if they were worried about their boats, and I was a welcome figure in the Alexandra, although I was careful never to drink too much. Unsurprisingly, the fishwives despised me, and spread all sorts of unkind rumours, but I neither cared about the women, nor what they said. Several men tried it on with me – I was nineteen years old and a bit of an exotic rarity among this group of fishermen and sailors – but no-one had any luck, and Jack's strong arms helped promote good behaviour among those whose advances grew troublesome. Spurned men like to find reasons for rejection, and many called me names, some of which were in fact close to the mark, but no-one ever really knew the truth. Apart from Jack, who I had to keep at arm's length, I had no real friend in the town, and no reason to confide in anyone, either. I felt as if my life was a little like two little sixpences, one of which I spent in the outside world, the other I kept hidden in my pocket. So with this half-a-shilling identity, Hull had become my home; but the town was still only one letter away from eternal damnation, and I was determined to leave it as soon as I was able.

When Jack told me, then, about another once-in-a-lifetime opportunity to travel *and* to earn money while doing so, I was all ears. Someone called Sir Ernest Shackleton was planning a trip in a ship called the *Endurance*, and he was looking to hire many experienced hands for the expedition. Jack said I should apply for the position of carpenter; he was going for the job of boatswain.

I was expecting to have to fill in lots of forms, detailing my qualifications for the job. Jack showed me his letter of application.

My name's John Vincent and I want to be boatswain on your ship, the Endurance. I am a trawler fisherman, and know my way around boats, you know, sails, anchors, rigging and the like. I am also a boxer and can handle myself.
Thanks, Jack.

That is actually the revised version; I had to improve some of the spelling, but Jack refused to let me alter it in any other way. He must have known what he was doing because he was invited to an interview in London; his characterless friend Willy Stephenson, too. I will never understand the British. One week later, while I was still waiting for my invitation, both of them received confirmation that their interviews had been successful and that they would be joining the British Imperial Trans-Antarctic Expedition. My own letter of application had run to a full two sides, and I was positively gushing about the chance to work with Shackleton. The day after Jack and Willy received news of their employment, I received a letter of rejection.

Dear Miss Dittrich,
Thank you for applying for the position of ship's carpenter. After careful consideration I regret to inform you that, on this occasion, your application has been unsuccessful. I would like to stress that you were one of several sporty girls who applied and, if it is any consolation, it was very hard to turn down the opportunities your qualities would have brought to the expedition. I wish you every success for your future.

With sincerest wishes, Ernest Shackleton.

That really made my blood boil. *Sporty girls!* I could swim better or at least as well as any man I knew, I could build a boat from scratch, and could use a sextant more accurately than any fisherman I'd ever met (I did have the best teacher). I was not some flighty girl, and Shackleton's letter not only made me angry, it made me determined to prove that I was as tough as anyone.

Jack was also angry or rather, perhaps, disappointed. He promised he would fix it. A few days after I received the letter, he told me his plan. The *Endurance* was due to set sail at the beginning of August, and he would sneak me on it. I would get my ride.

At first I didn't think much of the proposal, but I was still seething and willing to stick two fingers up at Ernest Shackleton; it would be a victory, of sorts. There was another reason to get out of Britain – Germany was becoming increasingly unpopular, and everyone thought I was German, even though I told them I was half-Polish and had never even been to Germany. No-one seemed interested in the details. I think the British just wanted the seas to themselves, and were upset about Germany becoming strong, but I didn't really understand what was going on. Besides, Jack said that the *Endurance* was leaving from London; I had never been there, and quite fancied a trip to this famous city.

"No," said Jack. "You won't be getting on in London. The boat sails to Plymouth and departs from there a week later. That's where you get on. It'll be much easier there than in London, where everyone will be watching."

Plymouth? I'd never even heard of it and could barely even say the word. Jack remained firm. He told me to make sure I was in Plymouth harbour on the night of the 7th August and to seek him out in one of the local inns. I could take only one small bag with me. What I put in it, was up to me.

I arrived in Hull Paragon Train Station very early. It was a huge structure, with five separate roofs held up high above my head by a network of steel girders. I couldn't even see how many platforms there were, as they stretched far beyond my line of vision and crowds of people thronged the concourse. Just a few days before, King George V had declared war on Germany, and the station was a hive of activity. Huge quantities of goods were being loaded on to freight trains: fish, textiles, coal, grain. Among the gathered hordes ordinary citizens and soldiers alike were strolling, chatting, checking their bags, running for their trains, kissing loved-ones goodbye; frequent shrill warnings blasted from the guards' whistles while deafening shrieks from hissing train stacks billowed choking smoke over us all. It was an intensely busy, ugly place, and I immediately thought of Albert and his growing exasperation at the destruction of earth's peaceful, natural beauty. I wanted to leave this place as soon as possible; if all went well, I hoped to be in Plymouth by nightfall.

I discovered that the cost of a ticket was quite prohibitive, about fifteen shillings. I didn't have that kind of money, so had no option but to try to travel for free. In any case, if I was going to hide successfully on the *Endurance*, I should better get some practice in first by hitching a free ride on the train.

About an hour into my journey I failed in my attempt to hide on the train. It was a rather lame bid, involving trying to shuffle past the ticket inspector as he headed my way. However, I still had no problem avoiding the fare. I played the confused foreigner card, speaking only a smattering of heavily accented English (I thought it wise to pretend I was Belgian rather than utilise my more credible German mimicry) to the ticket inspector, who nevertheless tenaciously persisted in helping me purchase a ticket. So I broke down into even more incomprehensible wailing. I knew the crazy English thought that the motions and sounds of a train could cause a person to become insane, particularly if that person were a weak and feeble woman. I used this to my advantage. It was very effective, and I arrived not one penny lighter in Plymouth (I genuinely found it hard to say that word, even speaking my best English) late in the evening. I set about locating Jack.

The first pub I saw was called the Fisherman's Arms. It was close to the station at which I had just alighted, and just a stone's throw from the harbour, too. I didn't expect to strike it lucky on my first attempt, but thought this sounded as good a place as any. To my surprise, Jack and Willy were indeed inside, sitting around a table with a group of men. I assumed they were all members of Shackleton's party, and decided I shouldn't draw attention to myself. I made to go back outside.

"Arrrggrhher, moi luvva, wha ye be doyn inner?" or something like that. I had no idea what the shaggy old fisherman at the bar rumbled at me; it sounded like an outboard sputtering into life. Whatever he said, it made almost every man in the pub turn around and stare, including the Shackleton group. I beat a hasty retreat and waited outside in the moonlight shadows across the street, wondering how I should make contact with Jack.

As it turned out, Jack had already spotted me. He must have made his excuses, for just a few minutes later he exited the pub, lit a cigarette and looked around. I stepped out from the shadows and waved to him. He wasted no time to get to the point.

"We've got to get you on board tonight. Tomorrow there's too much going on. Stay here, and when I'm done with the lads, we'll sort you out. We're lucky it's still on, because Old Cautious offered the *Endurance* to the war effort. Luckily the Admiralty told him to proceed with the expedition."

"Who's Old Cautious?"

"Oh, that's Shackleton."

"Is he in there with you?" I had vague notions of giving him a piece of my mind.

"No. I think he's still in London. He's leaving a bit later. We're meeting him on the other side of the Atlantic. Wait here; I've got to get back."

"Wait! Does Willy know about this?"

"Don't be daft. No-one knows."

That reassured me somewhat. Before this adventure I was apathetic towards Willy, but now he had somehow pirated a place on the *Endurance*, I actively disliked him. Although I amused myself with the thought that even if Willy had known about my plan and shouted about it while wearing an eye-patch, waving a cutlass and stamping a wooden leg, no-one would have noticed him.

It must have been about two in the morning when Jack finally came for me. I'm not sure where he had been all that time, as I had seen him leave the pub several hours earlier. But it didn't matter; he had kept his promise. Not to arouse suspicion, we walked arm-in-arm towards the docks; no-one would question why a sailor was out with a young girl late at night in town like Plymouth.

We arrived at Plymouth harbour where, Jack assured me, he would have no problem as boatswain in getting past the guard to gain access to the ship. While I hid behind a pile of fishing baskets, he showed a document to someone at port security and kept the man in the booth talking while I sneaked past and made for the cover of a small, upturned boat. I couldn't help noticing that it was in quite a state of disrepair. More importantly, I was through and there was now no-one to stop me boarding the *Endurance*.

44

Eventually, Jack strolled over to me, the security man returned to his newspaper, and we were in the clear.

The *Endurance* was just one of dozens of sailing vessels, but certainly one of the more impressive ones. It was a three-masted barquentine, about one hundred and fifty feet long. I had seen thousands of ships like her before and even worked on many of them, repairing leaks or broken masts or problems with the steering. Yet something about the *Endurance* made an emotional impression on me. I could tell that whoever had built her had devoted such care and attention to her construction, as a wife or girlfriend might in packing the bag of her soldier husband before he went off to war. Timber from a single oak tree was joined seamlessly to form the natural curvature of the bow and her black, shimmering sides were made from what I guessed to be Norwegian fir, a strong, durable and beautiful wood. I could see, just above the waterline, a sheathing of South American greenheart, a wood tougher than metal and so strong that I have broken many tools working on it. This was a ship built with diligence, built to endure. Her name was perfect, and after overcoming much trauma in my life, I felt an affinity with her immediately.

"She's no ordinary ship," I remarked to Jack. "I thought she was just taking you across the Atlantic and around the Antarctic, although I have to say her hull seems a bit too rounded for that."

"You know your boats, don't you? Anyway, she's taking us across the Atlantic, at first. But then she's taking us to Antarctica. She's got to withstand the sea ice there. And then we're going on foot to cross the continent."

I knew the ship was destined for the Antarctic, but had no idea about this expedition on foot. "Why didn't you tell me?"

"Thought I did. But don't worry, you're getting off in Argentina."

"Argentina?! I thought you said America!"

45

"No. Never said that."

"But I don't want to go to Argentina."

"It's still the Americas isn't it? You can travel up from there and see a bit more of the world. By time you're done, we'll have finished our expedition, and we can tell each other about it all back in Hull. You in, or not?"

I had got this far, and at the mention of Hull my mind was made up. I was getting out of Britain, come what may. "Let's go," I said.

We scampered across the deck and into the dark belly of the ship. Jack closed the hatch carefully, shutting out the night sky and enveloping us in pitch blackness. In this breathless, sightless moment I could hear the *Endurance* for the first time, murmuring in the faint harbour swell like an infant child might burble and gurgle in contented sleep. Despite the crushing darkness, I felt safe and reassured.

Jack lit up the cavity with a torch. "This way."

We crawled through a thwartship bulkhead, over the solid oak keel and past supplies the men would need for their journey, towards the bow of the ship. "We're in the front side pockets of the ship," explained Jack. He didn't need to tell me; I knew enough about boats to realise exactly where we were. "This is where we store all the lumber. Make a hideout for yourself in here. I'll come down once in a while to give you some food and water."

"What about... you know?"

"That bucket." It might have been embarrassing for me, but Jack was a tough sailor, and wouldn't be phased by that unpleasant duty.

"Okay," I said.

"Take this torch and this bag. There's a blanket in there, and some provisions to keep you going for a while. And if you get caught, I know nothing about this."

"Of course."

After Jack left me, I busied myself with creating the hideout. I rearranged the lumber so that I had a small space to crawl into, accessed by one large piece of wood, which, when in place, would keep me hidden from view. I could just about lie down, which is exactly what I did. It had been a long, exhausting day, and I fell swiftly into a long sleep. When I awoke, I knew we were moving across the sea.

57°52' South, 46°47' West

A large wave shook the MS *Schwabenland*, causing a potato to roll off my plate and drop to the floor before I could catch it. On my way to dinner with Kapitän Ritscher I had spotted through the window quite a heavy sea, and no sign of land. That meant Elephant Island was far behind us and we were now passing through the notorious Drake Passage. Here, within a few minutes, cobalt blue skies can be overrun by thick, angry clouds and from calm seas can rise monstrous waves that crave nothing more than to consume any boat foolhardy enough to confront them; I'm almost too afraid to ask what the Germans have renamed this stretch of water.

I left my seat to retrieve the potato.

"Leave it," smiled Kapitän Ritscher. "We've plenty more in the kitchen."

"Well, I think I've enough on my plate with this meat anyway," I said, returning to my seat. "It's delicious. What is it?"

"It's the finest Italian," he said, a smirk playing on his lips.

We were in the ship's canteen, just the two of us. He said he was particularly interested to know what happened in Argentina, as it was Germany's closest ally in this part of the world and that without their help in controlling the seas, Britain might not have yet capitulated in the Southern hemisphere.

"I didn't know Argentina and Britain were enemies," I confessed. "If they were, how come Shackleton's men were able to dock in Buenos Aires."

The captain shrugged. "Well, they've always been at each other's throats over the Malvinas, which of course Argentina owns now, quite rightly."

"I can't believe that everyone's been fighting for all this time. When I left, they said it would be over by Christmas."

"Over by Christ... Oh! You don't know! *That* war finished in 1918. We lost. Did you know at one time we had Britain, France, Romania, Russia, Italy, Canada, Japan and the United States all fighting against us?"

"Really? Why did everyone fight against Germany?" I asked incredulously. It seemed inconceivable to me that a country which was capable of giving the world Albert and my peace-loving father could be so hated.

"Because we had very different worldviews and on their own," he began to explain, his eye following a kitchenhand who had come to pick my potato off the floor, "they weren't strong enough to defeat us. Well, even Germany couldn't take on all these nations on its own, and their poisonous worldview prevailed. Look where that has got us! The Argentinians always respected our superior military might, which is why they finally agreed to join us in the second war. That's the one we're fighting now, and only the Americans stand in the way of complete victory. This time, we have a secret weapon on our side."

"Oh, what is it? Or aren't you allowed to say?"

"Of course I can say. Everyone knows about it, or rather him. The greatest scientist who has ever lived. We have Albert Einstein."

Another wave lifted the boat; I dropped my spoonful of peas, and they scattered in wild directions. Albert? *My* Albert? How could he have got himself involved in a war? I had to ask Kapitän Ritscher.

"Albert Einstein. You mean, the one who lives in Zürich, the mathematician."

"Lived in Zürich. And he's a lot more than a mathematician. Yes, the very same. I know. Many of us were surprised too, what with the accusations about his heritage and..."

"His heritage?"

Kapitän Ritscher put down his cutlery. "Heritage is the key to success. It's very important for the fatherland to know exactly who it's dealing with. I'm sure you understand that. That's enough about Einstein. Tell me, what happened in Argentina?"

I never actually set foot on Argentinian soil.

The journey there took two months; for almost the entire time I was holed up in the confined space right at the front of the *Endurance*. I heard and felt every wave thrown at this magnificent boat. Even though I knew that the bow and the sides which kept the ocean out were several feet thick and were put together with exceptional skill, I could not help but feel tense at each sudden jolt, each creak, each freak wave which lifted the ship many feet into the air before sending her hurtling down into the trough. I bounced around a fair bit, but cushioned the ride a little by positioning the lumber, blanket and my bag to wedge me in. Even then, I suffered the odd bruising bump.

It is difficult for those who have never experienced utter darkness to comprehend the range of sensations and imaginations that course through body and mind. I knew my eyes were open, because I could feel them blinking; I knew I was crouching, because I could feel the pressure on my back, my hands, the soles of my feet; and the sounds and scents of my environment made me acutely aware of my place in the world, because I could smell the fragrance of moss and oil, bark and soil mingling with my own earthy body odours, and I could hear the wood rasping and groaning with the stiff movements of my limbs and the heavy sighs of my breath. But there were many other things which confounded me and led me down some desperate paths in search of clarification.

I heard whispering; faint, swift, snatched conversations or comments which I could never quite grasp. I saw images of light, sometimes filling my entire field of vision, and I saw dark shadows moving within the black void around me. In these moments I would seize the torch and flood my hideout with blinding light, only hastily to switch it off again as my eyes recoiled in pain at the sudden exposure. Then I would be plagued by dancing phantasms which made my head thump in agony. It was not a pleasant experience.

Relief, both from the monotony of my confinement and the disagreeable stench which my circumstances naturally caused, came every few days or so, when Jack came to check up on me. I looked forward to those moments as if they were all I had to live for, wondering how many hours it would be until the next one. But he never stayed for long, and he never engaged in fulfilling conversation. Indeed, all I really got from him is that he hated all of his companions, and they hated him just as passionately.

After one such brief visit I sat in my hideout, munching on some dried biscuits and sipping water from a flask. It might not sound like much, but this was right up there in my list of highlights for the journey. I sneezed and dropped my biscuit. Cursing myself for my clumsiness, I reached for the torch, which I always stored in a ledge just above my head. As I grabbed it, I sneezed again, this time more violently. The torch fell from my grasp, hit my head, and clattered somewhere to the floor beside me. This time my cursing entered a new realm of vehemence, as did my sneezing. Before I knew it, my body was convulsing, my face exploding, my mind fiercely fighting to maintain control as I crawled over the floor and between the piles of wood in an attempt to find the torch. My hand chanced upon it, and without regard to my eyes, I swept the glaring flashlight over my wooden chamber.

Never in my life have I been overtaken with such terrifying fear as when the beam of light reflected upon two green, shining cat's eyes. Both the creature and I shrilled a note of horror and we unanimously launched ourselves into a panicked scramble about our tiny, shared space. I kicked the fortunately empty bucket over, I banged and crashed against the inner sides of the bow, and sent piles of lumber tumbling all over the place. Somehow in our constant whirring the tiger-striped cat managed to avoid all of these hazards, and we managed to avoid one another. I had only one aim: to get out of there by whatever means possible.

There was no lock on the door to this lumber room – what use would it have served? – and I darted out into another similarly cramped but blissfully cat-free storeroom. However, my sneezing was not subsiding, and I could feel the sides of my neck growing sore with a creeping rash. I needed fresh air. I retraced the steps Jack and I had taken in what seemed like a lifetime before, located the hatch that led to the deck and, without caring if anyone caught me or not, flung it wide open.

I was surprised that above me was neither filled with a bright blue sky nor scudding grey clouds, nor anything but the blackness of night. I had assumed that Jack always visited me during the day; I had no way of knowing and had lost all sense of time. But I didn't care. I raced to the side rail, grasped it tightly, drank in the exquisite freshness of the sea wind and delighted for a few, fleeting moments in my freedom.

"It came from over here."

Someone had heard me! I looked about hurriedly; I was too far from the hatch, which I could see still open several metres away. Rigging from the foremast was within hand's reach, so I grabbed a rope, flung my legs around it and hauled myself up to the lowest boom as speedily and as stealthily as I could. My urge to sneeze was great.

From my elevated position I saw two men approach the hatch.

"Who left that open?" said the one I had heard a few moments before. He had a distinctive New Zealand accent; I had heard many sailors from his part of the world in the docks and pubs of Hull.

"Dunno, Wuzzles." This man had a noticeable Yorkshire accent, with which I was even more familiar.

"Who'd be going down there this time of night?"

"Dunno, Wuzzles."

"Do you think Chippy's down there?

"Wuzzles, I just dunno."

"Come on, let's check it out." The one called Wuzzles moved closer to the hatch.

Just then, a third man appeared beneath me. "Hoo's it gaun?" From the near-incomprehensibility of his accent, definitely a Scotsman. I really needed this trio to go; my eyes were nearly popping out of my head from the pressure of keeping the sneeze in.

"Chippy!" greeted Wuzzles in surprise. "Have you been down here?"

"Aye, earlier."

"Ah, okay. Close it next time, will you?"

"Sorry, Wuzzles. Ah guess me heid's been in a fankle, what wi' this bampot rounded hull makin' us all boke. Mrs Chippy!" he exclaimed, as the cat which had tormented me emerged from the hatch and coquetted around his legs. Its name was almost the only thing I had understood the Scotsman say.

"It must've been the cat we heard, Wuzzles," explained the Yorkshireman.

"Yup." Wuzzles closed the hatch and the three men departed, thankfully taking Mrs Chippy with them.

When I could no longer see them, my body relaxed and the sneeze which had built up to almost volcanic proportions erupted from me and nearly hurled me from my perch. I clung on to the boom, held my hand to my mouth, and prayed no-one had heard me. None of the men returned, and when the coast was clear, and my sneezing fit was well and truly over, I clambered down and made for the safety of my hideout in the belly of the ship.

It was from Jack, a couple of days later, that I learnt who Wuzzles, the Yorkshireman and Chippy the Scotsman were. Wuzzles was Frank Worsley, the captain of the *Endurance*. Jack hated him, thought he was far too weak to lead them and called him a 'bloody kiwi'. I had no idea what he meant by that, so he told me that this was how everyone was calling people from New Zealand these days. Seemed odd to me. The Yorkshireman was another Frank, Frank Wild, for whom Jack had a begrudging respect on account of his strength, yet still didn't like very much. Chippy was Harry McNish, the carpenter; the one who had my job, so I didn't like him, and the fact that the cat was his, made me like his cat even less than I already did, if that were possible. Jack also said that Mrs Chippy was in fact a tomcat and was only called Mrs Chippy because he followed the carpenter around like a devoted wife. For a vulnerable moment this drew me to the cat a little, and made me cross with the other crew members: why did people insist on labels and terms, just for their own amusement? Why couldn't they just call her, or rather him, a tomcat name? But then I remembered that Mrs Chippy was, and would always remain, a cat; we would never be friends.

I thought I had been added to Jack's list of shame when I told him about venturing onto the deck, but his initial anger diffused fairly quickly, and he seemed to understand the reasons. He was very clear, however, that I should not do such a thing again. I ignored him.

The liberation I had felt out on the open deck was not something I was prepared to give up. I knew that the *Endurance* was large enough, and that I knew my way about ships well enough, to allow me to steal occasional moments of release from my confines, an instance of emancipation from my dark quarantine. I never told Jack, but over the next few weeks at sea and until we reach the port of Buenos Aires, I spent many hours on the deck, investigating the ship and eavesdropping on the men as they gossiped amongst themselves.

The main thing I heard was inane seaman banter, but I also picked up a few interesting bits of information. Worsley, it seemed, was well-liked but seen as ineffectual, and the men were looking forward to Shackleton taking over, as he, they said, would have a firmer grip on the crew. Jack, in particular, was viewed as someone who needed a stronger leader, as so far he had been able to bully his way into getting pretty much everything he wanted. Although I didn't begrudge Jack the chance to be on this expedition, I did wonder how he had been chosen in the first place. Just how this came to pass I picked up from Worsley; Shackleton's selection process for his crew had been very arbitrary indeed.

"Did you know he had over five thousand applications, and he sorted them all into three piles?" said the captain one night, while I was in the shadows of the forecastle.

"No, I didn't." I wasn't sure who this person was, but it wasn't Wild or Chippy, of that I was certain.

"Yup. He put them into three piles: mad, hopeless, or possible."

"Which one were you in?" laughed the other seaman.

"Very funny."

"What about the fourth pile?" asked the seaman, evidently on a facetious streak. He was probably the joker of the crew.

"Go on, then."

"The girly group. Weren't there some girls who applied, too?"

"Yup. Shame we couldn't get one of them to join us," grinned Worsley. I wasn't finding their humour at all funny.

"Would've made these long evenings more interesting."

They were both lucky to have survived the night, as I was minded to tip them over the railings there and then.

On another occasion two more men, neither of whom I recognised, were talking about Shackleton. It was evident that the leader of this expedition had made an impression on these men, and the closer we got to Argentina, the more they spoke about him.

"Old Cautious never got over it you know, losing to Amundsen in the race to the South Pole."

"Yeah, but imagine being the first to cross Antarctica. That's an even harder feat."

"I know. All the way to the South Pole, and then further. Do you think we'll succeed?"

56

"If we all work together."

"What is it Old Cautious said he looked for? Optimism, imagination, courage and... what was the other one?

"Patience."

"That's it. We could do with losing Vincent. He just causes trouble, that hot-headed brute."

It wasn't so much the description of Jack that troubled me: he *was* hot-headed. Rather I felt more aggrieved that I had not been selected for this expedition. As far as I was concerned, I possessed those four qualities as well as any of the men I had heard or seen on this ship, and I was a talented ship builder, too. I had been cheated out of something for which I was perfectly eligible, and I felt a desire to right this wrong.

When I was back in my hideout, I entertained the idea of stowing away for longer, until I was in Antarctica. Then there would be no turning back; Shackleton would have to take me. However, before this idea could really take root, Argentina was sighted. It was time for the next stage of my journey to begin.

Jack told me that the *Endurance* would be in port for a few days; there was much equipment to load and still a few hands to hire. As such, there would be a great deal of activity in and around the ship. Unless I wanted to risk being caught and perhaps even arrested, I had to wait for the right moment to make my departure from the ship and start my (South) American adventure.

It was on the third night docked in Buenos Aires that Jack gave me the all-clear. He came to my hideout with a bag of provisions and told me that the *Endurance* was due to set sail the next day, so the whole crew were going to the harbour for a few drinks and to say goodbye to warmth and dry land for a while. When they were gone, that would be my chance to leave.

I waited for several hours. It was difficult to know exactly when I should leave, but during the two-month Atlantic crossing I had developed a few tricks to determine where the crew were on the ship. I went to my secret spots, still in the hull, listening intently for footsteps or voices above. I could hear none. I fetched my belongings, checked all the locations one last time, reassured myself that now was the time to go, and carefully opened the hatch to the deck. I peeked through a gap before pushing the hatch all the way up, as I had done many times already. Deadly quiet. It seemed that the ship had been entirely abandoned.

My eyes were drawn to a dull glow radiating over the starboard side of the ship. Buenos Aires. I could not quite believe I had come so far from home, and a wave of excitement gripped me. I climbed out onto the deck and ran to the railings to get my first glimpse of this different world. It was hugely disappointing; the harbour was very much like any other I had seen. The same boats, the same cranes, the same smells and sounds. Apart from one sound. Dogs. Many barking dogs. And they were getting closer.

I quickly gathered my bags and headed towards the gangway. I reached it too late. The dogs I had heard were close to the far end. There were so many of them, led by several handlers. I could not possibly disembark without them seeing me. I was confused – was this Argentinian port security in action? It seemed drastically over the top and it was certainly very frightening. I stood at the top of the gangway, not quite sure what I should do, when my time for further contemplation vanished altogether. The dogs were boarding the *Endurance*!

I backed away from the gangway, ran up some steps, across the quarterdeck to the stern of the ship and hid as best I could. If necessary, I would jump into the sea from here; I knew I could easily swim to safety, but I would have to ditch my belongings. Faced with so many dogs, this would be a price I would have to pay. I had no idea how many of them there were. Twenty, thirty, maybe more, all piling onto the ship. Were they after me?

Human voices carried over the barking animals. I raised my head to gain a better view and saw that the voices belonged to the several guards I had just seen, each one of which was handling half a dozen or so dogs. I had no idea what these men were saying, but they sounded angry. However, if they were after me, they went the wrong way, for not one of them led the dogs to the rear of the ship. Then I realised that these were not guards hunting me, after all; the dogs were for the Antarctic expedition. Jack had told me about the plan to cross the continent, and they would need the animals to pull equipment across the ice.

It took some time for the dogs to be loaded and the handlers to leave, and I was getting concerned that the crew would return soon. I imagined various conversations, should Shackleton discover me here, and how, after I had dressed him down about his selection process, about his letter to me, about the quality of his crew, he would acknowledge that he could not possibly continue his expedition without me. I would be the ship's carpenter and that Scotsman, Harry McNish, would be my assistant. The idea of being the first woman to cross the Antarctic appealed to me. How's that for patience, optimism, courage and imagination?

But it was a fanciful notion, and now it was time to leave. Once again, I collected my bags and, treading softly so as not to set off the dogs, who had by now settled somewhere in the ship, I gingerly headed back towards the gangway. Everything was clear now, everything was quiet. I stepped backwards to take one last look at the magnificent ship that had brought me here.

"Ow, mind how you go, is it?" Those few backward steps had caused me to stumble into a man, trip and fall to the floor. I had been caught! "Here, let me help you up. Easy does it." A dark-

59

haired man offered me his hand. I looked at him with wide, wild eyes. I glanced to my bags. Should I try to grab them before making a run for it? "You, er… you won't tell anyone you saw me, will you?" His voice was kind, melodic. I had also heard this accent before but couldn't place it. I let him pull me up. "Please, I just want to join the expedition. I'm a great seaman," he said.

This was curious. "What do you mean?"

"Bakewell got on, but I didn't. Have you met him, yet? He's my mate, and we do everything together. I promise I'll work really hard. Please, just let me hide for a few days, then I'll come clean and tell Mr Shackleton."

"You want to stow away?"

"Well, only for a couple of days. I don't want a free ride or anything. Promise."

This was a strange turn of events. The man was young, really just a boy, and he had such an engaging nature that I immediately liked him.

"How old are you?"

"Eighteen. What about you? You look about the same age."

"Nineteen."

"You won't tell?"

"I'll do better than that. I'll join you. I shouldn't be here either."

After a brief explanation, we exchanged names, and grins sealed our secret pact.

Wales, that was where Perce Blackborow was from. It was clear to me now, as I had met sailors from all over Britain in Hull, and had heard many a Welshmen sing in the Alexandra. I joked with Perce that his accent was unusually strong; he said pretty much the same of mine. I was surprised, however, to learn that he wasn't alone in his stowaway plan. The friend he had mentioned, an American called William Bakewell, was an official member of the crew but was also in on the secret, as was an Englishman called Walter How. Both the American and the Englishman

60

wanted to help their young Welsh friend in his desire to be part the expedition, too; and now all three of them knew about me.

I never mentioned Jack to them. Firstly, I assumed that the newcomers would like Jack as much as everyone else seemed to, that is, not at all. Associating myself with him might not be advantageous. But more importantly, I wanted to protect Jack. He had taken a huge risk in helping me: if I were caught and Jack's involvement uncovered, he would almost certainly be thrown off the expedition. If anyone knew about our connection, I would be increasing that danger. So as far as William and Walter knew, I'd received no help and had managed to sustain myself by sneaking into the ship's kitchen. They commended me on my resourcefulness, but from now on, they said, they would come to me in my old hideout and take care of all my needs. Now that Jack would be assuming I had left the ship, these new benefactors were very welcome indeed.

From them I learnt more about the expedition. I had assumed it would involve trekking to the South Pole, then back again. However, the goal wasn't just the South Pole, but to be the first team to cross Antarctica. They were planning to land on the frozen continent in December, spend a few months trekking back and forth, laying supplies, then only start the mammoth trek in November, almost a year later, to arrive at the South Pole by Christmas in 1915. Meanwhile, a team from Australia would land on the other side of the continent, at somewhere called Hut Point, so called because many Antarctic expeditions had erected a hut at that point. From there the Australian crew were to place supplies at intervals for Shackleton's crew to pick up after they had reached the South Pole. When Shackleton's crew had crossed the continent, the Australian team would be waiting for them, and they'd all sail back together in March 1916, happily ever after. What a journey! The more I learnt about it, the more excited I grew about joining the expedition.

The *Endurance* left Buenos Aires and was scheduled to arrive at South Georgia about ten days later. Perce's plan was to come out of his own hideout, a clothes locker, after about a week. As it turned out, he only lasted three days because he was so uncomfortable in his cramped space that William and Walter 'arranged' his discovery by an unwitting member of the crew, whereupon Perce was marched to Shackleton, who was furious with the intruder.

"We've got limited provisions on this ship. Everything has been weighed and accounted for to the last ounce. If we run out of food, we eat you. Do you understand?" raged Shackleton.

"They'd get a lot more meat off you, sir," replied the young Welshman.

When Perce came to my hideout and told me this, I giggled and admired his audacity.

"How did Shackleton react?"

"Quite well. I work in the kitchen."

"Maybe I should come out of hiding now, too," I suggested.

"There's something else you need to know before you risk that."

Perce then divulged his initiation ceremony; Shackleton insisted that there be one. He was tied to the front of one of the lifeboats and lowered to just a few feet from the surface of the sea, at precisely the moment a pod of killer whales was taking an interest in the *Endurance*.

"They came right up to me, sniffed me, butted me with their massive heads. I can still feel their hot fishy breath on my face. I've never been so terrified in my life. I'm surprised you didn't hear my screams all the way in here. How was I to know that orcas don't eat humans?"

All the same, I decided to postpone my own big revelation to Shackleton until we were on the orca-free land of South Georgia.

I can't recall who told me now, but before we reached the island either Perce, William or Walter, or perhaps all three together, such was their apparent glee at the turn of events, informed me that Jack had been sacked. Just as I had feared, even in the short time these three men had known Jack, he had managed to annoy them. More ominously for Jack, Shackleton had heard too many

62

negative reports from too many members of the crew, so demoted my friend from boatswain to able seaman. I knew this would be a great personal bruising for Jack, so took this moment, and the risk, to tell them that it was actually Jack who had helped me stow away and that he had a good heart. I hoped this would soften their opinion of him, and asked if I could see him.

It was with great anticipation that I awaited his arrival the next day. I heard him approach, clattering through the bulkheads to get to me. Either he was in a hurry, or he was angry. I feared the latter. Although I was certain it was Jack, I took up my concealed position behind a screen of lumber. The door opened, a flashlight shone directly on to my hideout.

"Marianna?" It was that distinctive Welsh accent.

"Perce? Where's Jack?"

"He's not coming. We haven't told him about you. He's in a very prickly mood. As is Shackleton. Most of the crew are a bit tense, mind. News is, the ice in the Weddell Sea is not on our side. Let's not rock the boat, is it? We'll be in South Georgia in a few hours. We're laying anchor at Grytviken. I'll come and get you once everyone's ashore, and we'll work out how best to come out of the closet, as it were."

I was disappointed, but could see there was little reason, or time, to do anything about the situation now. "Okay. See you in a few hours."

It was exactly as Perce had said. A couple of hours later I felt the *Endurance* come to a stop. I pictured the men being ferried to and from the port, and Perce making some excuse to return to the ship on his own. His excuse, he told me when he fetched me under the cover of darkness, was that he had come to find Mrs Chippy. This deception was in fact true, for he had earlier prepared his alibi by locking the cat in the engine room, much to the distress of the carpenter Chippy, who had spent a whole hour looking for her.

"Told Chippy I'd seen her sleeping in the engine room and thought he'd taken her with him. Said I'd bring her for him,"

63

smiled Perce. I told him about my allergy. "That complicates things. I'll put her in a sack. Everyone's in the town having food and drink. We can let the cat out of the bag then," he said, giving me a wink. Then his face turned grave. "There's one more thing," he said.

Perce thought it wise that I didn't reveal the fact that I was female. At first, I thought he must be joking, that it was not something I could very well hide, but the seriousness of his expression told me otherwise. I was baffled by the suggestion. His reasoning was that as far as he knew, there was not a single female on South Georgia, and he would be worried for my safety among so many men. I had no papers; I had no right to be there. For the outside world, I didn't exist, and no-one would be looking for me. I might be fine, he said, but I was like a spark within a pile of dry wood; it wouldn't take much for things to flare up. It was a fair point, but I reminded him that I was used to a male environment and I could hold my own among them. I further told him about the time Jack had rescued me, and said that no harm would come to me with him around.

"Okay, just for the beginning, until we know the lie of the land," he proposed. "Just keep things as... quiet as you can. For instance, you don't have to say you're *not* a girl, but you don't have to say you *are* one. Let Shackleton get over the shock of meeting you first, before he has that to deal with, too. It might be an idea to, you know, well, you have certain... assets...," he waved vaguely in my direction, "that you can keep to yourself for the moment."

"Assets?" I enquired. Of course, I knew exactly what he was talking about, but I'd been cooped up on my own for so long that I felt a need to tease him.

"Yeah, like, qualities." He fluttered his hands towards me again, only slightly more accurately.

"Oh! You mean these!" I smiled, holding my hands in front of my breasts.

"Um... Yeah. You can just, you know, flatten things, and choose a name that could be male or female, like George or something.
64

But nothing too exotic. We don't want you to draw attention to yourself."

"George is no good. I think they'll know from my accent that I'm not English."

Perce took that statement as an agreement to the plan. "Great, you think of a name, then. Here, I've brought some scissors. We have to cut your hair."

He suggested that my hair be cut to within a few inches of my scalp. That, I told him with a firmness that made him raise his hands in defence, was never going to happen. Shoulder length, and no shorter. I hadn't washed in two months, so was already as mucky as a boy, and stank like one too; all it needed was a few adjustments to my clothing and I looked the part. I was surprised at how easy the transformation had been and was rather pleased with the results. For the name, I chose something that could be both male or female, as Perce had suggested, and moreover one that was shared by the blandest person I knew.

"Meet Willi," I declared to Perce as I revealed myself to him. "How do I look?

"Pretty convincing," he said, nodding in approval.

I'm not certain why, but in that moment Carmen flashed into my mind. "Do you think a girl would like me?"

Perce laughed. "Ha, I'm not sure. Wait..." He took off his fisherman's cap and pulled it over the top of my head. Then he adjusted it a little. "There. Now you're irresistible!" I blushed. "We'd better get going," Perce chirped. "I'll get Mrs Chippy. You know, you two have a lot in common now!"

Once outside, Perce gave me a thick coat, for which I was extremely thankful as the temperature on South Georgia was noticeably lower than in Buenos Aires. He rowed through the bay, which he told me was called King Edward Cove, and towards the shore, while I gazed upon the bright moon, reflecting off a crisp covering of snow on the mountains which shrouded this natural harbour. There was a raw, natural beauty to this island, and I instantly thought back to my life in Zürich. But the hissing Mrs

65

Chippy, safely bagged, brought my mind very much back to the present. I ensured that the sack containing this clearly very aggrieved cat stayed as far away from me as was possible on a small rowing boat. I had a big moment coming up, and I certainly didn't want it to make my grand appearance as a weeping, sneezing, coughing, spluttering, rash-red mess.

Perce beached the boat on an icy, gravelly shore, sprang out, and offered his hand to me. "Please give me a couple of minutes head start, so it doesn't look like we've arrived together," he said, while hauling the rowing boat further onto the shore. Then he picked up the bag with the growling Mrs Chippy inside and dashed off.

I took my first steps on land for two months. I glanced around at this alien world, and thought with its mountains, moonlight, calm water and sparkling snow, it really didn't look so very different to rural parts of Switzerland in the winter. If this was all there was to Grytviken, then it was indeed a tiny place. Lanterns hung from hooks on a cluster of buildings dotted around, but in only two were there any signs of life. In one, which looked like it might be a family home, lights shone from generous windows, but otherwise this house was silent. All the noise came from the other building, the one to which Perce had hurried. It was a large shed of some sort, and within its walls were dozens of feasting, drinking, uproarious men. This was it; this was the moment I revealed myself to Shackleton.

55°64' South, 39°13' West

I'm reaching the point in my story where

my past travels are almost crossing with my present ones. We will shortly be arriving in what is now known as South Chlodwig Carl Viktor Fürst zu Hohenlohe-Schillingsfürst, Prinz von Ratibor und von Corvey Island. Despite the occasional unsettling wave, it has been a far smoother ride through the Drake Passage this time, in my nice, warm, dry cabin, than it was when I left the island, thirty years ago in a Norwegian steam brig, scurrying after whales in cold, sodden oilskins.

Kapitän Ritscher seemed disappointed with me when I couldn't give him any information about Argentina. I'm not sure what he wanted from me. I was a teenage girl on a bit of a jolly – what does he expect me to know? I almost have the sense that it is *he* who is withholding something from *me*. He deflected all of my questions about Albert, saying he would fill me in another time, has never told me anything about himself but only interrogates me about *my* past.

However, there are things I need to know before I arrive in Europe. A few times now the captain has mention something about the sea level rising and the ice disappearing. I need to know what that is all about. Also, I want to know what life is like in Switzerland, and of course in my parents' home countries, Germany and Poland. What about Britain? Is it even called that anymore? I can't imagine the people in Hull would take very kindly to being run by a group of Germans, although they couldn't very well have made more of a mess of the town than the locals already had.

I had a strong recollection of that coastal, northeast English city now, and not only because of its fishing industry, which was evidently how Grytviken survived. It was more the deep impression that entering Alexandra Inn for so many years had left on all my senses: the dim yellow light dribbling through murky windows onto the wet street; the raucous clamour of drink-fuelled wit and remonstrance; the thick air, pungent with the odour of ash and unwashed fishermen; the tacky, syrupy film of spilled beer clinging to every surface; and that peculiar taste of freedom mixed with fear, of wanting to belong to this community of cheerful poverty, and of wanting nothing more than to be further from it. All these sensations rushed through me as I pushed open the door to the hut and, as I had fully expected, everybody turned around to face me.

I recognised a few of the men staring at me; in fact, in a way I recognised them all. They could have been any group of men in any tavern up and down the coast of England and, it seemed, the world over. However, there was no doubt which one was Shackleton. Middle-aged and of average height, one might be forgiven for thinking he cut an unassuming figure. Yet his broad shoulders were as strong girders, supporting a thick neck and a heavy head. Steely, grey-blue eyes and a mouth held in fixed, firm aspect across an iron jaw lent him a handsomely stern expression. He had an enduring, compelling countenance, and there was little doubt that he was the leader of this band of men.

"Is this boy yours?" It was another man, turning to Shackleton, who shook his head slowly in reply. The first man addressed me. "Who on earth are you, then?"

I was emboldened by the fact that the cap covering my scruffily cut hair, my dirty face and my generally unkempt appearance had at least fooled them into thinking I was male. I scanned the men scattered about the hall, searching for Jack. He, surely, would see through my disguise. Would he speak up? Perce, I noticed out of the corner of my eye, was raising his eyebrows, evidently urging me to proceed with our plan. Wherever Jack was, I prayed he would play along.

"My name is Willi," I said in my best German accent. "I stow away on the boat *Endurance*. I must escape my country."

If I harboured any suspicion that the man I had identified as Shackleton might not in fact be the expedition's leader, those misgivings were now blown away. His flat, titanium expression mutated into molten fury.

"You were on *my* boat?!" he thundered. I wasn't sure if I should respond; I wasn't sure if I *could* respond and fumbled to find some words. My faltering speech was, however, rapidly overwhelmed by another furious blast. "Where did you hide? Who was helping you? Speak, for God's sake! Speak!"

His rage subdued me entirely, smothering any possibility of defence. My heart was beating uncontrollably, my hands sweating and my mouth quivering. If I didn't speak soon, I was afraid that either Jack or Perce, or even William or Walter would intervene on my behalf, jeopardising their own position. In the end, the first man who had spoken to me came to my rescue.

"Let's take this discussion elsewhere. Ernest," he said, turning to Shackleton, "let's go to my house where we can speak to this boy here and find out what's going on."

The man, who introduced himself as Fridtjof Jacobsen, the manager of the whaling station, led me out of the hut, with Shackleton fuming alongside him. He took me up the path and into the soundless, well-lit house I had seen earlier. It resembled the villas I had been used to seeing in Switzerland.

"This is what everyone around here calls the *Slotte*, the castle. It's where I live with my family," Fridthof explained as he opened the door. "Take off your shoes and leave them there. My wife likes cleanliness."

A smartly dressed woman holding a baby appeared out of a room just off the corridor. She took one look at the three of us and, probably on account of Shackleton's face red with anger, mine white with fear, and her husband's blank with confusion, surmised all was not well and announced she would put Solveig back to bed. Fridtjof ushered his two guests into the kitchen and told us to sit down at the large wooden table while he busied himself opening and closing cupboards, retrieving crockery and glasses. When he was done, he placed on the table a plateful of flatbread stuffed with buttermilk, syrup, flour and cheese. He filled the glasses with some spirit.

"Akvavit. Will put some warmth back into those pale cheeks," he explained, noting my quizzical look. "And the snack is Møsbrømlefse, perfect after a day's work in the cold. Now, I think you've got some explaining to do."

The walk from the hut to the villa and the invigorating effect of the hearty food and bitter drink helped to restore my composure somewhat. Shackleton took a little more time to calm down and hurled many sharp remarks at me; none of which had anything to do with my German heritage, as I had half-feared, rather were focused solely on imperilling his men by stealing the valuable provisions on board his ship and putting my own life in danger. He understood, he said, my reasons for not wanting to be deported

70

back to Germany, which is what I claimed the British authorities were planning to do with me, but he disapproved wholeheartedly of my means of escape. He completely discounted my professed skills as a carpenter and potential ability to support his expedition. In the end, the whaling station manager, who had the final say in the matter, decided that I could stay in his house for two weeks until the next ship sailed for Buenos Aires. In the meantime, I would help his wife with the housework, as she had her hands full with their four children and could do with some extra support. I didn't have much option but to agree.

Klara Jacobsen, Fridtjof's wife, was a no-nonsense woman who accepted that I would be living with them for a couple of weeks and welcomed me into her family as if she had known me all of her life. I liked her. I was a little worried that my chores might involve looking after the infant girl I had seen, but Klara needed no help there. She happily showed me a framed document displaying 'South Georgia Birth Certificate No. 1'; the babe in her arms, Solveig, was the first and, the proud mother claimed, only child to have been born and registered on the remote island. Two other daughters and a teenage boy, just a few years younger than me, completed her family, and they were all remarkably independent.

"There's no room for stragglers here," Klara said, almost as much a warning to me as it was an explanation for her children's' self-sufficiency.

The boy, Karl, eyed me suspiciously on the first night when his mother told him we would be sharing a room. I was immediately concerned that he had already seen through my disguise or, in the close confines of his room, would quickly see me for who I really was. However, I was very careful not to let him see me in any state other than fully clothed, even as I was getting into bed, which no doubt he thought was extremely odd behaviour.

"Cold here. Not used to it." I said on the first night, justifying my strange bedtime habits as I slipped under the blankets on the mattress laid out on the floor.

71

Karl simply shrugged, rolled over and went to sleep.

However, he certainly warmed to me the next day when he saw the extent of my familiarity with boats and how I could, with almost no materials, fix even problematic leaks. He, in turn, wanted to demonstrate his knowledge, and eagerly showed me how to stoke the engine boilers on the whalers. Of course, I knew how to do this, but feigned ignorance and paid close attention, which he mistook for enthusiastic interest, so promised me a real treat on my second morning there. It proved to be anything but that.

A thick mist had enveloped the town, cloaking the *Endurance* out in King Edward Cove with an inscrutable haze of icy droplets. Hot steam churning from a number of seething metal machines set along the harbour front rose and swirled into the mist, as if the machines themselves were the instruments for this nebulous landscape. Every pinch of colour had been drained by a smothering, impenetrable greyness. If I had just glanced casually at the scene, I would have thought that a thirty-metre-long leviathan being pulled up the slipway from the water's edge by the clanking engines was an upturned boat, and the treat that Karl had promised me was to inspect the clearly damaged hull and help repair it. However, this was no vessel I recognised: it was too slender for a boat of that length; its sides were too soft and yielding; curious shapes extended where there should be none; and the surface glistened not just with the dampness of the cold ocean, but with the flush of hot blood. This was a blue whale.

I had never seen one live before, although 'live' was not exactly the correct description. But, even in death, the beauty and grace of this extraordinary creature sent a shiver down my spine. Then I shuddered in horror when I realised what was unfolding before me. Its enormous body quivered with each shuddering jerk from the winding winches which, ropes tied to the whale's rump, reeled the dead animal in, scraping it further away from the sea. Trails of blood seeped from many wounds and viscid gore oozed from one large gaping hole, blasted by the explosive harpoon

72

which still jutted from the beast's head. Finally, the whale was hauled onto the flensing plate where men, flensers with spiked boots and armed with crude slicing tools, jumped on to the carcass and began to flay it, cutting long slits into the blubber. The flensers peeled one strip away after another, the fat crackling like a spitting bonfire as it tore from the soft flesh beneath. One of the men punctured the whale with a large hook attached to a pulley, another steam winch hissed into life, a burst of hot vapour wrapped around the harbour, the body was twisted onto its flayed back, and the pale-yellow underbelly was stripped of the final chunks of blubber.

The whole process had taken no time at all; I don't even know how much time. I was as mesmerised as I was appalled, and time was numb to me. The flensers jumped from the carcass and slapped one another on the back, downed a dram and moved away to let three more men, lemmers, move in to butcher the whale further, slicing through its lips, removing the whalebone, carving the meat, tending to the entrails and feeding the bones into a steam-driven saw.

"This is my treat?" My voice was cold. Karl looked at me curiously.

"Well, no, I just wanted you to get an idea of why we need the steam winches. It's a very important job. They're bringing another whale in soon, and we can stoke the winch engines together. They're a bit different to the steam engines on a boat."

I didn't reply. I gazed at the remnants of the stricken animal, still being disseered, now barely recognisable as having ever been a living creature at all; the lemmers, knives in hand, trampling in its blood and guts. What would Albert have made of it all? He probably would have commented on how this whale, so magnificent, so awe-inspiring, so far-removed from the violent industry of human existence, laid bare man's visceral baseness even as its own innards were being exposed.

Again, Karl misread me and assumed I was held in happy captivation. "It is amazing what they can get from a whale, isn't

73

it? I mean, who would've thought under all that blubber there was so much useful stuff?"

"It's hard to know what's on the inside," I answered coolly.

The hot steam engines screamed again; another whale was being hauled up the slipway.

"Come on, let's go and help." Karl bounded towards the action.

I didn't feel good about stoking the steam engines; it somehow made me complicit in the brutality. However, the whale was already dead, regardless of whether I helped or not, and the heated physical exertion of the task was in many ways a welcome relief from the cold ruthlessness I had passively witnessed. As it happened, I didn't have to feel guilty for long, as a tap on my shoulder heralded a visitor who was to take me away from it all for a while.

"Jack!" I exclaimed in surprise, even forgetting my affected accent. Karl stopped shovelling at the intrusion and leant on his spade.

"You're Willi, right?" said Jack. "You need to come with me."

I knew he had recognised me, but if Karl considered asking Jack who he was, he wisely thought better of it. I'm not sure Jack would have taken kindly to being questioned by a sixteen-year-old boy. Instead, Karl scowled a little, so that Jack didn't see, and carried on tending the engine as we departed.

I followed Jack for several minutes until we reached the boil yard, where a dozen huge copper cauldrons, each the size of a small house, bubbled with boiling blubber. Men on ladders were tossing hunks of fat into them, while others were draining the rendered fat into barrels. Everyone was drenched with oil, dripping from their trousers, their shirts, their hair; and all were covered with the soot of thick, black, fetid smoke which discharged from these sizzling vessels.

"People have a funny idea of showing a girl a good time today," I remarked.

"Last I heard, you weren't a girl," responded Jack sullenly. "We can talk here. Are you going to tell me what the hell is going on?"

74

I told him as much as I dared; I feared for Perce, William and Walter if I revealed their involvement in my extended stay. I explained that during the course of my two-month solitude hiding in the *Endurance* I had grown attached to the idea of Shackleton's British Imperial Trans-Antarctic Expedition and wanted to be a part of it. I didn't think it was fair that I had been excluded in the first place, and I knew I could benefit the group. So I'd just stayed where I was for a bit longer and, when the time was right, decided to reveal myself. I was sorry to have deceived him, I said. That, at least, was true.

"Why the hell are you dressed as a boy?"

"Thought I'd have more chance of being accepted."

It sounded plausible, and Jack grunted in acknowledgement. "You should've warned me."

"Sorry."

"Anyway, you can forget the idea of coming with us. We're holed up here for a while as the ice in the Weddell Sea is much worse than expected. We need to wait for it to thin. You'll be long gone by the time we leave."

I hadn't really had the time or even the energy to process my situation in the two days I'd been on South Georgia. I suppose I had just gone with the flow. Even so, the news came as a shock to me, for it really did look like I was destined to be taken back to Argentina. Now that joining my fellow stowaway Perce and the others on their pioneering adventure was to be denied to me, I wanted it even more. However, Jack insisted that this was out of the question. He had, he said, already taken a risk in meeting with me here, since Shackleton seemed determined to find a reason to replace him. He could do nothing more for me now than to wish me good luck and remind me to find him back in Hull when I was done exploring North and South America.

Re-joining Karl didn't appeal to me, so I wandered away from Grytviken, up the foothills of the mountain range, and scrambled up onto a low rock, where I gained a view of the town nestled on the shore of King Edward Cove. Everything was still enveloped in a grey haze. Only now, from this distance, could I clearly distinguish between the two misty vapours which hung over this natural harbour. One was still, a huge, motionless, ethereal cloud of no apparent origin, resting on a frozen bay; the other, coming from the cauldrons and engines steaming at the water's edge, was a swirling, twisting, excitable miasma, constantly pushing at its larger, quieter cousin's boundaries, colliding with it, dispersing it, replacing it. At first I felt represented by the agitated vapour, desperately battling against an uncompromising, unmoving force; but then I found harmony with the more peaceful body, desiring nothing more than just to be, to hang around, with no explanation. I wondered what I should do now, which course I should take, or even if I were able to determine my course. I decided to find Perce. The stowaway. The man who broke the rules and triumphed.

My search for him did not last long, quickly ending in failure. It is difficult to lose someone in tiny Grytviken, and I soon established that he wasn't in the town. I figured he must have been on the *Endurance*, out of my view, performing one duty or another. I would have to speak with him some other time. The day was otherwise uneventful for me, and I spent much of it sitting around the Jacobsen family's kitchen table, mostly chopping vegetables brought in by the *Endurance*, and generally helping Klara and her small staff prepare food for the hungry men at the whaling station. She was very surprised that a teenage boy was not averse to kitchen work, and she wished her son would show more interest in such matters.

"The only thing the men can do here is skin the hide off a whale. But you ask them to cook the meat inside, and you'll be sick for a week!" she laughed.

"My mother died when I was very young, so my dad and I looked after each other," I explained. I thought it better to stay as close to the truth as possible.

Klara smiled at me. "You're such a sweet young man. You'll make some woman very happy one day."

76

I helped carry the food and drink from the family home over to the hall where I had first revealed my disguised self to Shackleton. The men were in a joyful mood, some already on their second or third drink. A man with piercing blue eyes and a mousy beard, who I did not recall having spotted on the *Endurance* during my nightly eavesdropping missions, called me over.

"Hey, boy, not seen you here before. You on the expedition?"

"Er…"

"No, he's not with us anymore. We just brought him here." The falling and rising cadence of an accent forged in the green valleys brushed my hesitation aside. Perce. "He's learning all about whaling before he returns to Buenos Aires."

"Ah, new blood! You English, boy?"

"No, German."

"German, eh?" The man drew in a sharp intake of breath and placed his tankard heavily on the table. He looked me up and down. "Listen, boy, there are no nationalities among whalers. The sea is our land, and our only foes are the monsters in the sea. Welcome! Tomorrow, you come with me. I'll show you true whaling before you leave us!"

That was how I met Lars Anton Anderson, and how I came to leave South Georgia.

54°28' South, 36°50' West

Seeing Lars Anton Anderson for the first time after so long filled me with mixed feelings. On the one hand, I was overjoyed to see someone I had assumed was dead and to lay my eyes on a face I could truly associate with my past; on the other hand, despite having already been back in the company of men for some days now, it brought home to me how truly alone I had been for thirty years, and, to a great extent, how that loneliness still persisted, for I was surrounded by strangers and my familiarity with the Lars of old had barely lasted more than a week.

Kapitän Ritscher had nearly fallen from his seat when I had mentioned Lars's name. "Shit!" he exclaimed. "He's on South Chlodwig Carl Viktor Fürst zu Hohenlohe-Schillingsfürst, Prinz von Ratibor und von Corvey Island now. We'll have to get you two together again!"

MS Schwabenland came to a stop in King Edward Cove, exactly where the *Endurance* had dropped anchor thirty years previously. I looked over the railings towards the town where I had spent a few memorable days, and could hardly believe my eyes. It was the middle of May, and we were just entering the coldest months of the year, yet the granite mountains cradling Grytviken were free from snow, no ice was forming in the bay, in fact it was a pleasantly warm, sunny day. I came to the only reasonable conclusion: I had completely lost track of time over the years.

Kapitän Ritscher set me straight.

"No, no. Frau Dittrich, you are quite correct in your timings. This is the new normal. Why do you think we wanted this piece of land so much? There have been some changes while you've been away. Wait until you arrive in Europe."

Not only had the landscape shed its snowy skin, but the town had changed beyond recognition. If I remembered rightly, the whaling station had been a collection of buildings on a relatively narrow, flat piece of land at the foot of some hills, behind which rose large, imposing mountains. Now, the harbour boasted no such gentle gradient. The town sat on the hills themselves, against which lapped the waters of King Edward Cove.

Moreover, it was apparent that Grytviken was no longer a small whaling outpost, but a thriving port with large concrete structures being built as I watched. Families were on a steep beach, a little further down the coast, some splashing around in the water. In the middle of winter, that was a remarkable curiosity. Also noticeable were the flags. I had seen similar ones on the ship already, and not thought too much of it. Here, they were everywhere: white ones bearing a black equilateral cross and a red canton bespeckled with several white stars; huge, scarlet ones draped vertically from tall buildings; others, too, all with varying combinations of stars and crosses in red, white or black. In the centre of every one, a strange, black, hooked cross. It certainly brightened up the place. Kapitän Ritscher followed my gaze.

"Those flags you're looking at – they're the symbols of the National Socialist Party, the government of Germany. We rule here, too. In fact, we're making Grytviken quite the holiday destination, as you can see. At the moment only for wealthy Germans, and the odd Norwegian who's lucky enough to have worked here before. But I'm sure it will be welcoming less fortunate people soon. Come, let's get on land and find your old friend."

Kapitän Ritscher took me into a building which resembled some kind of community hall, not unlike where the men of Grytviken used to drink all that time ago. But this one was newer, larger, grander. He spoke to a few men, from their military dress evidently soldiers of some sort, before one pointed over to a table. The captain nodded and gestured for me to join him and we walked over to a table together, where a man dressed in a smart brown uniform was sitting, looking through some papers.

"Shit! Look who I've found!" greeted Kapitän Ritscher.

The man looked up. If it were not for his distinctive beard and, above all, those penetrating eyes, I would never have recognised him as Lars. Lars looked at me, and his quizzical expression certainly suggested he had no idea who I was.

"Another one for the camp?" he proposed.

"No, no!" laughed Kapitän Ritscher. "This is Marianna Dittrich, who you used to know as Willi!"

I could almost hear long defunct synapses in Lars's mind firing up again, and I could see them flashing in the twitch of his mouth as it endeavoured to form my name, in the narrowing of his eyes as they scrutinised my face, and in the tug of his beard as he struggled to revive those almost forgotten memories.

"Willi... Marianna... from Elephant Island?"

I nodded. Tears began to trickle past my nose as I recalled those short, transformative moments spent with him.

"That's it!" rejoiced Kapitän Ritscher. "But we picked her up on Deception Island. What do you make of that, Shit?"

Lars looked from the captain to me. "How... but... How come you're here in South Georgia?"

Kapitän Ritscher rolled his eyes. "When will you learn, Shit, that we've changed the island's name?"

"Why do you keep calling him that?!" I flared. My outburst almost blasted Lars from his stool, and it flung the captain's eyes wide open. I was surprised myself. Kapitän Ritscher gathered himself.

"It's not an insult, Frau Dittrich. It's just that Shi... Mr Anderson keeps on getting himself in all kinds of shi... trouble – this is difficult to explain – and back out of... trouble. It's a nickname that's stuck."

"It's okay, Marianna, some things are not what they appear to be. I'm sure you understand that," Lars winked.

It was now Kapitän Ritscher's turn to look from one person to the other. "I can see you two are familiar with one another. I will leave you alone to catch up."

With the captain departed, Lars bundled his papers together, put them neatly in a brown satchel, and asked me to accompany him on a stroll around Grytviken. It was easy to strike up conversation with him.

"Your beard is greyer than I remember," I commented.

"For a man of your age, I'm surprised you don't have one at all," joked Lars. "Besides, it's not the only thing that has changed."

There were many paved streets and roads made of crushed granite now, and we had to be wary of speeding vehicles as we made our way through the town.

"What's happened to this place? It's so busy."

"Like I said, there have been a great many changes since you were last here."

"I can see that. Look at the mountains. Where has all the snow gone?"

"Melted, perhaps forever. For years it was as if the mountains were crying, water streaming down them all day, all year. Until they had no more tears to cry. I'm not sure the snow will ever come back. The only permanent thing here is the folly of man," said Lars, broodily. It didn't sound like the sort of thing he would normally say; those words were more suited to Albert. I wondered if he had anything to do with all of this transformation.

"Have you heard of Albert? Albert Einstein? The captain mentioned him on the boat and said he was key to some kind of secret."

We had reached the outskirts of the town, which with its concrete paths and roads was beginning to encroach up the surrounding mountains like tendrils. Lars stopped and grasped my shoulders. "He's right, Marianna. Einstein is key. When we met, in 1914, no-one had really ever heard of him. But he became a celebrity, made science fashionable. Suddenly everyone wanted to be a scientist. You should have seen the developments back then, especially during the 1920s."

"Developments?"

"Technological advances. Things were being invented that your wildest fantasies could not have imagined. But there was a downside. Soon the scientist realised that all this progress came at a cost: with all the heat these new industries were creating, the earth was warming up. That's what's causing the seas to rise. In a roundabout way it also helped the Nazis come to power in Germany, as suddenly everyone began talking about land and where people were going to live."

"Is that why there was a war."

"Among other reasons, yes. You came here with Ernest Shackleton and his jingoistic crew, right? Back then, everyone was saying that the war, the first war, would be over before Christmas. Well, it wasn't over before Christmas. It lasted a bloody long time. There was peace, for a few years, and then it all started all over again, in the second great war. Well, Albert Einstein's making sure it won't drag on this time. He's saving the world, and he's the reason I'm wearing this brown uniform."

In early November 1914, although the realities of the war and stories of unimaginable suffering in the trenches in Europe were beginning to filter through even to South Georgia, no-one living on the island then could have foreseen that one day uniformed soldiers would be stationed there too. I certainly would not have believed that Lars Anton Anderson would ever be seen in military attire; I had known him as a thoroughbred whaler who dressed and smelled accordingly.

When Lars promised to show me what true whaling was and we met in the harbour, the war felt so very far away that I doubt we were even thinking about it. The fog from the previous day had lifted, and the snow-capped mountains were just visible through the numbing sleet which soddened my clothes. It had been, as Jack had already told me, a particularly chilly winter, and the icy conditions which prevented the *Endurance* from embarking on its mission still bit into this late spring morning.

Despite the gruesome spectacle I had witnessed the day before, the prospect of hunting a whale did not perturb me; I understood matters well enough to realise that the fishing industry, in all its various forms, was a necessity; indeed, my own skills depended heavily upon exploiting the ocean for all it had to offer. It was, moreover, critical to my hopes that I showed how useful I could be, for I had not given up on the idea of accompanying the Imperial Trans-Antarctic Expedition. If I could impress Lars, and word got back to Shackleton, then it was reasonable to assume that he might, after all, take me along. Besides, spending another day with Karl, as harmless as he was, did not thrill me with excitement.

"You're not going out to sea in those clothes, boy," snapped Lars when he saw me. "Go in there and fetch yourself some waterproofs. Meet me over there," he said, pointing to a large whaling ship. I could still hear him grumbling about my unsuitable attire as he stomped away.

I opened the door to the small shed he had directed me towards. It was full of stinking, half-rotting oilskins, tossed

83

carelessly in a pile among an assortment of other unloved items: ropes, nets, hooks and baskets. I rummaged through, in the hope of finding something that would vaguely fit. Fortunately, anyone around seemed preoccupied by the whaling ship moored at the end of the jetty, so I could change without fear of being spotted. All the same, I still closed the shed door and scrambled into the foul-smelling outfit as quickly as I could, and not just because it was freezing.

As I exited the shed, I very nearly knocked over Harry McNish, the carpenter. I hadn't spoken to him before, and, after apologising for my clumsiness, assumed he would continue on his way. However, McNish grabbed me by the arm.

"Ye the stow'way, eh?" he said.

"Yes, Willi," I replied, holding out my free hand. He ignored it.

"Ah should gie ye a skelpit lug, ye skinny malinky!"

"What?"

"For stoun on *Endurance*."

I thought I understood that. "Yes, sorry." I decided to keep my responses to a minimum and hope he would soon pass.

"Ah, nae mind. I'm a wee crabbit. Mrs Chippy, me cat, dun a bunker."

"Erm…"

"The eejit dogs are aff their heids wi whale scran an Mrs Chippy's feelin' peely-wally. Canny find her."

"Dogs?" I hazarded, and I wasn't so certain I had even heard that word correctly.

"Aye, on *Endurance*."

My ear was drawn to the centre of King Edward Cove, where the *Endurance* had been anchored since arrival. The dogs, I now realised, were being driven to near madness by a ton of whale meat which was hanging up in the rigging and dripping blood onto the deck below. Through the blanket of sleet I could just about make out the shadowy forms of humans moving about on the ship, their voices appealing for calm, but the dogs' frenzy was intensifying with every new spattering of blood. Suddenly, a

84

splash quelled the hysteria, but only momentarily, for someone yelled "dog overboard!" and the barking and yelping began anew, with the men now shouting with increased concern. I pointed towards the commotion.

"Dogs?"

"Ah, ye dinnae understand. I speak slow for thee. Hae ye seen me cat? She ran away."

"No, sorry. I've seen no cat. I must go now." Even if I had seen it, I'm not sure I would have helped him or his cat. I still hadn't forgiven him for taking my job, and I had no intention of looking for any cat.

"Ach, I'm scunnered. It's a dreich day! Off wi thee, then."

He left me, making strange noises through pursed lips as he resumed the search for Mrs Chippy. I was quite pleased to have reasonably got through the baffling conversation.

The whaling vessel, a two-masted, square-rigged steam brig named the *Sandefjord*, was similar in size to the *Endurance*. I didn't like these ships. For me, a ship should be either a sailing ship or a steam ship, but not some hybrid version of both. This boat did not benefit from modern steam ship design, which made them far less likely to capsize than sailing ships. In addition, upwind, this boat would use up more fuel than a steam ship because of the increased wind resistance. It would also be slower because of all the coal needed to power the engines, and it would still have the high maintenance and expenses of a steam ship. I relayed my misgivings to Lars, who laughed in response.

"She's got a powerful harpoon on the bow. That's all that matters. We're hunting whales, not entering a beauty contest."

I helped the men carry supplies and various equipment onto the ship, some of which was standard for all expeditions: a wooden keg for drinking water; bread; tobacco; a sextant; lanterns and a piggin to bail out water. However, some of it was specific to whaling, and Lars explained the purpose of each one.

"That piggin there is also used to wet the line attached to the whale. Those beasts can move pretty fast, and the friction can

85

cause the rope to smoke. That thing is a dragging float, to make it harder for the whale to swim. And if that doesn't work, we use this," he said, holding up a spear-like object. "It's a fluke lance, to sever the tendons in the whale's tail so it can't swim away, and it cuts a nice neat hole which we can use to tow it back."

I pointed to five large wooden tubs. "What's in there?"

"Ah, each one contains three hundred metres of hemp line, perfectly packed so it uncoils without kinks. If you get your leg trapped in that rope when the harpoon's in the whale, then you'd better start praying. And these," he added, "don't need any explanation." He pointed to a jumbled collection of knives, spears, harpoons, hatchets and barbs dumped on the deck. "You can sort them out. And after that, be sure to put those supplies in each lifeboat, and secure them tightly," he said, indicating three heavy-looking chests.

"What's in them?"

"Rations, drinking water, sextant, compass, flares. You know, the kind of thing you need in lifeboats. It doesn't hurt to be prepared. While you're at it, check the boats are in order."

This task kept me occupied. In one boat, the canvas had been blown partially off by the wind. After putting the chest in, I secured the canvas. In another boat, I noticed one oar was missing, so I had to locate another. In the third boat, someone had left some flesh to rot. I almost gagged clearing it up. In addition to these jobs, it also took me a while to heave the chests into the three lifeboats. My outward appearance may have resembled a young man, just about, but I couldn't fool my muscles into believing they were manly. However, what I lacked in physical capacity, I made up for in mental strength, and I managed to lift all the chests into the lifeboats. Besides, I cheated a bit; I emptied them first.

Eventually we weighed anchor and set off at low speed, leaving the sheltered King Edward Cove, past the stationary *Endurance* and out into Cumberland Bay. The rugged Barff Peninsula, with its many coves and icy crags, stretched its long arm starboard side.

86

We reached its northernmost point, the *Sandefjord* swung around the headland, turned southeast into the open ocean, and, when the order was given to hoist the sails, the main and foresails were raised and braced to capture the westerly wind. Although I didn't think much of these ships, to be on one in full sail was a breathtaking experience, and, despite the medium swell, we skimmed away from the peninsula and across the ocean as if it were a sheet of glass.

The hunt began immediately. Lars told me to be a barrelman. I assumed this had something to do with beer and asked him where the barrels were kept. He pointed skyward.

"Up there. The barrelman stands in a barrel and looks out for whales," he explained.

Fortunately, the days of standing in barrels were over; it was now a slightly more purpose-built construction known as a crow's nest, which to me sounded even worse. I had to accompany a seasoned sailor to the top of the foremast, climb into the crow's nest, some twenty metres above the deck, and scan the ocean for signs of the tell-tale plume of vapour caused by a whale breathing. Heights did not overly concern me, but being in a basket sitting on top of a long mast, on a boat rising and falling with the ocean swell, pitching to one side and the next as waves crunched against the ship's side, and with chilly sleet sharpened by a biting wind stinging my face, I very quickly desired to return to the deck again. However, I kept my thoughts to myself, and gripped with white knuckles on to the basket's railing and tried to look through the sleet as best as I could – my hope of joining Shackleton's expedition hinged on my ability to endure the trials at sea.

We were up there for two hours, at the end of which my body was numb with cold. Not once did we spot anything resembling a whale, or any other kind of life apart from some large skuas which took offence at our ship and flew angrily towards my head, causing me to duck and fear falling from the crow's nest. One of them decided to rest on a spar, from where it looked crossly at us before flying off again. I couldn't even say that the harsh conditions were made more tolerable by the company of the sailor I was with, for the only conversation I had with him during those two hours lasted just a few minutes, during which I managed to extricate from him that we were heading towards the South Sandwich Islands, where a few volcanic islands attracted an assortment of wildlife, both on land and in the sea, and it was often a good place to find whales. I didn't even find out his name.

Lars kept me busy all day, scrubbing, inspecting the sails and rigging, and, when he found out I could use a sextant, double-checking our position with this instrument. For my willingness to work and my versatility, I was quickly accepted as one of the company, and the men dubbed me 'Willi Wunderkind' as I seemed capable in so many areas. No-one cared I was new, no-one cared I was (apparently) German, and no-one knew I was really female. I was enjoying myself.

The ocean was kind to us, too, for these could be the most dangerous seas on the planet, and within an instant a storm could descend upon a ship and overwhelm it. Before we turned in for the night, the whalers related many tales about their encounters with waves as large as mountains and comrades they had seen swept overboard, never to be found again. These bedtime tales did not help me get to sleep, but at least they kept the men occupied and allowed me to pretend to doze off fully clothed. Later, when everyone was snoring like hogs, I changed into a fresh set of clothes, ready for the next day.

I was put to work in the *Sandefjord's* crow's nest at first light, which at this time of the year was very early indeed, at about three in the morning. My untalkative companion reached new levels of taciturnity under the grey skies of the South Atlantic dawn. My initial greeting was repelled with a grunt, and any further comment received no acknowledgement at all. I set about the business of scanning for whales.

About halfway through our shift I spotted them – whales up ahead on the horizon. The silent Norwegian was looking the other way so I tapped him excitedly on the shoulder.

"Look! Look! Over there!" I pointed. "Whales!"

The sailor turned around, followed my finger, then looked back at me with such disdain that I might as well have been a smear of skua dropping that he'd rather wipe away. He continued his unsociable watch astern.

"But... whales... isn't that what we're supposed to be looking for?" I despaired.

"Hmm."

I glanced again at the whales. They were still there; several of them. "But..." I gestured forlornly at the opportunity that might be swimming away.

"They're islands, you fool."

Of course they were. He'd even told me we were heading towards them. Now I wished only to crawl into a hole and pull a large slab over me to cover my embarrassment. But there was nowhere to hide; there was never anywhere to escape among this crew of men. It sometimes felt like a choking, stifling oppression, following me everywhere. Now, on top of a stick over twenty metres in the air, my humiliation couldn't have been more exposed.

I looked glumly at the islands for five minutes, hating them, hating whales, hating the person next to me. I didn't even care what his real name was now, for in a fit of petulance I had decided to call him James Moody. It was the name of a sailor who had come to the Alexandra every now and then. Unfortunately for James he was assigned to the *Titanic*. James was nice and luckless, but for his surname would live on in my grumpy companion.

Then I *did* see them. A group of whales, their backs slipping in and out of the sea, probably one nautical mile away. There could be no doubt, yet still I hesitated to disclose my find. James Moody turned around and spotted them immediately.

89

"They're whales!" he exclaimed excitedly. "Let me see…" He leaned forward, as if the thirty centimetres he gained in this manner would make all the difference. "Ahh! Minke whales!" he asserted with confidence. Apparently those thirty centimetres *were* significant. "There she blows!" he bellowed, stretching a sea-weathered finger towards the whales I had been the first to see.

His shout immediately drew the attention of the men below. Several of them ran to the railings; Lars ran to the foremast and called up to us. "Where is it? What is it?"

"Two miles leeward. Minke whale pod," yelled Moody back down to him.

Lars barked instructions, men appeared from everywhere, scurrying around like disturbed ants, then, without a word Moody sprang out of the basket and, holding on to a rope, glided skilfully down to the deck. I presumed my job was done, and with a little more circumspection in my descent, joined the frenzied crew below.

Without knowing quite what I should do, I decided to join Lars at the bow. He was already priming the harpoon gun, a formidable steel weapon, over a metre high and over twice as long. The battle scars of flaking blue paint on the heavy cannon and the sturdy metal mounting were testament to many encounters with the giants of the sea we were now chasing.

"Ah, Willi. You can help. This gun's set up for larger whales. I've got to get this harpoon out and put one of those smaller ones in. Give me a hand, will you?"

He passed me the harpoon shaft he had just removed. It was as tall as a man, and by my reckoning weighed almost as much, too. It very nearly knocked me from my feet as I took its full weight, and I struggled to secure it among the others on the ground. As if it were as light as a matchstick, Lars picked up a shorter shaft. It was still a fearsome looking missile, as tall as me, the arrowhead as long as my forearm, with four hideously hinged barbs, wired to slice and anchor onto the prey when the arrow exploded into its

90

body. With practised skill, Lars loaded the gun, fixed a rope into a groove that ran down the length of the shaft, slid the rope down to the front and secured it. The gun was ready to fire.

With sail and steam, the *Sandefjord* was closing in on the whales fast. The bow wave swelled before us, a mass of rushing water clearing a path through which the ship could charge towards the creatures, still oblivious to the hulk bearing down upon them. Lars had the pod in his sights; now he had to fix his aim on just one of the whales. He trained the gun on his target, bent his knees and turned his head to the side to speak to me.

"You have to strike before they gally and sound!" he shouted. I had no idea what he was talking about.

"Okay!" I shouted back.

He faced forward. I could see the tension bristling in his shoulders. "Now!" he yelled.

An explosive charge propelled the harpoon forward, the rope trailing, twisting in its wake. The missile slammed into a whale's side, and instantly the sea around the creature reddened with gushing blood. Lars whooped in delight, but then cursed just as loudly.

"The others are diving. Quick, get another harpoon!"

I heaved one from the pile and dragged it to him. Within a few moments Lars loaded, trained and fired the gun again. Another direct hit. "Gunner Anderson does it again!" Lars fist-pumped the air.

The whale-line attached to the harpoons fizzed past me as the two Minke whales rolled and writhed, tugged and struggled, desperately trying to pull away. They were like two husky dogs, harnessed by cruel spears through their guts to a mobile slaughterhouse, pulling it along while blood seeped into the cold around them. The whales' fight to survive lasted far longer than I cared to watch. Their energy drained into the grey sea, yet still they battled to escape the monstrous colossus *Sandefjord*, which could move faster through the ocean, attack with outrageously more powerful weapons and hold on with unnatural force. It was a contest the whales could not win.

I turned away, just as a kink in the whale-line shot from the large wooden tub, coiled around Lars's ankle, and yanked him with terrible velocity from the ship and into the ocean. I screamed for help and rushed to the railings. Lars was in the foaming sea, his body dashing above and below the water. With each fleeting break to the surface he wrestled with the rope, perhaps trying to free his foot, perhaps trying just to grab on to it. Men joined me and grasped the situation immediately.

"Don't let go of the rope!" yelled one to him.

Suddenly, I realised the danger. If he freed himself, he would tumble into the sea, the *Sandefjord* would be on him in an instant and he would be crushed. However, if the whales dived, or sank, he would have no choice but to let go.

"Get the whales!" shouted Lars back, his determined voice rising above the din of the calamity.

Even more men rushed around, the sails were swiftly lowered, and someone bellowed the full astern command, to bring the ship to an emergency stop. The effect on our propulsion was immediate, yet still the *Sandefjord's* momentum carried it forward for many agonising minutes. I was pushed away from the bow while two more men hastened to load the harpoon gun. They didn't bother attaching the rope, firing the deadly spears within just a few feet of their stricken comrade. Two, three, four harpoons flew past Lars and ruptured through the whales' flesh, each one blasting a new gruesome hole into their bodies.

The thrashing of the whales eventually stopped and soon after the *Sandefjord* stopped, too. The hunt was over. Grinning like a naughty child as he scrambled up a ladder which had been lowered over the side, Lars ordered for their catch to be reeled in. The great bodies were winched from the sea and dumped on deck, just as some killer whales were beginning to gather.

"These are small, what, maybe seven and a half, or eight metres long; but a good start," stated Lars as he removed one harpoon and inspected the shaft as if nothing had happened. "We'll start processing them here and chuck the waste into the sea." He called one of the men over. "Show Willi how to strip the blubber." Lars gave me a comradely slap on the back, which nearly took the wind from me. "Good fun, eh?"

54°28' South, 36°51' West

I was desperate to hear Lars's tale, as
he was to hear mine, and he suggested we walk to Gull Lake, just
a ten-minute stroll from Grytviken, to avoid being interrupted.
The lake, Lars told me, had recently been purchased by a German
entrepreneur and was rapidly undergoing development as a
tourist attraction, with an ice-cream stall, beer hall and water
rides all planned. It was a far cry from the bloody whaling station I
remembered.

We sat down on a rock and absent-mindedly observed the
builders at work. Before we talked about his escape from
Elephant Island, I simply had to know how Albert was saving the
world. I had been in contact with my eccentric friend for all these
years, through the radio I had found on Deception Island, and not
once had he mentioned anything remotely akin to such global
heroics.

"That hill there is called Brown Mountain," said Lars, indicating
the low peak which overlooked the lake. "In the winter, when I
worked here, it was covered with snow."

"What's that got to do with Albert Einstein?"

"Everything. While you've been away, the ice has been
retreating all over the world. You must have noticed it yourself.
That hill will probably never have snow on it again. Its name
announces as clearly as anything else how much things have
changed." I nodded thoughtfully, recalling how my icy prison for
thirty years had indeed changed over that time. "Well, Einstein
and some other scientists identified the cause, and determined to
do something about it, before the whole world floods."

"Due to the melting snow?" I asked.

"Exactly. You see, for years Einstein had been lamenting the destruction of the natural world. Then in the 1930s a movement began in Germany, and one of its key concepts was the need for *Lebensraum*, or living space. By this time it was clear that the seas were rising, so our living space was shrinking. These people, the Nazis, offered a solution."

"What was it?"

"Reduce the number of people. It tied in quite closely with what Einstein had been preaching for at least a decade. He teamed up with them and developed some pretty radical ways to achieve that goal."

"Like what?"

"By getting rid of the most unproductive people. Have you seen how in Grytviken everyone looks athletic?"

"No, I've not really noticed it. But now that you mention it, yes, I suppose they do," I admitted. "But you can't just *get rid* of people. No-one would allow it."

"You'd be surprised. And, well, let's just say that those who disagreed with the Nazis, and there were many – the Norwegians, the French, the British, the Americans, to name just a few – they soon learned that opposing Einstein was not a very clever thing to do."

As we gazed upon the barren, brown mountain, overlooking the glittering teal lake, Lars told me what happened next. Death, destruction, devastation on an unimaginable scale. The earth was being saved, I thought, but what about its people? What had happened to my kind and gentle Albert? Lars continued his harrowing narrative. The very sky had wept with a torrent of falling bombs, obliterating the people below. Millions upon millions of lives lost; men blasted into fragments, women and children slaughtered; communities, towns, cities wiped out. I could barely hear any more. With tears streaming down my face, I ran away from this appalling revelation, ran up the bare mountain and, when I reached the summit, I fell to the ground, my tears seeping into the dry earth beneath me.

On board the *Sandefjord* in 1914, we had our own gory battle to
contend with, namely trying not to fall overboard as a result of
slipping on the blood and bile oozing from the two whales.

The crew crawled all over the carcasses, like flies on a half-eaten
piece of fruit, and made short work of butchering the animals.
The blubber was stripped, the baleen removed, the bones
collected, and the meat harvested. When they were done, the
sloppy rest was cast into the sea for the hungry killer whales to
feast on. My job was to scrub the deck clean again, and soon the
Sandefjord set sail westward to scour the seas for even larger
prey.

The wind, having picked up in strength, had inched around to
the northwest, and was driving straight into my face as I took
watch in the crow's nest with Moody. Just as the previous day, an
annoying skua harried us for ten minutes or more, flashing white
streaks on the ends of its wings with each indignant sortie, before
taking up residence on the same spar on the mainmast, from
where it glared at us with beady eyes. I concluded, quite
arbitrarily, that it was the same bird who was visiting us, and

decided to name it Carmen. This wasn't intended as a slight to my erstwhile friend in Switzerland, rather the bird's brown plumage reminded me of Carmen's hair, and in any case I was almost thankful for the bird's appearance, for at least she provided a distraction from the freezing monotony of my task.

The quartering sea was steadily rising, fuelled by a waxing wind. Carmen probably wished she had not joined us, for now she was far from land in a gale against which even her strong wings would not prevail. She swooped down from the spar to take shelter somewhere on the ship. I was looking forward to the same after my watch had ended, but my new assignment provided no relief from the weather, as I was ordered to stay on deck to clean, check and sharpen the tools earlier used to kill and butcher the whales. I am not sure why I couldn't have done this inside, but there were many things about sailors I didn't understand. After that we had to check the rigging and the sails for possible wear or tear, as they had been lowered in such haste to save Lars, but all was found to be in order. The day seemed to drag interminably, and my body ached for rest. I assumed that the increasing gloom above me was the ascent of night, a signal for the end of my chores. However, the skies deceived me, for they stubbornly clung on to the light, as, I later discovered, they always did at this time of year. They were not being blackened by approaching nightfall, rather by dark and threatening storm clouds.

The captain was as loathe to be caught in a powerful storm as any of us were and set a broad reach course, heading directly south. The wind was increasing to gale force, driving the Sandefjord onward, away from the threat behind us, but straight down the throat of a new danger lurking further south: icebergs.

They emerged dotted along the horizon, scattered haphazardly like a unit of soldiers in disarray. They bobbed up and down with the swell, and while we were fleeing the storm to the north, the icebergs were far off to the south and posed no immediate threat. Yet in no time at all these giants of the South Atlantic were upon us, some seemingly singling us out for a ship-destroying

97

charge. To press further south into this mêlée would have been lunacy, and the captain changed tack to escape it.

On rotating iceberg watch and with the sails once again lowered so as not to impede our progress, we steamed westwards all through the night, skimming a fine line between the destructive violence of a powerful storm and that of the column of bergs. We prayed these forces would not unite. Sometimes the icebergs seemed to be going one way, then all of a sudden, as if under the sway of some drunken pilot or despotic divinity, they altered course, forcing us to steer one way or the other in order to avoid a collision. With the constant meandering of the ship, the heavy swell, the whistling winds and the necessary vigil we all had to share, none of us had much sleep.

Fortunately, the following day brought a slight improvement in the weather, although the *Sandefjord* now found itself far away from its intended hunting ground, and lone wandering icebergs continued to terrorise the ship. Lars told me that our new course would be to head just a little further west, for we were now not too far away from the South Orkney Islands. After that we would head back north to South Georgia and might intercept any whale crossing the Drake Passage.

The swell was heavy and the wind, now sharpened by a biting chill, was still strong, yet I had to resume my post with Moody in the crow's nest. I didn't expect the lack of sleep to have made him any chattier, and I was correct in this assumption. Carmen braved the conditions and materialised from some hidden place to settle on her spar on the mainmast. She didn't attack us this time, although I was sure this was more due to the strong gusts deterring offensive intentions rather than a change of heart towards us. Nevertheless, I had come prepared for her this time, and when Moody's eyes were fixed on some distant spot on the open sea, I threw some pieces of bread to her. She caught them on the wing brilliantly and returned to her spar to gobble the snack down.

For a couple of days very little happened on the *Sandefjord*. The gales had largely blown themselves out, the sun had dispersed all but the most stubborn of the drab clouds, and in the relatively calm conditions we ate, slept, set sail, washed the deck, stood watch, checked the harpoons, prepared the whale-lines, and generally found tasks to keep ourselves busy. I didn't mind the chores at all, as they kept me out of the cramped crew's quarters which by the hour accumulated fresh filth, grease, rotting food, smoke, and other foul compounds emitted from the sailors' bodies. When I had a spare moment, and when no-one was around, I tried to give the cabin a quick clean, but it was rather like trying to hold back the sea: no sooner had I brought a semblance of order to our shared space, than another grubby wave of squalor would roll through it all.

I was now trusted to be in the crow's nest alone; James Moody had evidently put in a good word for me. I thought about changing his name in light of this development, but decided against it as he was no more charming on deck as he was on top of the foremast. It was a cold, long but strangely fulfilling task which I looked forward to, and I regularly took on extra shifts. Most of all, I enjoyed watching and interacting with the skua, Carmen. Her plumage fascinated me: soft and speckled brown; her wings were like an Indian chieftain's war bonnet – at once delicate and intricate, while streaks of gleaming white flashed innate confidence, provoking the world to notice her. When I called out to her, she responded with squawking sonances which I convinced myself were some attempts at communication, and I even engaged in conversation, but only when I was sure that nobody was looking. She never failed to fly to her lofty perch when I was there, and I never once heard the other sailors mention her. I didn't talk about these encounters either, for fear they would readily add her to a stew, but quite where she was lodged when she was not on the spar I never knew, for she disappeared like sea spray when she grew tired of scowling or squawking at me.

99

While on whale watch, I thought I spotted a monstrous iceberg up ahead, still several miles away. I warned those on deck. However, and a little to my embarrassment, the mass I had seen was in fact the South Orkney Islands. There was no danger of them drifting into us, and our captain was quite capable of steering around them, I was told by some laughing shipmates.

As the never-setting sun reached its zenith, we crossed over the circle of latitude that marks the northernmost border of the Southern Ocean, the sixtieth parallel south, and our passage was heralded almost instantaneously with a thunderous boom from ranks of dark clouds banked on the white horizon further to the south. The seamen, wary of portentous omens, exchanged nervous glances. However, to the north, west and east, the weather was fair, so there was little reason for immediate concern.

The captain decided to take us around the group of islands, in the hope that, as with the South Sandwich Islands, the food-rich waters in the coastal regions would draw the whales. That hunch seemed to be upheld when, from my elevated position, I was certain that further to the west and not far from the land I had mistakenly believed to be icebergs, a sparkling reddish-brown swell heaved within an otherwise grey blanket of sea under the bright sun. This could be indication of huge swarms of krill; and where krill gathered, whales would feast. The *Sandefjord* steamed towards the patch of water.

There was no doubt that the sea was teeming with an abundance of krill, and before we could reach the area, other wildlife were already dining on the bonanza. From the air, packs of cormorants were launching from sheer sixty-metre ice cliffs, dive-bombing with terrific speed; from shingle beaches and rocky outcrops, Adélie penguins were catapulting themselves clumsily into the sea, then ejecting with colossal velocity to thump, fully fed, back on land; from the sea, leopard seals patrolled the waters, the younger ones gorging on the hapless krill while the larger ones thrashed the bodies of penguins unfortunate enough to be seized by sharp seal jaws. The *Sandefjord* stood off, waiting for its prey to arrive at the dinner party.

It was an astonishing display, one which Carmen flew off to see and probably also participate in. I was sorry to see her go. Yet it captivated the remaining audience on the ship for only a short time; they soon grew restless at the no-show of the expected star of the spectacle. For several hours we all waited, long after the natural marvel was over, anchored to our anticipation that the long days might end with some reward. But there was to be no such dividend; no whale came, and soon we had our eyes on an even larger concern. The dark clouds from the south had drawn closer; the wind was whipping up the ocean; we had another storm to evade.

It was a strange feeling; we went in an instant from being the all-powerful observer, lying in wait to pounce on our unsuspecting quarry, to being the hunted, chased by a force so powerful it could drive winds faster than we could run and hurl giant waves over our masts. Our only option was to flee.

The storm was coming from a southeasterly direction, so the captain took the ship further west, aiming to turn northwards once we had rounded the South Orkney Islands. The captain did not see, at this stage, the need for extra steam power to aid our flight, as the wind was in our sails, and he was confident of outrunning this latest threat. In any case we still had to be wary of icebergs, for just to the south in the Weddell Sea we could see the contours of the unusually thick icepack that was, so far, delaying the *Endurance*, and chunks of floating ice, some as large as houses, had wandered this far north, impeding any speedy retreat.

We skirted past the southern coasts of the islands with ease, and brilliant blue skies welcomed us as the *Sandefjord* turned northwards after passing the western tip of Coronation Island and began to sail towards South Georgia. I felt a surge of pride in my achievements over the last few days and was looking forward to returning to Grytviken where Lars could tell Shackleton about my usefulness. The Norwegian whaler had told me that my industry and readiness to learn had not only impressed him, but the rest of the crew too. He even said that I could stay with them on South Georgia, if Fridtjof Jacobsen agreed.

"But you have to relax a bit. The men have said that you cover yourself up day and night. Maybe it's a German thing, but we're all men here, Willi. If you're going to make a good whaler, then you've got to get used to being one of the boys."

I said that he was right, it was a German thing. I said I would try to fit in next time. I only had to get through a few more days of my deception, then, if all went well, I would soon be a fully-fledged member of the Imperial Trans-Antarctic Expedition and, once I was on the *Endurance* with no possibility of turning back, I would reveal myself. Not literally, of course.

"There she blows!" screamed the barrelman from the crow's nest. Suddenly, the storm to the south was forgotten, and the crew saw their chance of making a killing. The barrelman cupped his hands to his mouth and shouted down to the deck. "Due west, in a direct line to the Inaccessible Islands. Four miles or so. It's a blue whale, I'm sure. And a massive one at that. Only a huge whale can produce a spout that high!"

With such a prize within reach, there was no question of heading back up through the Drake Passage just yet. The *Sandefjord* swung its nose to the west, and the chase was on. Just a short time later, we reached the spot where the whale had last been seen. The barrelman scanned the ocean; I was sent up to join him. Lars said my younger, sharper eyes might be better able to discern the traces of a blue whale swimming near the surface: the column of mushrooming vapour; the long body, gently breaching the water; the small, triangular dorsal fin towards the back of the whale; or, if we were lucky, a slap of the tail which would alert us all to its whereabouts. The two of us in the crow's nest, and dozens of pairs of eyes peering over the railings on both sides of the ship scoured the ocean for any one of these signs. But there was nothing.

After ten minutes or so, Lars called up to us. "Which direction was it going?"

"How should I know," shouted the seaman back down to him. "It was miles away."

"There!" I called. "Did you see that? A spray of water behind those rocks?" I pointed to the Inaccessible Islands.

No-one had seen it. Those on deck could probably not see beyond the remote precipitous islands some five miles away, and the man next to me had been looking the other way. But I was certain that I had seen a tiny spray just to the side of the islands. After a moment's hesitation, the order was given to head further west.

The closer we drew to the islands, the more doubtful I grew that I had indeed seen a spout of water. The sea was growing increasingly heavy, and it could just as easily have been waves crashing against the rocks. However, I kept my misgivings to myself, and we pressed on, past the islands, for another ten miles or so.

"This is normal," said Lars, climbing up to the crow's nest. It was very cramped with the three of us inside. "It's as if the whales are playing some kind of cat and mouse game with us. The beast's sure to be out there somewhere. Keep your eyes peeled."

The only thing my eyes saw, however, was the approaching storm. A squally wind was now blowing through the sails, thrashing them with such force that the sailors had to shout to be heard. Every now and then Lars or the other sailor shouted "There!" or "Over there!" or "There it is!" and the ship would adjust its direction slightly. As soon as we thought we were practically on top of it, the whale would appear some two miles away and the chase began again. This game of cat and mouse, or ship and whale, or life and death, whatever it might be called, drew us away from the South Orkney Islands, far into a night in which the sun refused to sleep.

I imagined our ship as one element in a predacious chain: the whales hunting the krill; the *Sandefjord* chasing the whale; the

103

storm pursuing us; what monstrous entity would be behind the tempest, driving it with such ferocity across the sea? Onwards we pressed in this arrangement, for three or four hundred miles, skirting the northern boundary of the Southern Ocean, the sky gradually darkening with black and grey clouds. It was not a place to engage in games, yet the further westwards we sailed, the closer the storm approached, and the edgier my nerves grew.

I wasn't the only one feeling anxious. As a precaution, the captain ordered us to batten down the hatches, secure all the doors and stow away any loose equipment. The fore-course and main-course sails were furled, and for a while we combined both the hunt for the whale and the flight from the storm by harnessing the wind in the topsails. But it was clear that we were neither going to evade the storm, nor catch the whale, and our attention shifted solely to the tempest bearing down upon us. The large waves pushed the ship around, and there was real danger they would slew us broadside, so the captain swung the *Sandefjord* around to face the storm, enabling us to move at slow steam into the oncoming waves. The remaining sails were lowered, leaving only the jib at the front of the boat because the waves crashing over the *Sandefjord* precluded any possibility of furling it now.

Within just a few hours the ocean world around us had taken on a very different and very menacing character. The sun had been completely routed, as the clear blue heavens in which it had sat so blissfully to the north had now been entirely overwhelmed by a rushing pack of angry clouds. Their lumpy, jagged formations heaved and surged, like an upended ethereal mountain range in the genesis of creation, the entire billowing rank electrified by streaks of lightning. The sea rose to the intimidation from the skies by transforming to liquid onyx, unleashing huge waves from the bottomless abyss beneath us and hurling breakers, their crests seething with white fury, to fracture over the deck of the *Sandefjord*. Not to be outdone, the wind raged through the ship, screaming like a frenzied banshee across the deck, buffeting the masts and ripping off the jib, carrying it far across the ocean.

The sailors began to strap themselves to their beds, so I did the same; it was the only way to avoid being flung from one side of the cabin to the other. At times the ship rose almost vertically as we rode up the face of an enormous wave, then raced down the other side into a trough, and we were plunged into watery darkness as the sea engulfed us. Each time I thought that this would be our final moment, yet each time the *Sandefjord* sprang back out again, to face another daunting onslaught. To reduce the speed of our descent down the waves, the captain ordered the ship to hove-to, and the engines were reduced to dead slow, providing just enough power to steer the ship into the wind and waves.

We were barely in command of the vessel, our hopes and fears rising and falling with the vagaries of the unpredictable storm. The men tried their best to maintain a sense of control as the ship toiled on the ocean: some compared the experience to previous adventures; some told jokes; but whatever they said, their words were invariably swallowed by the deafening slam of a giant wave or a stomach-churning pitch to the side, when the ship seemed certain to keel over. I remained silent throughout.

Suddenly, it all stopped, as if a dancing, hissing candle flame had been extinguished by an arbitrary breeze; the howling, the pounding, the yawing was stifled in an instant.

"It's over," sighed one of the men.

"Or..." began another. Then *Sandefjord* began to climb. "No..." he added. His dread, everyone's dread, had become real. We were mounting a wave so monstrous, the very wind hid in fear behind it. Higher we ascended, the ship almost vertical. We would surely be flung back down the face of it any moment, tossed and smashed and scattered about the ocean.

In these fleeting seconds I thought of my father, of Albert, of Carmen, of all the men I had met in Hull and all the crew of the *Endurance* and the *Sandefjord*. I had felt restricted, limited,

105

governed by many of these people in one way or another, and in particular since arriving in South Georgia. I looked at my body, my weak, masked body and felt a sense of shame for the mimicry of the life I had led. This person who was about to perish was not me. At least in these final moments, as we rode a giant wave to heaven's vaults, I screamed to be myself.

"I'm Marianna!" I yelled.

As the final tremor of my proclamation still vibrated through the cabin, the *Sandefjord's* bow pitched forward and for an instant the ship was perfectly level. The wood creaked and groaned; we held our breaths. Then the inevitable; the ship leant forward and slingshot down the back of this liquid leviathan. We hurtled with unimaginable speed to the depths, to our doom, bracing ourselves for impact.

It came far sooner than expected. Foamy seawater smashed through the glass window of our cabin door. If we had not been strapped to our beds we would surely have been swept away; as it was, we were tied to our fates, drowning in our beds as icy cold water swirled and roiled around us. I fought against all temptation to release myself; I knew that would spell the end. As quickly as it had surged in, the water rushed back out of the window. I saw a flash of colour drift past me – a leg, I think, of some poor sailor who had either freed himself or had been pulled from his tethers – the sea had taken him as a small reward for its onslaught.

I'm not sure how the *Sandefjord* managed to come up for air once more, but rise to the top of the ocean she did, battered and broken. We had no time to process our condition, as suddenly the door to the cabin swung open and sea spray carried on a whistling gale showered us all. Lars, barely able to keep his footing, grasped on to the door, water dripping from his face, his eyes wide in alarm.

"Out! Out! Out!" he screamed. "She's going down!"

The men didn't need a second warning. They scrambled to unstrap themselves and raced out of the cabin. I was the slowest, and last to leave, but throughout Lars clung on to the door, one arm hooked through the broken window, until he saw me safely exit.

With the squally gusts and powerful waves lashing the *Sandefjord*, it was treacherous enough to be out in the open, but with the ship listing heavily and the wet surfaces icing over in places that could not even be seen, scrambling to the lifeboats was akin to running a gauntlet of death. I am sorry to say I saw several men slip to their doom.

Lars and I reached one of the two lifeboats on the port side; due to the pitch of the *Sandefjord*, this was the safer side from which to launch the boats. It seemed as if the entire crew were here. The men had already torn away the protective canvas on the lifeboats. Lars took one look at them and barked a command. "There's too many of you. You five, come with me. We'll take the other boat." Without looking around, he raced off to the opposite side of the ship.

The men he had spoken to either ignored him, or in the screeching gale had not even heard him, for they continued to prepare the two lifeboats. I took my chances with Lars. More than once my foot slipped and I was in danger of sliding from the ship and into the sea; more than once the Southern Ocean hurled its raw weapons at me, battering rams of immense power, attempting to drag me into the depths; but I held on to anything I could grab – dangling halyards, fallen spars, even flapping fragments of fabric which offered only the smallest service. They all helped to keep me on the ship, keep my footing, keep myself upright, and allow me eventually to reach the starboard side. By the time I arrived at the lifeboat, Lars had already removed the cover and security wire and rigged the bowsing gear to hold the lifeboat in place. Now he was throwing bags of coal into the boat.

"Where are the others?" he shouted, raising his voice above the tempestuous din.

"I'm the only one," I yelled in reply.

He looked behind me. "Get in!" he ordered.

I jumped into the boat; Lars waited a few moments more, concluded no-one else was coming and that our time was running out, then lifted the winch brake and, as the lifeboat lowered itself into the icy sea below, sprang aboard. We hit the choppy seas with a jaw-jarring jolt. He unhooked all the lines attaching us to the doomed *Sandefjord* and instructed me to row hard away from the ship.

"Row as if your life depends on it," he said, "because it does."

I was surprised to see that the wooden
church was still standing, exactly where it had been when I had last been in Grytviken. Whereas before it had stood on open ground behind the factory, it was now surrounded by apartment blocks and the shore had migrated to within a few metres of the steeple tower.

My accommodation was the very same room I had shared with Karl Jacobsen, in the *Slotte*. I think Kapitän Ritscher had somehow arranged this; the irony of it seemed to appeal to his humour. However, although it was the same villa, it was not in the same location. Years ago it had been disassembled, plank by plank, and reconstructed further up the foothills. Apparently, the Jacobsen family had not relocated with it, and the house was now occupied by officers and their guests. In fact, the family that had warmly taken me in had completely disappeared.

I asked around to find out what had become of them all: Fridtjof, his wife Klara, Karl, baby Solveig, and the other children, whose names I could not remember. But no-one seemed to know; the whole family had simply vanished soon after the Germans had arrived. Only Lars could shed a little light on the mystery, telling me the rumour was that they had all gone to work in some kind of factory in Europe after there had been an argument over the conduct of services in the church. It seemed to me like an extreme reaction to a disagreement. I decided to ask Kapitän Ritscher about it.

We were sitting at the same wooden table in the same kitchen where Fridtjof had given me akvavit and the delicious flatbread. This time, I was offered a colourless, tasteless spirit called Korn and a plate of salty sticks. I preferred Norwegian hospitality.

"The Jacobsens. Yes, that was unfortunate," said Ritscher, swirling the ice cubes around in his glass.

"What was unfortunate?"

"Well, I think you've seen for yourself the trouble the world is in. We Germans can't fight the battle against the earth on our own."

"What do you mean, against the earth?"

"You know what I mean. We have more people, we need more space, and that is one thing the earth is taking from us. If we don't all pull together, then there is no hope for us. For *any* of us. The Jacobsens... they weren't willing to do what was necessary. They saw things... differently." He chomped on a salt stick.

"How did they see things, then?"

"They looked to God for salvation. You know, even when the very church they helped to build was in danger of being overrun by the sea, they still put their faith in prayer. They were unhelpful, to put it mildly. There was no need for them here."

"So they left?"

"Yes. Maybe God can help them in their new residence." Kapitän Ritscher downed his drink and set the glass on the table.

Prayer was all we were left with, helplessly exposed on the Southern Ocean. Rowing seemed ludicrously ineffective as our small boat was shoved from one wave to the next. However, Lars insisted we keep at it, despite the wind and rain lashing our faces and making it almost impossible to keep our eyes open. We had to keep facing the oncoming waves, he told me.

Now I understood why Lars had laden the boat with bags of coal. It was to act as ballast, to try to keep our boat stable in the heavy seas. Yet it was still dangerously unsteady, tottering up one wave and careering down the other side like an out-of-control cart. With draining energy and hands numb with cold, I grasped on tightly to the oars, forcing them through the water in the hope I was making some difference. A thumping wave struck us broadside, and our boat spun around just as another wave began to drag us up to its crest. We were moments from being rolled, but somehow, be it through luck or the vigour of our efforts, we managed to turn the bow.

"This can't go on!" yelled Lars. He pulled his oars into the boat, so I started to do the same. "No, keep rowing!" he ordered. "I'm going to deploy the sea anchor." Lars crouched down to his haunches and reached under the rear seat. "What the...?" He turned around to me. "There's a sodding dog under the seat!"

"What?"

"A dog. Is it yours?" he asked.

"What on earth are you talking about?"

Lars grumbled something about having to deal with the mutt later, then rummaged around under the seat and retrieved the sea anchor. Another heavy wave rocked the boat, knocking Lars over; he banged his head painfully.

"Are you al...?" I began.

"No!" he blasted, picking up the sea anchor and treading past me to the bow.

With practised proficiency, Lars threw the trip line into the sea from the bow, and a few moments later tossed the parachute-shaped anchor after it. The effect on the boat was instantaneous.

111

As if a calming hand had been placed around the vessel, we ceased veering to the whims of the sea; the sea anchor held us rigid, headlong into each wave.

This did not mean the danger was over; this did not mean we no longer battled with every swirling second, bailing out water in a Sisyphean struggle to stay afloat; but it did mean we felt a surge of hope, and this hope gave heat to our cold and tired bodies. It was impossible to know how long we fought with the sea; just a few minutes lingered indeterminably, yet, at the same time, barrelled by in a flash as each passing threat was replaced immediately with a new peril.

Time wore on, the skin on our blistered hands wore away, but the storm finally wore itself out. The sea heaved and sighed, like a wearied sprinter after a gruelling race, and the swell eventually subsided.

"We've done it," I said, letting my oars rest in the oarlocks. "We've won!"

"No," replied Lars gravely as he pulled the sea anchor back in. "You're showing your naivety, Willi. You can *never* win against the sea. You can only hope to avoid defeat. We've got to use this breather to our advantage."

We had probably been awake for over twenty-four hours, with no time to process anything apart from the immediacy of the moment, but now, as the boat bobbed on an exhausted sea, we could turn to other matters.

"We should send out a flare," I suggested, "to try and locate the others. Maybe there's another ship nearby."

"You're right," agreed Lars. "They're in the box you stowed. It's under your seat."

I didn't really have the stamina to tug the heavy chest out. I was completely spent. Lars noticed my weakness before I'd even left my seat.

"We've not quite made a seaman of you yet, I see. Come on, you deserve a rest. Let me do it."

112

"Thanks." I moved across to his seat so he could slide the chest out under mine.

"Eh, what's this? No!"

The chest was on its side, the lid off, its contents spilled, including, among other things the metal box which contained our meagre rations of biscuits and milk tablets, which could have sustained the two of us for four days. But there was no trace of any of the food. Lars looked at me accusingly, evidently believing I had not stowed the chest properly. Then his face twisted with anger, realisation, recollection, it was difficult to say which emotion contorted his expression, but his next word left no room for doubt as to where the guilt for this disaster lay.

"Dog!"

So consumed were we by the raging storm, we had both quite forgotten about Lars's odd discovery hours before; I hadn't even seen the animal for myself, yet. I bent down to take a look under the rear seat. Sure enough, a bedraggled rag of fur cowered there silently, its sky-blue eyes fixed with crippling nausea and rigid fear. I sneezed immediately.

"Hello you. What are you doing there? Have you been a naughty boy?" I said.

It was far too friendly a greeting for Lars's liking. He put the scattered objects back in the chest and ran his finger along the blade of a sharp knife.

"The blasted animal has eaten everything; drunk all the water too. I'm starving. We'll eat the darned thing."

I suddenly found myself very protective towards the dog. "No! It must be the husky that fell overboard from the *Endurance*. But how on earth did he end up here? Let's send up a flare to contact the crew on the other lifeboats. They'll have some supplies."

Lars held up the two flares for me to see; he had already realised that this plan was not going to work. The rubber seal was broken on both waterproof casings; they were useless. "That dog probably did it. Chewed through everything. I'll slit its greedy throat and it will taste all the better for it!" he threatened.

113

"Don't be stupid. You can't eat raw dog."

Lars showed me a Primus stove. "The Swedes have devised a way to eat anything, anywhere," he grinned. "Let's kill the dog while the weather's calm."

"Wait! Maybe the flares will dry out. Let's find out where we are, before we do anything else. Give me that sextant."

The sun was only dimly visible, a blurred patch of light through a nebulous sky, and I could at best take an approximate reading of our location. I put us at around 61°30′ South, 54°80′ West; I was not confident at all. Lars had a go, but didn't really know what he was doing, so passed the instrument back to me.

"I'm a gunner, not a navigator. Where does that put us, then?"

I had absolutely no idea, but I hazarded south of a group of islands I had seen on a map while helping the captain on the *Sandefjord*. I told Lars.

"You probably mean the South Shetland Islands. You think the storm could've taken us all the way there?"

"We were chasing that whale for ages. We probably made most of the journey before the storm."

Lars thought about it for a minute. "Okay. If the others have survived, they will make their way to the islands. And we definitely need to get to land; we might not be so lucky in the next storm. If the weather clears a bit, we should be able to see the peaks. Clarence Island can be seen for miles around. North you say?" he said, looking at the compass he had retrieved from the chest.

"Probably."

"Let's get rowing then. If you slacken off, I'm feeding you dog." That was enough to reenergise my flagging limbs.

By now a light southerly wind was breezing the boat along the very course we desired to go, but it still wasn't enough to disperse the sea fog which hid any land from view. On a clear day, if we were within one hundred miles of Clarence Island Lars believed we would be able to see its highest elevations; we could, however, barely see more than the length of a medium sized

114

sailing ship. So while we were rowing north with determination, eager to reach land, the uncertainty over whether this was in fact the correct course made us extremely nervous and kept us silent.

Occasionally, a giant berg loomed out of the mist, like an inquisitive giant coming to peer at a tiny bug skidding across the water. Each time the sudden appearance of the icy juggernauts made us scramble out of the way, and, when we felt we were in safety, we had to take a new reading on the compass.

Every now and then I checked on the dog. It amazed me that the animal could have remained under there during the storm, and not even yelp a little, but then I thought about my own feats on the *Endurance*, where concealing myself had been so much easier than coming out into the open. However, each time I bent down to look in on the dog, not only did I get a scowl from Lars, but I also started sneezing. The mixture of sea and canine air clearly didn't agree with me, so I kept these cursory inspections to a minimum.

I was a good rower – years of practice on Lake Zürich had given me the necessary technique; but I was not built like Lars and after another couple of hours of strenuous effort I was reaching the limits of my endurance. I had already forced myself through many barriers to carry on, but now my body was tightening into a ball of constricted agony. Nowhere was spared affliction: my neck was stiff; my shoulders aching; my arms were heavy; and cramp was shooting intense barbs through my legs; my feet were numb; my hands were raw; my throat was seared with thirst and my mind was fatigued by my failing body's ceaseless physical demands upon its mental resources.

Lars powered on with his rowing throughout, encouraging me as best he could. "Think of a time in your life when you felt your happiest, when anything seemed possible. Let that thought give you strength," he urged.

There had been only one moment when I had truly felt such a release of energy that anything had seemed possible: the moment I had first seen Carmen play the piano. But try as hard as

I might to recall them, those heavenly notes would not rise above the soughing wind or calm the waves slapping against the wooden boat, and I was too aware of my own helplessness to draw upon further reserves. In a quiet voice I told Lars that if we were going to get to land, then it would be down to his efforts from now on. It was just then that Carmen appeared on the gunwale of our boat.

I had seen her too many times to be mistaken: the chestnut crown leading to her plush, hazel-flecked nape; her confident, tall stance with that long, slender back, bearing her speckled breast. As if greeting me, she spread her majestic wings, and those brilliant bars of white glared bright even in the dull grey mist which enveloped us all. I reached out to stroke her, but she responded with a piercing glare and an ear-splitting screech; I quickly withdrew my hand. Carmen ruffled her feathers, emitted another guttural squawk, then took flight again. I watched her fly away, feeling disappointed. What did her sudden appearance mean? Then I knew.

"She's going to the island! She's showing us the way!" I exclaimed, grasping both oars. "Let's go."

"You've lost it! I'm not following some dumb bird!" protested Lars.

"Look! She's heading north, just where we want to go. And you don't think skuas spend their life on the wing, do you? There must be land that way."

Lars grumbled that the sea madness must have gripped me but, as we had planned to go that way anyway and seeing that at least now I had found the energy to row, he agreed to play along with my fantasy. I smiled and thanked him, and silently thanked Carmen.

Whatever misgivings Lars harboured dispelled just an hour into our chase after Carmen, although I thought she had led us straight into another storm when a low blare rumbled from somewhere within the mist.

"A foghorn!" exalted Lars. "There's a ship out there! Your bird's done it."

We rowed on, and soon the singular quaking foghorn became two distant bellows, then three, then soon thereafter developed into a cacophony of claps, slaps, grunts and barks, growing louder with each strike of our oars through the ocean. Lars looked perplexed, then he looked dismayed.

"Seals," he groaned. "No ship."

We had heard Elephant Island before we had seen it; and then we smelled it, too. A rising stench of ammonia and rotting fish wafted over our lifeboat. The smell was so offensive that I thought it would have been more preferable had Carmen led us into a storm after all. Then the mists parted like a retracting curtain to reveal the noisome showpiece: flocks of squawking, squabbling petrels nesting in the cliff face and a bustling, burping rookery of elephant seals bickering on a rocky beach.

"At least it's land," I said, feeling partly guilty for bringing us here.

However, it was hardly inviting land, even discounting the hundreds, perhaps even thousands, of seals with their grunting, butting, belching, wind-breaking infliction. Far more disconcerting were the bleak, black headlands which stabbed into the sea, their steep, jagged sides under constant destructive attack by a ceaseless charge of seething breakers. Towering cliffs impeded any approach by boat, and at the sheer frontier of ancient glaciers, huge chunks of ice were flung to the frothing sea below, exploding into smaller fragments and blasting an icy spray high into the air.

We rowed northwards along the coast, trying to find a place to land. Foolishly, I hoped Carmen would come to the boat and point with her wing, or at least call from some safe haven on the shore, but neither of those things happened. Our sense of urgency was increasing, too, for we could see with each passing minute the window of calm was closing, and the heavens were filling once again with brooding clouds.

117

Lars stood up many times, believing he had spotted some secluded shingle beach, but each time he sat back down again, disappointed. Finally, we decided that we had little option but to land near the elephant seals; a prospect that made us shudder not only due to the wretched conditions, but also by the size of these monstrous animals.

The approach to the cove where the seals were gathered was obstructed by a shallow reef with turbulent combers reeling over it. Elephant seals patrolled both sides of the reef and they kept a watchful eye on us as we assessed how to navigate the crossing. The motions of the sea were not routine, but there was some predictability about when and how the waves would roll through the reef, although the actions of the seals were far less certain. After studying both waves and seals for some time, we felt we were ready. The manoeuvre had to be timed perfectly for us to ride on the back of a wave while avoiding any passing seal; one wrong move could easily capsize the boat. Lars said that when he gave the signal, we were both to row as hard as we could.

"Go!" he screamed.

With focused minds and energy, we propelled the boat forward. I was surprised at how quickly we got it moving, and with precise synchronisation the wave lifted us to skim over the reef and rest in the relative shelter of the cove. Lars was triumphant, leapt from his seat and fist-pumped the air, just as when he had speared the whale. Also just as then, the seas did not take kindly to being outdone by him and retaliated in the way it knew best: a long grey body swept towards the boat, buffeted it with tremendous force, and sent the jubilant Lars nose-diving into the chilly water.

My impulse to laugh was tempered by the presence of the monsters swimming all around us, and I quickly raced to the side to help haul him back into the boat. It wasn't easy, but after cursing and swearing to destroy all life on earth, Lars managed to scramble back in.

"You have a habit of doing that," I quipped, smiling. Then I saw his arm, hanging limp at his side. It looked badly broken.

"Bastard seals. Row over there," he instructed, indicating a spot slightly apart from the rookery. "I've got to get this arm set."

Apart from when he had deployed the sea anchor, it was the first time I had rowed the boat without Lars's strong muscles aiding me, and now I realised just how much he had been thrusting us forward; on my own, it was very laboured. There was no clear reason why the seals should be avoiding the tiny patch of shingle Lars had seen. It was slightly cut off by a rounded bluff from the rest of the beach, and maybe the seals enjoyed arguing with one another so much that they did not want to feel secluded here. Whatever the reason, I rowed the boat to a crunching halt and jumped out, eager to get my feet on land for the first time in many days. I offered to help Lars climb out of the boat, but he brushed me aside. Try as I might, however, I couldn't coax our silent canine companion out of his hiding place. I was sure the animal would be close to death by now and thought the only thing to do was to leave him to die in peace.

"We've got a lot of work to do," Lars said, surveying our tiny patch of shingle. "Let's pull the boat out of the water, kill a seal and melt some ice so we've got something to eat and drink. Then we'll get some sleep. Tomorrow, we build a shelter. It could be some time before help comes. But first, help me get my arm straight."

He told me to rip a strip from a blanket stored in the chest and showed me how to devise a sling from the material. After making his arm as comfortable as possible, Lars and I waded through the water around the bluff to look upon the rookery. The animals were huge; they were fast, too, even on land, and I saw many a bull charge with terrifying speed at a smaller male unwise enough to come too close. I couldn't possibly see how the two of us could kill one. Far more likely was that they would be having us for dinner if we got too close.

119

"We'll get one of the smaller ones that's been separated from the rest. They've almost certainly never seen humans before and won't see us as a threat, so we should be able to walk right up to one," explained Lars. "You stun it with a rock. I can't pick up one heavy enough with my arm like this. But I'll finish it off with my knife."

"I can't bash one of those poor things on the head!" I protested.

"Well, then I guess I'll just have to eat the dog, or you," answered Lars, showing me his blade. There was something about the crazed look in his eyes that told me he wasn't joking.

"Let's get it over with."

It worked *almost* exactly as Lars had predicted. The dear little seal pup looked up at me with such trusting eyes that I couldn't bear to bring the rock smashing down upon its skull. In addition, our presence had not gone unnoticed, and hundreds of seals were watching our every move. How could I kill one of them under these conditions? I threw the rock to the side and walked away. Lars despatched the animal himself. Quite how, I don't know, but he did say to me that the seal suffered far more because of my gutlessness, and if we were to survive until rescue came, then I needed to man up. That was the first time I nearly told him the truth about who I really was, but, instead, I just walked away from him sullenly.

It took some time before Lars could get the Primus stove working, using waterproof matches stored in the lifeboat and the blubber oil from the seal as fuel. The coal which had almost certainly helped to keep our boat upright during the storm was far too wet to use. The thick black fumes from the burning blubber were almost as repugnant as the stench coming from the beach, but the heat was very welcome, and the meat Lars cooked on a flat stone was delicious. We melted some ice in the metal box that had held the food before the dog had eaten it all and drank greedily.

"Let's toast our success," said Lars, downing some hot water. "And give our new home a name."

"Good idea," I replied. "What shall we call it?"

"How about "Lars and Willi Point?" he suggested. "Or even Willi and Lars Point. I'm not that precious over the hierarchy," he chuckled.

That was the second time I nearly told him, but he seemed in such a good mood, and I didn't want to spoil things. "Um... What about something more fitting to this place. I mean, it existed before we got here, so let's call it something that it's always been."

"Okay. What do you suggest?"

I gave it a moment's thought. "Stinker Point?"

Lars guffawed. "Brilliant. I love it. Here's a toast to Stinker Point." We began to tuck into our meal, snatching the tasty black meat avariciously with our salt-blistered fingers. "Calling this place Stinker Point has reminded me of something," said Lars, who seemed remarkably cheerful given the circumstances.

"Oh. What?"

"My grandparents used to make soap from blubber. They lived in a small coastal town, and they collected kelp, mixed the ash with the fat, and sold it."

"Sounds like horrible soap," I said.

"Better than smelling like an elephant seal, though."

After we had eaten our fill, there was still plenty of seal meat left over, so I took a chunk of flesh to the boat. If the dog could eat, maybe it could survive.

"Hello doggy. Look what I've got for you," I said, leaning into the boat and wafting the meat in front of the seat. A black nose appeared; it sniffed my offering. "Do you want so...?"

The meat was promptly wrenched out of my hand; he evidently did want some. I figured my weakened body must have made me sensitive to dog hairs, too, for I sneezed as soon as I was near him. Nevertheless, I returned with more meat, and when he had finished eating that, I poured melt water from the metal box where he would be able to reach it. After a little hesitation, the nose appeared again, a tongue darted out and the dog lapped up the offering. But he never ventured from his sanctuary.

While I had been tending to the animal, Lars had begun to gather some stones in a semi-circle by the cliff, using the four oars as supports either side of the wall. He instructed me to help him.

"A windbreak," he said. "It'll do for tonight. Not much, but every little helps. We need to sleep in shifts, so that someone can tend to this little fire." The fire was burning in a rock he had found, partly hollowed out by the sea so that it almost had the shape of a bowl. "If you put something flammable around the edge of this stone, like these feathers I've found, and keep them soaked in blubber oil, then it will never go out. It's a trick I learnt in Norway. We've got plenty of blubber to keep this small flame going for the night. It won't give off much heat, but, like I said, every little helps."

I admired Lars for his strength of character. We had both been through so much, perhaps as close to death as a fickle flick by a rogue wave or a gust blowing in an unexpected direction. Despite having now broken his arm, he was still fighting for our survival, feeding us, providing shelter, planning the next move. "You've done good, boy, now get some sleep," Lars said, as if reading my thoughts.

That was the third time I felt an urge to reveal my identity, but I wavered once again. "Thank you. You, too. Um... good night, Lars."

Despite being in damp, cold clothes and exposed to the elements, I slept immediately on my hard bed of shingle. But I woke up abruptly when Lars shook my body.

"Up! Up! Up! Get up!"

"Wha... is it my turn already?" I groaned wearily.

"No. Look!" he pointed out to sea. I squinted, rubbed the sleep from my eyes, but couldn't see anything remarkable. "The ship!" he exclaimed.

"What? Isn't that a star?"

"It's overcast, you fool. And it's summer. You wouldn't see stars that bright this time of the year. Quick, get dressed!"

"I am dressed."

"Right, sure. Let's get the boat in the water. That ship's our ticket out of here."

We hurriedly scampered to the boat and heaved it back into the water. Lars told me to go to the cliff and break off as much ice as I could while he got everything else ready. After I'd thrown in several large blocks of ice into the boat, and he had retrieved two of the oars and placed some of the cooked meat inside the chest, now packed with ice, he told me to board.

"You get in first, it'd be easier with your arm, while I hold the boat."

"What? I'm not coming," he stated matter-of-factly. I was too shocked to reply. He saw my stupefaction. "I can't row. I'm just extra weight that'd slow you down. You've got to get out there as fast as you can. The current's in your favour, as the west wind drift will drive the sea north at this point past this island before continuing westwards. The ship's, what, a mile away? You can catch it that easily. Come on, there's no time to lose!"

"But, what about you?"

"Well, you're not going to leave me here to rot, are you? Come back and get me. Tomorrow we'll both sleep in a nice warm cabin."

"But…"

"No more buts. Get going." He pushed the boat into the water, and I drifted quickly away from him. "Start rowing, boy!"

I couldn't leave it like this. I had to tell him. In this moment of his complete trust in me, I had to end the deception.

"I have to tell you something." I called to him. I had to raise my voice as the breakers behind me were already beginning to make themselves heard.

"Wait till you get back," he yelled in return.

"No. I have to tell you now." I paused, then summoned the courage. "My name's not Willi. I'm not even a boy. My name's Marianna, and I'll come back to you, I promise!"

Lars shouted something back, but the waves drowned him out.

After Lars's terrible revelation at the foot of Brown Mountain I didn't feel like talking anymore and, once my sobbing had stopped, left him there. Kapitän Ritscher's additional news later that evening about the departure of the Jacobsen family had not done much to cheer me up, either, so I was pleased when, the following day, I learnt that we were departing on *MS Schwabenland*, restocked and refuelled, for our next port of call, Cape Town: I was only too glad to see the back of this sad island.

However, I still harboured one great regret about leaving the island formerly known as South Georgia, namely that I never got to hear how Lars had escaped his island prison. Now, with *MS Schwabenland* steaming northwards to a new continent and Lars still in Grytviken, I would never learn how he had accomplished that remarkable feat. When, then, someone knocked on my cabin door this morning, Lars was the last person I had expected to see. But there he was, full of surprises.

"Lars!" I squealed, throwing my arms around him.

"Marianna," he smiled. "I've brought you breakfast. Mind if I come in?"

My cabin was tiny, so we both sat on my bed. Lars noticed the book on my bedside table.

"Didn't have you down as a Biggles reader," he remarked.

"Well, there's a lot about me you don't know,"

"Just like the old days," he smiled.

He placed four bread rolls, some ham slices and a block of cheese in the space between us. Neither of us was concerned about the lack of plates or cutlery, and we each ripped open our rolls and shoved some ham and cheese inside.

"Eating with our fingers is also just like the old days," I said. "Guten Appetit."

"Guten Appetit," he replied.

"I was just thinking about you this morning, and that you never managed to tell me about what happened on Elephant Island after I left. Did that ship come back to get you?

"No, it was far more bizarre than that."

"Please tell me."

Lars chewed on a mouthful of breakfast, contemplating how to start. Then he began.

"I'll never forget what you said to me, your big revelation, nor the moment I saw your boat disappear past the bluff, heading in the wrong direction. I thought, that poor mixed-up girl is dead, and soon I will be, too. I was so cold and tired, and injured of course, that I was sure I wouldn't last long. But somehow, I got through the first few days, and then the next few days after that. Before I knew it a week had passed. And so it went on, day after day, week after week, driven by a few basic needs: food, water, shelter, warmth.

"When, after a month or so, the elephant seals left, I thought my days were numbered, but then I remembered the birds nesting high on the cliffs. I thought I could either sit on my beach and starve to death or fall from a high cliff trying to survive."

"You could never give up," I said, remembering how I had admired his resilience all those years ago. "That's why the captain calls you…., you know. He thinks you get out of your scrapes by luck. But it's not. It's planning and determination."

126

"Maybe. In any case, the birds proved to be my saviour, in more ways than one. I raided their eggs, I ate their chicks, I used their feathers, and I'll tell you in a minute how climbing up to these birds eventually helped me find a way off the island."

"Like Carmen helped us!" I exclaimed.

"Who?"

"Oh, you don't know her. I'll tell you later. Go on."

"The birds kept me going for a while. One morning I woke to a tremendous sight, and an even more tremendous noise. Stinker Point had been colonized by thousands of chinstrap penguins. They were everywhere; several of them had even waddled into my makeshift home of stone and seal hide, warming themselves by my little fire. Well, now I had all the food I could wish for again. Just like the seals, the creatures didn't see me as a threat and they practically walked into my knife. I have to say, Marianna, there's a reason we don't eat penguin. It tastes awful. Imagine…"

"I know what penguin tastes like, Lars. I've been away a long time, too, remember?" I interrupted.

Lars laughed. "Well, I soon got pretty tired of that fishy, oily taste and learnt how to spice things up with limpets, seaweed and the occasional scavenger bird which I lured with some penguin meat."

"Me too!" It seemed we had some shared experiences.

"Did you also build a shelter? I managed to fashion some form of dwelling using rocks and large blocks of ice, which, over time, I became pretty skilled at cutting. I also used sheets of penguin or seal skin, stitched together with twisted seaweed. It stank, it was permanently wet, it ripped, chunks fell off, and the whole thing needed constant repairs. But it protected me from the worst of the elements, it kept me busy and it kept me alive until…" Lars broke off and looked at me.

"Until what?" I urged.

"Until Shackleton arrived."

Had I known that Shackleton's crew would also end up marooned on Elephant Island, I would have stayed with Lars. At the time, however, it seemed that our only chance of help was the ship currently heading towards the north-western edge of the island.

But there was one huge obstacle in the way: the reef. In our haste to launch the boat, neither Lars nor I had considered it. The combers crashed over it with forceful regularity, and I doubt that even if Lars had been rowing with me, we could have generated enough momentum to pass; on my own, I had no chance. However, if I did not try to reach the ship, we might never leave our island prison.

The boat faced the reef; I looked back forlornly to Lars. I could see him waving his arms, urging me forward. Perhaps he had still forgotten the reef, although even from his position he must have been able to see the breakers impeding my progress. I decided to give it at least one attempt.

I backed the boat some ten metres away from the reef, took a bite of some cold seal meat in the hope this would give me instant extra strength, and began to row with all my might. My advancement was disappointingly slow, and with my back to the reef, I could not possibly see or time my arrival. I braced myself for a crushing, icy impact with a tumbling wave and prayed it would not capsize the boat.

Then, suddenly, my speed picked up, and I hurtled forward at a velocity even Lars would never have been able to generate. I barely had time to process whether I had been caught in some rip tide when the boat barged through a wave as if it were nothing but a weak ripple and burst through to the open ocean on the other side. I had been soaked by the spray, but I had done it.

Lars rejoiced, jumping up and down on his little beach. Then he pointed northwards, and I knew I had no time to lose. I turned around to look at the shimmering light of the distant ship, but my attention was grabbed by something much closer. There, sitting on the bow, was Carmen.

"How did you...?"

"Squawk!" and she flew off.

Then, far more curiously, the big grey head and ugly snout of an elephant seal popped out of the sea, just by my boat. A large scar ran down the left side of its face; evidence, no doubt, of a violent encounter with a rival male. The bull opened its mouth and gave a lusty roar, almost like a laugh, spraying me with musty, malodorous steam. Then it disappeared.

I shook my head and turned to the pressing matter. I could just about make out the silhouetted shape of the ship. It looked like a couple of miniature blocks conveying a tiny lantern across the sea. Encouraged by my success over the reef, I set to a steady and determined pace. A slight northerly headwind made the going tough. Only by glancing at fixed points on the rugged shore could I gauge my progress, yet the discouraging early indications were that I was making little headway, so I elected to check only infrequently to avoid losing heart.

129

The next time I looked I shrieked with distress: I was further south than when I had started, further from the ship and further from the reef. I had not been riding a current north, as Lars had predicted, but south, and the wind had exacerbated the problem. There was no chance I would ever catch up with the ship. I gave up trying; I now had to get back to the island.

I redoubled my efforts, but I had already been rowing the best part of an hour, and was flagging. No matter how hard I rowed, I inched further and further away from Elephant Island, now so far out at sea that I couldn't even be sure exactly where Stinker Point was anymore. Soon I had drifted so far past the most southerly point on Elephant Island, that I had an uninterrupted view of the distant peaks on Clarence Island, fifty miles to the east.

It is hard to describe the feelings that overwhelmed me in that moment. I couldn't even say that I was engulfed with despair, more a sense of utter disbelief at my sudden situation: powerless to save myself; doomed to die on this little lifeboat; nobody would ever know where I had perished, nor indeed would even I know the precise location of my death. I believe it was this last thought that troubled me most. There are few certainties in life, but unless you are met with a violent end, there is at least one certainty in death – that the final moments will be spent with people who know who you are. All I knew was that I'd spend it alone, somewhere wet and cold.

For an indefinite time I sat with my arms wrapped around myself, watching Elephant Island dwindle away, my boat bobbing aimlessly on the ocean. Then the island vanished forever, disappearing behind a thin veil of fog. That was the moment the dog chose to peek his nose out of his underseat den.

"Why do I keep forgetting about you?" I said, forcing myself to smile. "Are you hungry?"

It was comforting having him here, but I wanted to see him properly. I threw a slab of meat in the middle of the boat. His nose twitched, and very gradually his snout emerged from the hiding place. He was probably hoping he wouldn't need to leave the security of his hideout. But I remained firm; if he desired to eat, he would have to come out completely.

Little by little, a shaking, nervous head peeked from under the seat, then shoulders, back, and eventually hind legs edged warily towards the centre of the boat, closing in on the meaty prize. I could now see the husky in full view for the first time, and it was a sorry sight. Quite how he had managed to become so filthy under there I do not know, but his tangled and matted fur barely hid a wasting body; apart from the food I had given him, he had only eaten the meagre rations in the lifeboat to sustain himself, and must have been severely dehydrated, too, having only had a small amount of water in all that time. I scolded myself for not thinking about his plight, and gently placed a large block of ice next to the meat.

His eyes had lost none of their penetrating fierceness, and he looked at me suspiciously, as if I intended to replace the meat I had put there with the unappetising ice.

"They're both for you. You can lick the ice," I said, breaking a chunk off and giving it an exaggerated lick myself. "See. Yum. Although, I admit, it's better when it's water." The mistrust seemed to melt a little, the dog's sharp blue gaze softening. He cocked his head sideways. "I'll make it easier for you." I broke off some more pieces of ice and scattered them on the upturned lid of the chest.

Either through my words or my actions, the husky felt emboldened to approach the meat and start wolfing it down. He made very short work of it. Then he started on the ice, and that soon disappeared, too. He looked at me, and I knew what that look meant: more. I had plenty of meat in the case; quite why Lars had given me so much I was not sure, but I was glad he had.

Then a thought occurred to me: had Lars engineered this situation? Did he desire the island for himself? Did he suspect I would be swept away by the wind and currents, and to assuage his guilt had given me some sustenance for my final days? If Lars had done this to me, I was furious with him; much as I was furious

131

with Shackleton for denying me my rightful place on the *Endurance*. I could not tolerate men deciding my fate. Lars was a survivor, and perhaps abandoned all scruples when it came to saving himself.

However, even if Lars had not deceived me, I was still mildly angry with him; he should have known, great seaman as he claimed to be, that the currents would take me in the wrong direction. Of course, I couldn't be certain of anything, but I couldn't believe he had planned it; I couldn't possibly see what advantage it would bring him. He was injured; I had the boat; I even had a dog, which would probably be useful for something on a deserted island. I turned my thoughts back to the creature in my boat. One thing was for certain, it wasn't his fault, poor mangy thing. I reached out slowly to pat him on the head.

"No, it's not your fault... dog." He flinched, but allowed the contact while he noisily ate. "I can't keep calling you *dog*. Let me see." He had survived against all odds; the ultimate underdog. He'd endured the ferocious storm, had been deprived of food and water; even his choice of den fitted the bill. "*Underdog*. That's a good name. Hello Underdog!" I chirped. But he didn't look up; I wasn't surprised; even if he could have understood the meaning of the word, he probably wouldn't have like its associations with failure. I wouldn't have looked up, either. I decided to call him something else. Then I had the perfect name: he stank, he looked awful, there was water all around and he gobbled down his food in much the same way as ill-mannered English fishermen. "Hull!" I trilled. Immediately the husky glanced at me, his tongue hanging loosely from his mouth. "Hull the husky. It's perfect! And while I'm at it...," I added, patting the boat on gunwale, "I'd just as well name you." A few appropriate names came to mind for the boat; in the end I settled for the *Galicia*, the place of my maternal roots. "Yes, you'll get me home, won't you?"

That was the moment I determined to get Hull, to get us, out of our predicament. I would not let the dog down; and if the sea and wind were minded to take us southwards, then south we would go. We had food, we had water, we had company, we had…

"Miaow!"

We had a cat.

It's dawned on me, as we cross the point

which separates the western from the eastern hemisphere, that my Antarctic expedition really is over. When *MS Schwabenland* found me on Deception Island, when we steamed past the South Shetland Islands, if that is what they are still called, when we went to Grytviken and I was reunited with Lars – all of this seemed a continuation of my previous incredible adventure. But now we are just a couple of days from Cape Town, far away from the life I have lived for thirty years. Perhaps now I only have memories; perhaps this is the reason I am so keen to spend time with Lars, to keep alive a story which is gradually mutating into little more than dry ink on paper.

Our breakfast in my cabin had been interrupted by a messenger, informing me that Kapitän Ritscher demanded an audience with Lars. He made his apologies and promised to tell me the rest of his story at some later point. Now, a few days later, I have just returned to my cabin having just had dinner with Lars in the canteen. I must say, his tale is every bit as astonishing as mine, and I am keen to tell it.

Lars told me how one day in April 1916, after almost a year-and-a-half of living alone on Elephant Island, there had been a violent storm which he felt lucky to have survived, but which had all but destroyed his shelter and carried off his precious stores of food. At the first opportunity, he began to rebuild his lonely existence. First of all, with the seals and penguins absent, he needed to climb up to the nests again to source some food. While there, he looked out across the sea and was convinced he could see three small boats towards the east; some distance from him, but close to the island. They were all heading northwards. He soon lost sight of them, but was sure they must have been searching for somewhere to land. Lars had long assumed that I had succumbed to the sea and his only hope of salvation would be from a passing ship. He could not let this small chance of rescue sail away from him, so resolved to find the boats.

Elephant Island is a harsh, mountainous island, fifty kilometres long and thirty kilometres wide; not a terrain one can easily traverse. But neither is Lars a man easily thwarted. He took several days to prepare himself well for the search, taking food, tools and shelter in the form of a feather-lined sealskin sleeping bag that he had carefully created. After a couple of bruising weeks of scrambling, sliding, and slicing his way up and down ice-covered cliffs and mountains, checking out almost every inch of coast along the way, he found the men he had seen in the boats, camped on a spit of land almost one hundred metres wide. It looked like luxury compared to Lars's tiny camp at Stinker Point. There were twenty-two of them, some in terrible shape. They had once been among the twenty-eight men with whom I had travelled from Buenos Aires to South Georgia; they were the crew of the *Endurance*.

Shackleton and Jack had left with four others just the day before Lars's unexpected arrival. Realising that no-one was going to come to Elephant Island, they had decided to risk the perilous journey back to South Georgia in the only boat they had which might possibly be up to the task. Lars and the remaining men from the *Endurance* had little choice but to sit it out in the *Snuggery*, a crude shelter fashioned from two upturned lifeboats, and pray that Shackleton's daring bid for rescue would succeed.

Lars was treated like a celebrity, although the twenty-two sailors were probably simply ecstatic to have someone else to talk to after similarly having been at the mercy of the Antarctic for so long. The ice, they told Lars, had frustrated their attempts to cross the continent even before they had set foot on it; the *Endurance* had been crushed in the Weddell Sea, and they had been battling for sixteen months to stay alive on crumbling floes until they had landed on Elephant Island.

Fortunately for them all, Shackleton, Jack and the others cheated death in the Drake Passage, reached South Georgia, and four months after their arrival on the island that had kept Lars alive for so long, a rescue ship came to save the castaways. If I had stayed with Lars, who knows how my story would have turned out?

I sneezed.

A clap of thunder; a whale's dying scream; the rumble of a giant wave; never have I heard a more ominous sound than the fragile mew of a cat I could not see. It froze me stiff, far more effectively than the full might of the Antarctic chill could ever do. Perhaps I had misheard. Perhaps it was the creaking wood of my weary boat.

"Miaow."

Hull's ears pricked up. He grabbed the remaining meat, lumbered back to his hideout and, with a shake of his head, tossed the now quite unappetising morsel to the hidden recess under the seat. Could there be a cat under there, too? Could two creatures have taken shelter on the lifeboat and remained unnoticed? It seemed absurdly impossible, yet, despite the risk of an allergic reaction, I had to check.

Whatever Hull's loyalties to any supposed animal may be, he could not suppress his natural instincts when his belly needed filling, and I managed to coax the husky out with a particularly fine-looking cut of seal meat. With him out of the way, I knelt down and peered under the seat. There, feasting on scraps of seal flesh, I saw what was for me a nightmarish vision of dully reflecting lime-green eyes stuck on a scraggly shock of fur. I had seen those eyes before, and I knew they recognised me. Those were the eyes of Mrs Chippy.

What was she, he, it, whatever, doing there? I sneezed at the vile creature; it hissed at me; I backed away and returned to my seat in the middle of the *Galicia*. What was I to do now? I certainly could ill afford an allergic reaction out here. Fortunately, it appeared that the sea breeze, the very thing that had conspired to blow me off course, was now coming to my rescue, preventing any fine hairs from reaching me. I just had to stay away from that back seat and somehow give Hull a good wash as he was surely caked in the offensive fur.

Before I could contemplate my predicament any longer, a dull thud from the bow behind me alerted me to a potentially new concern. I turned around, worried what awaited me. It was not, thankfully, a block of ice, one of those low growlers which prowl the ocean and pose an even greater risk to boats like mine than mighty icebergs which can be seen from some distance. It was only Carmen, a relatively friendly face, although, scowling with furrowed brow at the *Galicia's* stern, her countenance was not exactly welcoming. I think she knew Mrs Chippy was back there as she never took her cross eyes off the rear seat.

Her presence was strangely reassuring, allowing me a moment of calm reflection. First of all, I thought, the dog had come out of its hiding place, the cat had cried out to announce its presence, so there was no reason why I should not also take part in this moment of release; it was time for me to remove the band that had been wrapped tightly around my chest for days. It hadn't even occurred to me to do this before now. I'm not sure why, but I still looked about me before I unbound myself. What freedom! I had put the sense of constraint that I had been feeling since arriving in South Georgia down to being in the constant company of men, with barely a second to myself. But, while that may have played a part, now I realised that the physical compression I had placed upon my body had been far more constricting. Now I was free of both limitations and already felt happier.

Mrs Chippy, having finished her dog-chewed scraps, came out from under the seat. She was probably wondering where Hull had got to. He was turning in round slow circles in the middle of the boat, then curled himself up into a ball. Mrs Chippy blinked at him, narrowed her eyes at me, then noticed Carmen, just behind my shoulder, and gave a disapproving growl. Carmen proved she could be just as catty as this feline foe by responding with a spitting call so piercing, it nearly rendered my ears in two and made both of Hull's go bolt upright. She beat her large, dark wings and rapped her sharp claws on the gunwale, presenting a formidable sight. Mrs Chippy backtracked to her hideout.

I smiled. I had already determined to head south, and there was nothing about my situation which had changed. I grabbed the oars, turned the *Galicia* so that I could row with the wind, and started at a steady pace.

After several hours, the threatening clouds which had precipitated our hasty lunge over the reef on Elephant Island and had lurked ominously in the sky ever since were starting to thin.

Although the sun barely set at this time of the year, I knew enough about its arch across the sky to estimate that it must be near the middle of the night. After all of my recent exertions over the last few days, I was utterly exhausted. Hull was sleeping peacefully, and I regarded him with a hint of jealousy: how I wished I had a layer of fur to ward of the chill that seeped into my bones, whenever I stopped rowing to rest. Perhaps, I thought, he wouldn't mind if I lay next to him.

The boat was damp, it was uncomfortable to lie in, but Hull's warm body and the rocking motions of a sluggish sea quickly lulled me into a deep sleep. Judging by the high position of the sun when I awoke, Hull and I had stayed that way for around twelve hours. At some point during our slumber Carmen had joined us, for she was nestled in the nook between our two larger bodies. It must have been very snug for her. Fortunately for me, if there were any cat hairs on Hull, they did not affect me, and Mrs Chippy herself had remained aloof under her seat; perhaps the presence of Carmen had kept her at bay.

The sextant was with Lars on Elephant Island, so there was no way of knowing how far we had drifted, or even in which direction, for there were no landmarks from which I could take a sight. There was simply nothing but the vastness of the grey ocean all around, interspersed with countless icebergs of varying heights, spanning the radius towards the far-flung horizon which encircled me. It was as if the bergs were grotesque imitations of chapels, churches and cathedrals, springing up in a vast open plain, only the plain itself was forever fermenting and foaming, and the structures which moved across it could at any time flip over, crushing anyone who got too close.

My situation seemed hopeless, yet I had a few things I could be thankful for: the seas were comparatively calm; the wind was light; it was not raining; I had food and water; and I had company, which provided me with both mental and physical relief. Thus in a state of tragic contentment, I floated through my icy bethel for several days, not knowing when, where or how it would all end. Then, however, things became very different.

As so often in this part of the world, the storm came without any warning. From one moment to the next, as all four of us were enjoying some cold seal meat, the sea heaved a huge sigh, the wind snorted through the boat and a thunderous clap boomed above us. The Southern Ocean had awakened.

I had already lived through one dreadful tempest, and did not relish the prospect of enduring another, especially now as I was on my own. Then I remembered Hull, Carmen, and even Mrs Chippy. I was far from alone, and I had a responsibility to get them to safety.

"Quick, quick! Get under there!" I shooed Hull back under the seat. Carmen refused, instead opening her wings and flying off. I had no time to see where she went.

Within a few minutes, the waves were larger than the *Galicia*, lifting her up and spinning her around like a toy. More waves crashed into the sides, shooting stinging sea spray metres into the air. I remembered how Lars had deployed the sea anchor into the wind in the rough seas, and how this had steadied the boat and most likely kept us from being overwhelmed. I hastily did the same before the sea grew even heavier.

The anchor yanked the *Galicia* to face the waves headlong, setting her position in the ocean. For an instant, but only an instant, the tension eased from my body; then a rumble unlike any I had ever heard before filled me once again with extreme dread. At first I couldn't be sure where it was coming from: it was a distant, crunching, tumbling turbulence, and it was clearly getting closer.

Then I saw it: an iceberg, no, a frothing, foaming wave, hurtling towards me between port and stern, a direction which should be entirely impossible when the windward force of the brewing storm was directly in front of me. What was more, the wave was not even very wide, perhaps ten metres or so; just one, rogue wave, in course, colour and composition entirely separate from
140

the rest, coming straight for me. It held me spellbound, even as I knew its impact would devastate the *Galicia*. I think in that moment I had truly submitted myself to my fate: with the power of the unstable ocean railed against me, the tides of fortune had decreed to end my continued endurance. It was over.

As if resigning itself to my destiny, the long rode of the sea anchor slackened, and the *Galicia* instantly began to sway. In a moment she would be turned, rolled over and capsize. I held on to my seat and closed my eyes. Then the boat surged forward, just as it did when I had crossed the reef on Elephant Island. This time, the force of the jolt threw me astern and almost overboard. Awkwardly splayed on the floor of the boat, I clung on to the seat under which the animals cowered as the *Galicia* inexplicably picked up speed, tearing through the ocean far faster than I could row. What mysterious agency was propelling us along?

The roar of the rogue wave was growing and I allowed myself to glance over the back of the boat. I wish I hadn't. A wall of churning ice several metres high was just metres from us, swirling and roiling, desperate to champ down upon us and draw us into its seething violence. And yet, by some unknown power, the *Galicia* remained ahead of it, perhaps, I thought, riding on the bow wave of this monstrous entity behind us.

Each second seemed like a minute, each minute like an hour. So I could not say how long this race against death lasted, but in this immeasurable time, while still submitting to my fate, no longer was it a surrender to unavoidable doom, but an acceptance of a destiny. My mother's premature death, the relocation to Zürich, the chance encounter with Albert, my father's job in England, meeting Jack, and all the rest of it; everything had brought me here, to the outer edges of Antarctica: I was never intended to join Shackleton's British Imperial Trans-Antarctica Expedition; I was always meant to do this journey on my own.

No sooner had I reached this conclusion, than the *Galicia* was flung out of its path, the icy, grinding wave subsided, melting into the sea, and the storm which had threatened to overwhelm me from all sides died down. Then, ahead, I saw land.

The probable explanation for the unlikely

singular wave of ice, Kapitän Ritscher explained, was a rip current which had collected a mass of brash ice. He seemed very keen to show off his impressive knowledge on the topic.

"They're becoming more and more common, you know, as warm deep water currents strike a column of rock and shoot upwards, then out across the ocean. We're getting these warm water currents in quite unexpected places, these days. Where you were is littered with undersea mountains, so I'm not surprised you got one there. What you experienced was quite rare back then, but now a fairly regular phenomenon."

"What about all the ice, if it's warm water?" I asked.

"Ah, good question. Of course, because the ice is melting so quickly, there are huge areas of fragmented ice where there used to be floes. The rip currents pick them, tossing and turning the ice along the way until the ice melts, or the strength of the current dissipates. It's quite fascinating. But there's one thing I find more fascinating than that."

"Oh?"

"How you managed to ride this current and then be ejected from it. I've never heard anything like it."

I had my theories, of course, but I couldn't tell him all of them in case he thought I was mad. I only told him one of my explanations, the least far-fetched one.

"I think I was simply somehow propelled forward by the wave itself, and then maybe my sea anchor caught hold of another wave and ripped me away to safety."

This, at least, was my working theory after the storm, as I drifted on the becalmed seas of the Southern Ocean and beyond the white of wandering bergs saw the golden glint of a distant peak, surely a beacon of hope. I hauled the sea anchor in, returned to the seat and prepared myself to row towards land.

What further nasty surprises did my adventure have in store for me? I certainly did not expect this one: in my anxious haste at the storm's onset, I had failed to secure the oars properly; one was now missing. How was I to row towards the shore with a single oar? Tired, wet, cold, with arms sore from so much rowing, it would have been difficult with both oars. Now I had constantly to switch from one side of the boat to the other, three strokes port, three strokes starboard. It was more than twice as taxing, and my aching arms could barely maintain the effort. Even more maddening was the current, sweeping me further along the coast, too far away to reach it, but close enough to see it skating past.

I didn't know the name of this frosty island that I desperately desired to set foot on, but it seemed to stretch on indefinitely and had an icy determination to keep the *Galicia* at bay. No matter how hard I tried, the faraway rocks never rose higher, the definitions of the shore never grew sharper, the birds flitting about the cliff face always remained as distant flakes. It was as if a giant hand was pulling me back, pushing me along sideways, allowing me to see but not touch; and after a day and night of struggling against this stubborn island guardian, I gave up. The golden peak which had given me such optimism had deceived me with its shimmering aspect. It had not been a promising symbol at all, rather one of glaring mockery. My hope slipped away, the fight slipped from me too, and exhaustion cast me into a fitful sleep.

When I awoke, I was once again being warmed by Hull's furry body; the animal was lying prostrate over me like a blanket. I patted him on the head. Mrs Chippy had also dared to come out and was tucked between the husky's back feet, far too close for comfort for me. I shooed her away with a sneeze-ridden profanity. The chilly wind blowing through our open boat spared both my nose and her ears from further unwelcome reactions.

It was, of course, impossible to know how long I had been sleeping, or how far we might have drifted. I stretched my sore limbs, rubbed the sleep from my eyes and looked about me. I was greeted by a tempting, teasing sight. Some five or six kilometres away, fluttering in and out of view through swirling mists, another elusive island was coasting by. Once again, I ignored my protesting body and, after throwing some seal meat towards my stowaways, committed myself to reaching land.

Every now and then I glimpsed a towering ice-capped mountain emerging through the fog. I wondered at how something so imposing, so dominant over this landscape, could also remain so illusory. My battle to reach it, however, did not last as long as the

145

previous day, and my heart and mind gave up before my body gave out; I knew it was futile to carry on rowing with my single oar.

I sank into the *Galicia*, leaning against the side and drawing my knees up to my chin; I didn't want to see the island taunt me anymore. Hull approached me and placed his head on my bent knees. He whined a little and every few seconds looked up at me, as if checking I was still there. I couldn't tell if he was asking for food or empathising with my melancholy; either way, I liked it. Even Mrs Chippy, jumping up on the seat above her hideout, came to look upon me. She stared at me expressionlessly, never looking away, blinking occasionally. I didn't it like nearly as much, but as we were quite literally all in the same boat, it felt mean to cast her away again.

"How *did* you two get to be on this boat, anyway?" I asked, stroking Hull absent-mindedly between the ears. I looked from one animal to the other, and imagined how Hull, after falling from the *Endurance* and paddling for his life to the shore, must have chanced upon Mrs Chippy and given chase. I could see in my mind's eye how she ran up the gangway to the *Sandefjord*, then sprang into the *Galicia*, with Hull doggedly pursuing her. Their fates were sealed when I brought the chest to the boat and secured the canvas, locking them in together. "Ah, but I forget. You're not a *she*, are you, Mrs Chippy? You're a *he*." Then I imagined the same scenario, only with the roles reversed and a cross Mrs Chippy harrying the bedraggled husky right up until I arrived. Then the two had no choice but to become friends. "Yes, I think it probably happened that way around."

Only one of our crew was missing. I hadn't seen her for some time. Perhaps she'd flown back to Elephant Island and was now keeping Lars company. That thought cheered me, although I would certainly have preferred it had she decided to stay with us. More likely Carmen was out fishing; for her the ocean was not the deathly threat it posed to us, but a larder full of tasty promise. For

146

us unfeathered souls on the boat there was only cold seal meat to share, and that had almost run out, too.

I pushed Hull gently from me and strained to my knees to check on our meagre supplies. *On my knees*. It was the most appropriate expression for my condition, which, when I glanced over the boat, became that instant inordinately worse.

A giant iceberg loomed directly ahead, so large that its outer edges disappeared into the sea fog. It was a wonder I hadn't noticed it before, but I had been so focused on reaching the shore which had now almost fully slipped by, that I hadn't paid any attention to where the *Galicia* was actually drifting. Now, I had three choices: evade it on the left flank; evade it on the right flank; or keep drifting towards it. I even considered the last option as a potential solution. The berg was so massive I might be able to camp on it for a while. However, I dismissed the idea almost as quickly as it had come to me; I had seen enough of these icy leviathans keel completely over in the sea to know I did not want to be on one, or even near one, when that happened. The route to the right, in the same direction as the unreachable islands, had proven frustratingly impassable. This left me with no real choice at all; I had to get around the left flank.

Gradually the mists shrouding the berg cleared, and I soon came to suspect that it wasn't an iceberg at all, but an island, although the remarkably sheer, linear front edge did not resemble anything like the jagged contours of the islands I had spent the last couple of days drifting past. I allowed the boat to float closer, and my suspicions were confirmed: it was an island, yet with such steep cliffs rising straight out of the sea there was no prospect of beaching anywhere. I began to row further to the left, as I certainly did not wish to be dashed against the rocks.

The closer I approached the island, the sharper its features grew. Three stacks of varying sizes jutted out from the far edge which I was trying to clear: one tall and slim, closest to the cliff face; furthest away was a smaller, squat rock; and in the centre, a bulky mass which was both taller and wider than the other two.

147

Despite or perhaps as a direct consequence of my precarious position, I couldn't help comparing the three rocks, here on the periphery of an impenetrable island, to the three bodies set adrift in the *Galicia*. It was clear which one was Mrs Chippy: the hunched one on the outermost edge; but what about the other two? It took me a few minutes to decide.

"I'm the thin one and you're definitely the big one, Hull," I declared to the dog lying at my feet. He looked up at me lovingly. "If you keep eating meat like you do, you'll be as fat as that rock." Hull whimpered and put his head back on his forepaws.

It was far easier, working with the current, to steer the *Galicia* past the three stacks, than it had been rowing in the opposite direction, and as soon as we turned the corner, the topography of the coast changed. Gone were the sheer, forbidding cliffs of ice, instead rugged crags glowered back at me, but they offered no greater chance of landing. This was an island which refused to give up its secrets. I rowed further, hugging the uninviting coast as closely as I dared.

The *Galicia* passed another bluff, and I thought I could perceive a break in the cliff face, a mile or so ahead. Perhaps there would be a shallow beach there, somewhere we could land, somewhere we could, albeit for a short time, gain some respite from the unrelenting motions of the sea. As we neared, the break widened until the crags parted entirely and I saw that, far from being one solid line of rocky cliffs, the crags in fact comprised two facing peninsulas which allowed a slither of the sea to flow into some as yet concealed part of the island. I rowed towards this cleft.

Ahead of me was the aspect of the southern headland; it was an horrific sight. As if an army of advancing hellish beasts had at once been seared and petrified, the layers of mangled rock piled high in grotesque configuration giving testimony to some ancient and terrible seismic violence. The blackened beach beyond did little to quell the dreadful scene. All I had desired for days was the chance to set foot on land once more, but I would have preferred it were not here amidst this monstrous setting.

148

A huge stack, rising perhaps forty or fifty metres from the sea, stood at the entrance between the two peninsulas. It resembled a stone sentinel, gazing impassively out across the ocean, waiting dormantly until some unsuspecting mariner awakened it from its eternal watch. There was even the trace of a heavy arm running down the monolith, ending in a thick lithic fist which, by chance of nature or forces unknown to me, seemed to be clutching its last petrified victim. I took no chances and quietly asked the silent sentinel for permission to enter. Hull scrambled to his feet as if in salute to the island's defender; either that, or the husky thought I was speaking to him again.

Just past the stone guard, the northern end of the steep craggy headland soared to well over one hundred metres high and just as wide. It was a rock-ribbed formation that echoed the design of a majestic cathedral organ, complete with an ornamental screen of stone and ranks of tall pipes. The contrast of this breathtaking composition with the raw disfigurement on the opposing headland could not be greater. I stroked us onwards, hardly breaking the water for fear of unleashing whatever held these paralysed forces in check. But I wasn't careful enough.

No sooner had I entered the narrow gap between the headlands when a vigorous gust rose quite literally out of the thin, cold air. As if the pipes on the stone organ themselves were speaking, a whistling wind from nature's bellows took hold of the *Galicia* and propelled her further forward. A great swell then lifted up the boat to carry her onward still. Fearing I might be flung into the sea, I sat on a seat and rather lamely tried to steer us with the oar, yet a wave or some other instrument of unknown origin took hold of the *Galicia* and pedalled her along with even greater speed. My solo efforts to conduct our progress were ineffectual against this mighty choir of wind, wave and swell; I put the oar on my lap and awaited the conclusion of this movement across the water.

The boat passed through the two headlands, and as soon as I saw the inner depths of the island, I knew it was somewhere magical. It opened up before me, a huge, tranquil bay, many miles long and wide, encircled by a ring of protective mountains that kept this place hidden from anyone who failed to find the narrow passage I had stumbled across, or baulked at the daunting approach. I had thought this island was an iceberg; I was wrong. I had thought that it offered no safe landing spot; I was wrong in that, too. And now I was in this Antarctic paradise, a place where penguins thrived on the many beaches; a place where mountains sheltered birds from ferocious winds; a place where even plants could flourish in spots of greenery; a place untouched by human hand.

But, in that final point, I was also wrong. Just off to my right, tucked behind the peninsula and in a smaller bay carved directly out of the huge one in which I found myself, was the unmistakable evidence of human activity: buildings, boilers, beached boats and the rotting carcasses of thousands of whales.

"You're very lucky to be arriving in Cape Town at this time of the year," said Kapitän Ritscher as *MS Schwabenland* was completing its docking manoeuvres. "There are violent storms in the winter, and the window between the rainy season and the muggy summer months is open for such a small time these days. This is just about as perfect as it gets."

I looked at the brilliant blue sky, cloudless apart from one that seemed to have been pulled from the heavens and draped like a blanket over the flat-topped mountain which overlooked the port city. The same red, white and black flags that covered Grytviken abounded here too: the boats, the cranes, the wharf, the buildings, scarcely a centimetre was left untouched by the Nazi symbols.

"Couldn't they find a flag large enough to cover the mountain, and had to use that white fluffy sheet instead?" I joked.

"Is this a serious question?" enquired Kapitän Ritscher.

"Um, no." I had forgotten that Germans were not known for recognising sarcasm.

"Oh. Shame. I like the idea. I will put it to my superiors." He rubbed his chin thoughtfully, probably imagining what the mountain could look like.

"So… how many days are we staying here?" I asked, wishing to change the subject.

"Just two nights. Enough to revictual, then we're heading straight up the Atlantic and we'll have you back in Europe in no time. In the meantime, enjoy the city."

Lars had promised to show me around. He had been here a few times before and each time, he said, it was noticeably different.

"You know that odd-looking cloud up there?" he said, pointing to the one I had seen from the ship as we made our way through the busy harbour market. "Well, they call it the tablecloth here."

"I can see why."

"Legend has it, that it forms on the mountain when the ghost of a pirate has a smoking contest with the Devil. They can both smoke so much that plumes of smoke soon envelop the whole mountain."

"I wouldn't be surprised if it were true. I've seen some things in Antarctica that defy rational explanation, too."

"You'll have to tell me about them. Well, here in Cape Town, that's not the only contest going on right now. There's a battle raging right beneath our feet."

"Oh?"

"They've been trying to expand the city. They can't really build on the steep sides of the mountain, so are reclaiming land from the bay. But the sea isn't letting them. In fact, if anything, the sea is taking land from the city, just like in Grytviken. Last time I was here, I'm sure the harbour front was further out."

I looked down at my feet. The concrete pavement seemed firm enough; it was hard to imagine that the stalls all around me might one day be under water.

"Hey, take a look at this!" Lars had begun to rummage through a book stall and had found something. "You like this sort of thing, don't you?" He held up a book, its dust jacket showing two planes flying over a rural landscape. The mountain in the picture looked very much like the one we had just been discussing. The book was called *Biggles in Africa*.

"Well, I'm not that keen on them. Some of the sailors lent me a few to read. Not really my thing."

Lars was already leafing through it. "This one was published in 1936. That's before the Nazis took over all of Europe. Most of these have been burned. Johns writes only pro-German stuff now. This one's a collector's item, or a ticket to the camps."

152

"What do you mean? A ticket to the camps? The books have been burned? What's going on?"

"Anything that doesn't fit in with the Nazi world view is removed – that goes for people as well as books. Although as far as I can tell, this is just an adventure story set in Africa. Still, they wouldn't like the picture on the cover."

"Why ever not?"

Before Lars could answer, our conversation was interrupted by loud and angry shouts coming from somewhere within the market; the cries were growing stronger by the second. Then, crashing through these yelps and screams and curses, came charging some kind of wild beast, skittling bystanders aside in its panicked flight. I craned my neck, trying to see through the stalls and past the flurry of fabric and fleeing shoppers, but could only make out something large, dark, and evidently bolting from a group of uniformed men hot on its heels.

Instinctively, Lars grabbed hold of my arm and yanked me to the side, just as the thing turned and headed in our direction. Within an instant it clattered through the stall directly in front of me, knocking me off my feet. I looked the poor creature straight in the face; it wasn't an animal, but a man, clothed only in a pair of shorts, sheer terror in his eyes and sweat dripping from his obese body.

"Sorry," he said, offering his hand to help me up.

Our fingertips barely touched when a voice barked from just beyond the crowd: "Stop!"

The man withdrew his hand and bounded away. He did not get very far this time, and his large frame fell just metres from me. At first, I feared he had been shot dead by an armed officer who had come right up beside me. His gun was still trained on the man, who was, thankfully, not dead, but writhing around on the ground, groaning in agony.

"Stay down!" snapped the officer.

The crowd had parted like the wake of a ship; the officer at its helm, the wounded man at its bow. The man mumbled, then stumbled to his feet. "I said down!" screamed the officer. "Hit him again."

A second officer stepped forward, raised his weapon and fired. Immediately the man crashed to the ground, his heavy body convulsing violently. Then I noticed thin wiry strands leading from both officers' guns to the man, where they were attached to several silver barbs protruding from his back. From nowhere, many more officers appeared, all dressed in grey uniform with the same red armband sporting the hooked cross that Lars wore. They swarmed around the man and, between them, hauled him to his feet and dragged him away.

"What was that all about?" I gasped.

"Did you see the size of him?" asked Lars.

"What?"

"Marianna, I told you in Grytviken. Fat people aren't tolerated. God knows where that lump of lard has been hiding out. Pretty quick on his feet, though, wasn't he?"

"What will they do to him?"

Lars forced a smile. "What do you think? What did *we* do with whales?"

I was at once both appalled and overjoyed. The stench from the carcasses rotting on the beach was unbearable, yet the sure feeling of land under my feet filled me with such overpowering happiness that I fell immediately to my knees and, again and again, scooped up piles of the dark, gritty debris, trying to embrace it as if it were my dearest long-lost friend.

My long-lost, *warm* friend. Whether my exuberance injected some imagined heat into this long-desired land, or whether it was a physical response to being adrift at sea for so many days, I couldn't tell. But it didn't matter what the cause was: the warmth, real or imaginary, enlivened my spirits and I lay down in the heated sand, whirling my arms and legs through it and giggling like I was five years old again. Hull, who quite possibly could have been five years old, enjoyed it, too. He skipped and rolled around and covered himself in muck to such an extent that, when he finally exhausted himself and lay down, panting with excitement, it was only from his drooping tongue that I could see he was a dog at all. Even Mrs Chippy ventured out, at first hesitating on the gunwales, then leaping down and tentatively pawing at the sand until, after satisfying herself that all was well, finding a nice warm spot in which to rest.

Thirst. Hunger. The words made me sit bolt upright; it was time to stop the frolicking. I stood and surveyed the beach properly. Rocky hills leading to ice-covered summits rose dramatically from the beach. The formidable peaks enveloped the entire island, like an amphitheatre gazing down upon a glassy stage and dwarfing the small settlement that someone had erected here.

The collection of buildings was situated on the beach at the tail end of a lumpy mountain slope which resembled a gargantuan seal, slumped with its head buried in a mountain of snow. The place reminded me of Grytviken, only stripped to the bare essentials. Several wooden buildings were clustered together on the beach directly in front of me; off to the right and not too far from the rotting corpses, huge rust-red drums, each the size of a church, towered over an adjacent barn. To the left, on its own

155

and some distance away, was yet another wooden construction. All of the buildings were similar: low-storeyed warehouses with sloping roofs. None would have ordinarily looked inviting, but for me, each one promised to be a palace of abundance, and I relished the prospect of exploring them.

"Come on Hull," I called, heading to the few huts directly ahead. "Let's go and see what's inside." He hastened to his feet and bounded to my side. "Mrs Chippy, you stay there." She didn't even acknowledge my instruction.

The first hut opened into a generator room. The machine was as tall as me and I guessed that it was used for powering some kind of whale-pulling winch. Piled high next to it was a large amount of coal and there were sacks, too, filled with potatoes, rice and other goods. This was a very bright start. A small, curved corridor led from this hut into the adjoining building. This was divided into a series of rooms. In the first was a small kitchen, complete with stove, pans, cupboards and an overflowing bin; from the state of the food remains I could tell that no-one had been here for quite some time. If I'd been anywhere else, I would not only have turned my nose up at the mess, but also ridiculed the awful yellow and green painted décor. But here, after seeing a world sapped of colour for days, I could not have found the interior design more appealing.

The few shelves and kitchen cupboards yielded some surprising treats stored away in various tins and boxes. Although everything was in Norwegian, I could tell that among the provisions were dried peas, beans and fruits, packets of hardtack biscuits, jars of molasses and numerous bottles of akvavit. Hull wagged his tail in anticipation, but I resisted the temptation to open something now, instead putting everything back where I had found it.

"Let's not rush into things, Hull. We don't know how long we'll be here." Hull dropped his tail.

Entering the adjoining room was like stepping into another, futuristic realm. Gone was the jumble of crockery, assortment of tins and garishly painted walls and cupboards. Here, from nickel-
156

grey floor to brilliant white ceiling, was the most modern technological equipment I had ever seen. I vaguely recognised this achromatic room as a radio station, fully equipped with transmitters, wires, knobs and dials and many devices which were wholly alien to me.

"Hey, Hull, maybe the generator runs this. All we have to do is power it up, twiddle a few buttons and someone will come to get us!" The dog's tail started wagging again. I can imagine he thought that if we were going to be rescued soon, we'd just as well return to the kitchen. "Let's see what's in the next room," I said. Hull looked disappointed, again.

In the next room, the table, chairs, and shelves filled with games and books suggested this was for eating and recreation. From here I entered what must have been a dormitory. Around the bunkbeds lay sheets, clothes, boots and all sorts of personal items. Judging by the state of the place, the residents had either left in a hurry, or were a slovenly bunch who did not much care for order. Either way, there was no indication that anyone had been here recently. I wondered where everyone had gone, and if the war in Europe had compelled them to leave.

I decided to head towards the building standing in isolation some distance away. On the way I noticed another shelter which I had missed before and peeked inside. It was a washroom and toilet. From its revolting state I deduced that it had never been frequented by a female before, and I had no desire to change that now. I quickly moved on.

The large building on its own excited me greatly. Just outside were a couple of wooden boats, completely broken and probably irreparable. Inside the building, I discovered several hardy tents and all kinds of tools and instruments that would be of interest to any boatbuilder: quite apart from the compasses, sextants and stacks of neatly cut timber, there were tools for sawing and sanding, tools for cutting and clamping, planing and pressing, tools for scraping and stripping, bevelling and blocking, marking and measuring, tools for carving and curving, tools for shaving
157

and shaping; tools I was familiar with, tools I had never seen before. No wonder the Norwegians were famed the world over for their craftsmanship. It was a boatbuilder's paradise and I spent so much time in here that I quite forgot about my hunger and thirst, and about Hull until he started to bark. I glanced over in his direction, and the husky gave me a glowering look.

"Okay, Hull. That's enough for the day. Let's get something to eat."

We walked back to the main hut, giving the toilet a wide berth. These unpleasant water closets were something I would have to sort out sooner or later. For now, all I wanted to do, all Hull wanted to do, was sit down, eat and rest. But the island had two more surprises for me before I could relax.

Lying on the beach, not far from where I had moored the *Galicia*, was a large elephant seal. Even from this distance, I could see a large scar on the left side of its face: it must be the same animal I had seen in the sea by Elephant Island. Had it followed me all the way here? Then a thought occurred to me: the rush through the reef; the inexplicable surge away from the bloodcurdling wave of ice; the self-propelled motions of the *Galicia* through the narrow passage to access this island – could it all be the work of this powerful animal before me? Was he helping me because I had refused to attack the seal pup? It seemed absurd, yet, for whatever reason, the creature was indeed here. I approached it with caution.

Hull followed, snaking around my legs, whimpering and growling with increasing intensity the closer we advanced. With a swiftness which belied its bulk, the huge seal shifted on its belly to face us full on. I had seen these creatures move before; they could cover ground astonishingly quickly. Then, just as in the sea, the seal thrust its neck towards the sky and bayed so loudly it seemed the very mountains shook; it was like a guffaw, reverberating around this forsaken amphitheatre of ice. When the last echo fell into the glassy bay, the seal dropped to his chest and stared at us with those jet-black eyes. He blinked several times, then placed his
158

head and extraordinarily long nose flat on the black sand. I couldn't be sure, but I think he promptly fell asleep, his deep breathing resonating through the sand like an idling engine.

"I think he was saying hello, Hull," I said, squatting on my haunches and rubbing the husky up on down on his thick coat. The dog was shivering noticeably, whether from the cold or from fear, it was impossible to tell. Either way, I decided to leave the seal in peace and head inside.

The seal was the first surprise. The second made me squeal with delight. Waiting on the ridge of the hut housing the generator stood a proud skua, looking this way and that, ruffling its feathers. Just like the seal and its welcoming roar, the skua greeted me in the way it knew best, with an ear-piercing squawk.

"Hello Carmen!" I rejoiced. "Well, it seems everyone has come for dinner. I suppose I'd better invite Mrs Chippy, too. Let's see what I can rustle up."

The kitchen stove was wood-fired, and on the broken boats alone there was plenty of spare material to fuel the stove for months. I melted some snow and cooked a huge feast of peas, potatoes and the last chunks of seal meat, washing it all down with hot tea. I think it was the most delicious dinner I have ever had. Hull thoroughly enjoyed it, too. I even made a dish for Mrs Chippy and Carmen. The cat left the vegetables, but greedily ate the rest. Carmen sat on the windowsill and looked at her dish suspiciously, before flying off to get something more delectable. She returned five minutes later with a very fat fish.

I thought about the large seal and peered past Carmen to see if he was still on the beach; he was. It didn't seem right to exclude him, but it seemed more wrong to offer him a dish of seal meat. What did elephant seals eat, anyway? The answer lay in my field of vision: Carmen's fish.

"Um, Carmen. Would you mind if...?" I pointed to her meal.

For a creature whose expressions do not change a great deal, she pulled off a very convincing glower, then flew off, leaving a half-eaten fish carcass on the windowsill. I took it to the elephant seal.

I announced my arrival before I got too close; I didn't want to startle the scarred colossus. When I was near enough, I threw the fish towards him; it seemed pathetically paltry next to his enormous head. The seal considered the small offering for a moment, then snorted it up into his great mouth and looked at me expectantly.

"Sorry, that's all I have. Hmm... everyone else has got a name; what should I call you?" I weighed up the options, and very nearly settled on 'Lars' when, in a moment of inspiration, I recalled something Albert had said to me when I last saw him. "The scar, the journey over the sea, the cleverness in helping me when I was in trouble. I have the perfect name for you: Odysseus!"

I'm not certain Odysseus took to his new name, for no sooner had I announced it, than he wrenched his huge frame around, lumbered off down the beach and slipped into the water. Or perhaps the fish had whetted his appetite and he simply went off in search of a more substantial dinner.

What a strangely dramatic couple of days it had been: the near-death experience of the ice-wave; the despair of failing to reach the shores of distant land; the danger of the narrow entrance to this bizarre, hidden horseshoe island; and now the delight of comfort in a well-equipped home and companionship among an odd mix of animals. In reality, my situation was still desperate, alone on an abandoned island somewhere in Antarctica, yet I only felt unremitting hope and joy as, exhausted from the tribulations of my experiences, I collapsed into one of the bunkbeds to sleep more soundly than I had for as long as I could remember.

Our next port of call, further up the African coast, was a relatively small harbour town called Walfish Bay. Despite the deep water bay, which allowed even large ships to dock, Kapitän Ritscher was extremely disparaging about the place.

"Hot, desolate, nothing to do or see," he complained as we gazed at the flag-bedecked town on our approach from the sea.

"There seem to be a lot of birds," I remarked. Huge flocks of pelicans, flamingos, and many others I had never seen before and had no hope of identifying colonised the coast, the sand spits and the skies.

"Great. Birds. Who's interested in them? For me this town represents everything that went wrong with the old Germany."

"How come?"

At that moment, Lars joined us.

"Ah, Shit, have you been here before?" I winced at Kapitän Ritscher's name for my friend.

"Just once. Not much here," replied Lars.

"See! This barren place is what Germany was left with when Africa was divided by the European powers, while France and Britain got more than half the continent between them. Just look at it," he said, sweeping his arm across the bay. "Nothing but desert. What were we ever going to do with this?"

"Bird-watch?" I hazarded. I don't know why I kept forgetting the captain's complete lack of humour.

"Anyway," he said, ignoring my comment, "at least we managed to get rid of the local population entirely."

"Where did you move them to?"

Lars coughed at my question. The captain looked at him and smiled. "They're all dead," he said coolly.

"You killed them?" I gasped.

"We allowed them to die by *almost* natural causes, put it like that."

"Why?"

Kapitän Ritscher's emotionless explanation shocked me, and Lar's apparent silent support of it all was just as ghastly. The captain told me how the people who lived here, or near here, were driven by German soldiers to the hot, inhospitable mountains further east, where survival was almost impossible. This, they were instructed, was where they were allowed to live. The Germans then poisoned any water wells they could find and shot anyone who strayed out of the territory. It had been more than two years since the last living local had been seen.

"So, I think you can say, they're extinct, and what little this awful place has to give is for us alone now," concluded the captain.

"They're doing it a bit more efficiently in Europe, though," added Lars.

"Of course. We do everything more efficiently in Europe."

Given his disinterest in birdlife and his loathing of desolate landscapes, I am quite certain Kapitän Ritscher would have gone quite mad had he found himself in my position on the horseshoe-shaped island.

If it were not for a very informative catalogue of the flora and fauna on the island which I had found in the abandoned base, I would not have been able to name any of them. As it was, I not only discovered that the island I had stumbled upon was called Deception Island, but also, over the first few months in which I spent there, I became quite the expert in identifying animals and plants, even from quite some distance.

There were birds everywhere: skuas, petrels, gulls, terns, penguins. Apart from the penguins and the brilliantly white snowy sheathbills, a lot of the other species resembled Carmen, although for me she always stood out, and I could spot her among her many feathered friends as they frolicked in the sky. One thing was certain: Carmen was kept very busy away from us on the beach, interacting with the other birds, and sometimes those interactions even seemed peaceful. Odysseus was occupied, too, when it suited him, as there were almost as many types of seals to connect with as there were birds for Carmen: elephant seals, Weddell seals, crabeater seals, fur seals, leopard seals. He was the boss of them all, however, and whenever he felt another creature was getting too close, he would bounce towards it with his mighty bulk and send the terrified pinniped dashing for the safety of Port Foster, the large bay which the island encircled.

Naturally, there were no other cats or dogs. I don't think Mrs Chippy was bothered at all; she enjoyed her own company too much and seemed to detest that of all others. Nor did Hull seem put out. He liked everyone, whatever they looked like; although I think I was his favourite, probably because I was the one who fed him.

The necessity of feeding Hull and Mrs Chippy, and of course myself, soon made me overcome any reservations about sacrificing an occasional penguin or seal. Both animals regularly
163

came to our beach, and it was simply a matter of going out to collect them, rather like picking mushrooms from the forest floor, just a bit bloodier. However, I still baulked at the idea of killing penguins myself, so opened the door for Hull and told him to go outside and fetch one. I stayed inside; I didn't want to see him attack the helpless creature. Just a short time later I heard the familiar scratching of his paws against the wooden door. There he was, a limp penguin in his mouth, looking very pleased with himself.

"Well done, Hull! You did it!" Then I saw past him. "Oh no! Hull! What have you done?!" He had slaughtered them all. A penguin massacre, their bodies littering the beach.

All of a sudden there was far more penguin meat than we possibly needed, so I buried what could still be salvaged in the snow on the nearby hills, and Odysseus had a fine couple of days gorging on the surplus. I didn't let Hull out by himself for some time after that, until I had trained him that one was enough. A sharp command after he had killed one and a rap around the ear if he ignored me was all that it took; he soon learnt not to repeat the slaughter. So we had no shortage of food; water was bountiful, too, as I simply had to cut snow blocks and take them my 'melt tanks' – pots or buckets – in the kitchen or generator room.

As for my own social well-being, I was too preoccupied with my situation to miss human contact. I spent the first few days, and then weeks, mainly with trying to figure out how to operate the radio station. I realised that, first of all, I had to get the generator working. That was the easy part: just by looking at the machine I could see that that I needed to put coal in the furnace and ensure there was enough water in the tank to provide steam for the turbine. Once the generator was fired up, I had to experiment a little, flicking various switches to find the one which turned the electricity on. When the lights came on in the radio station I leapt for joy, kissed Hull on the nose and ran outside screaming with sheer delight, with the husky spinning in circles as he followed me.

I had accomplished so much during my first few days on Deception Island, that I was fully convinced rescue was imminent. How wrong I was. For one thing, the controls in the radio room were baffling: at first, the machine emitted only squeaks and pips. No matter which dial I turned, no matter which direction, I never heard anything more than hisses, buzzes or whines. I spent many hours in that room, speaking into a microphone, asking if anyone could hear me and giving my location in case they could. But I never had any indication that my calls were being received. At times I would convince myself that a crackle was a faint voice, struggling to break through the interference. In those moments I would grab the microphone and plead, beg for someone, anyone, to repeat the message. But it never came to anything.

Over the ensuing weeks I developed a routine of spending a miserable hour in the morning and another in the evening in that room, idly fiddling with the knobs and switches, increasingly convinced I was wasting my time. Gradually, like chunks of ice melting before my eyes and seeping into the soil, the elation I had felt upon arrival ebbed away until nothing remained but dark pessimism. Hull remained ever hopeful, or at least it seemed that way, as he seemed to be permanently happy, but the futility of the task caused me occasionally to skip one of the shifts, and, months later, sometimes I didn't bother going into the room all day.

Where the radio station became the den of my despair, a closet where I allowed the deepest melancholy to gain full sway, outside that space I led a cheerful, fulfilling life, as remarkable as that may seem given my circumstances.

From the various books and magazines, I discerned that the British, the Norwegians, and North and South Americans had all been here at some point, exploring, researching or whaling, and they had left a wealth of information about the island. Quite why they were not here now, I did not know, but I put it down to the

165

war and hoped that, should my attempts to contact the outside world continue to fail, someone would return some day.

Until that point, I determined to discover the island for myself. I learned from the many folders that the base was built on a stretch of land called Whalers Bay, and the warm sand was due to heat rising from deep below my feet; the island was in fact an active volcano, its horseshoe shape the result of a monumental explosion in the distant past. Indeed, just next to the base, hot springs fed into a lagoon, and Hull and I spent many hours bathing in the balmy water, which was a pleasant change from the constant cold; even though it was now high summer, the ambient temperature barely rose above zero degrees.

Just a few days after the summer solstice it was Christmas, and I wanted to give all my companions a gift. Hull received a whalebone from one of the rotting cadavers, and Mrs Chippy got a fish, which Carmen had caught a few days before and deposited on my windowsill; perhaps she thought I was her chick. For Carmen, I had fixed a perch to the hut by the radio station room window; for a personal touch I wrote her name on a sign and dangled it from the perch. Days later I removed the sign, as I think it spooked her when it moved in the wind. I didn't really know what to get Odysseus. What do you gift a three-ton animal that just lies around all day? In the end I moved three large rocks to his favourite spot, one for each time I believe he had aided me in the sea.

My Christmas treat was to be a glass of wine in the lagoon. In fact, I took the whole bottle, but didn't intend to drink it all. Hull followed me in with his bone, and we thoroughly enjoyed splashing around with one another, until he dropped his bone and it sank to the bottom of the lagoon.

"Don't worry, Hull. The lake's shallow and I'm sure I can get it. If not, there are several thousand more just over there."

I swam over to where I thought he had dropped it, then saw to my utter consternation Odysseus shuffle along the bank and lurch into the lagoon. I felt at ease with him on land, and had even patted him on the head on many occasions, but here in the depths I was at his complete mercy. Hull had spotted him, too, and paddled away wide-eyed towards the opposite bank. Odysseus was upon us in seconds, circling around. I was certain he would attack.

But he did nothing; or rather, he merely played with us. Even in the shallow lake, Odysseus was able to keep his huge body hidden from us until the moment he chose to reveal himself. Every now and then his head popped above the surface, at times in front of us, at times behind or to the side. Each time he snorted, before diving down again, leaving me to guess where he might next emerge. I was beginning to enjoy the game. Then things took a sinister turn: Odysseus grabbed my leg and pulled me under. I knew intuitively that this was no aggressive act, but the huge seal was incalculably stronger than I and could have crushed the bones in my leg without any effort. I fought to overcome my instinct to struggle free and instead twisted my body so I could stroke the side of his face. Never is time more relative than when you are under water in the mouth of an elephant seal. Those few seconds, twenty perhaps at most, just two or three metres down, lasted as long as my entire life had up until that point. Then Odysseus let me go and I quickly swam to the surface and to the safety of the bank. I didn't feel quite in the mood to play anymore, and Hull had already made good his escape. I returned, my heart racing, back to the base, where I downed several glasses of wine from a new bottle.

Before the weather turned too severe, I determined to hike to the highest peak on the island, Mount Pond, convincing myself that if I could reach the most formidable summit, I could overcome any challenge on this island. I remembered seeing the peak from the *Galicia* when I had first approached the island, and I had seen it every day since, looming over Whalers Bay. It had been an ever-visible challenge from the moment the island had come into view. The charts that previous occupiers of my base had left behind revealed to me that the peak topped five hundred metres, and that the easiest approach to the peak would be from another cove, about eight miles further along my branch of the horseshoe.

A few weeks after the Christmas incident, I decided the weather was fair enough to go. The sky was murky, covered with one lumpy grey cloud, but the days were still long at this time of the year, and I figured I could row to the cove, hike up and down the summit and be back again within ten hours. It was the farthest I had ventured while being stranded here and I was feeling anxious, even though I had plenty of suitable equipment that I had found at the base: spare oars, a sturdy backpack, gloves, a hat, hiking boots which almost fitted and warm clothes, some of which I had to shorten so that they didn't droop over my feet and hands. I didn't look elegant, but I looked the part.

Hull jumped into the *Galicia*, and Mrs Chippy strolled down to the water's edge to see us off; she had no intention of joining the expedition. Odysseus eyed us suspiciously, but when I pushed the boat into the bay and began to row, he entered the water, too. His presence was reassuring. I scoured the sky for Carmen but couldn't see her anywhere.

I rowed on the calm waters of Port Foster, skirting the dismal cliffs and rocky hills along the coast. Under sunlight, Deception Island shone with an awe-inspiring beauty, the rays gleaming off icy cliffs and the harbour shining radiant blue. But today, the water was grey, the snow lifeless, and the rocks dark and brooding.

The beach at Pendulum Cove, where I would begin my hike, was with its black, gravelly sand similar to the one at Whalers Bay. A towering rock-red hill, perhaps one hundred metres high and reminiscent of the stone sentinel watching over the entrance to this island, guarded the southern aspect to the cove. Steam rose through the dark volcanic ground and drifted in wispy clouds with the vagaries of the breeze. Out of interest, I dug a small hollow in the sand, and it quickly filled with boiling water. It smelled terrible, but Hull must have thought I had prepared some kind of

168

soup for him and he moved to the edge of the hollow to begin his feast.

"No, Hull. I don't think you can drink that," I warned.

I set off and the husky followed, turning around every few metres to glance at the tasty stew he thought I had made for him in the sand and then, bafflingly, denied him.

We climbed a prominent, ice-free ridge and I gained an unobstructed view of Mount Pond. I had imagined a steep-sided, ice-covered, mountain-like peak; it had certainly struck me that way when I had seen it from the sea or my base. But, much like many elements of this island, that appearance was deceptive. From this angle, Mount Pond revealed a gradual ascent leading to a relatively flat summit, sprayed with pockets of ice and snow; the whole elevation resembled an enormous gateau with white sprinkles scattered around it.

"Now *that*," I declared to Hull, "does look tasty."

Nevertheless, it was far from an easy, afternoon stroll. I had to choose my path with caution, taking care not to take the immediately most obvious route, which might later lead me to an area with even greater challenges. I opted for an initially taxing climb, then the gradient levelled off and we reached the cold, windy summit reasonably swiftly. Someone had kindly pitched a sign here, so there was no mistaking we were at the highest point of the island. Green lichen clung to yellow rocks and volcanic vents hissed nearby, again demonstrating how the island's harsh, forbidding, icy front belied its other side of warmth and colour. We approached a vent to benefit from its warming air.

"This is our home, Hull," I said, crouching down next to him. "Just look at that magnificent view." I don't think he was impressed; perhaps he was still thinking of the warm stew on the beach.

For me, however, it was breathtaking. I was on top of the world and the full expanse of the horseshoe-shaped island presented itself to me. It was as if the island had been welded together in three separate segments. In almost matching symmetry, ice hills

169

rose opposite one another on the two outer branches of Deception Island, linked in the centre by the third piece, a largely ice-free strip of rock; each of the three sections was perhaps ten miles long. All around the inner edge, but particularly in the centre section, shimmered a number of inlets colonised by seals, penguins and a variety of seabirds. Steam escaped from vents not just here on Mount Pond, but around the entire ring, and hot mist swirled in the numerous coves. There was just one entrance, the narrow gap between the two peninsulas I had come through, the portal complete with its citadel guardian. Deception Island was an Antarctic fortress, a place forged by the hands of an ice-god, a stadium in the remotest part of the world that was intended to be hidden from human intrusion. Shame, deference and a sense of privilege coursed through me in equal measure. I had a strong sense that I had no right to be here, yet circumstance had allowed me to observe this beating heart of nature in its rawest form, and to see from my elevated position the scope of its serenity, its beauty, its life and its volcanic fury.

"Is that why the people left?" I mused out loud. "Did an eruption scare everyone away, or even kill them?"

We stayed on the mountain much longer than I had intended. If Albert had been with us, he would have possibly mentioned something about being lost in the moment of time. But this affected Hull far less than me, and I knew I had to get us both back to the base before either of us grew too cold, tired, or hungry.

Seeing Lars, someone who had saved my life, the only person to whom I had entrusted my identity all those years ago, had been a great source of comfort to me as I transitioned from my life in isolation. Now, with his indifference to the plight of the Africans, I felt as if I barely knew him at all and didn't feel inclined to see him as we travelled up the West African coast, back on board *MS Schwabenland*. But avoiding someone permanently on a ship is no easy task, especially when they come knocking on your door.

He came, smartly dressed in his uniform, gift in hand. It was the same book he had seen in the harbour market in Cape Town. I thanked him for the gift, threw it on the bed and said I was busy.

"Marianna, stop ignoring me. What have I done wrong?"

"If you don't know, then there's no point discussing it."

"You've been off with me ever since Walfish Bay."

I sat down next to the book, picked it up and inspected its cover. "It's not just what you told me there. It's everything." I said, without looking up.

"What do you mean?"

I sighed, placed the book on my lap, and fixed my gaze on his. "Tell me and tell me clearly. What did you mean, back in Cape Town, when you said those guards chasing the man would do the same to him as we used to do with the whales?"

"Okay. You're going to find out sooner or later, anyway." Lars sat down next to me. "We don't catch whales anymore. That's banned."

"Good."

"Yeah, I suppose. But we still need to get our things from somewhere."

171

"Things?" I queried.

"Yes, things, and stop interrupting me. Listen, there are simply too many people on the planet, and rather than just let those who no longer have a place get buried or burnt, it makes much more sense to use them. The dead don't need their bodies anymore."

"What?!" I covered my mouth in horror.

"It's the right thing to do, Marianna, if you think about it. Those millions and millions of bodies, that's a massive resource."

"But... but... what...?" I could barely articulate my disgust.

Lars misunderstood my stammering. "Well, medical research for one, making soap for another. That's what I meant about the obese man in Cape Town. Did you know that eighty kilogrammes of human fat can produce more than twenty-five kilogrammes of soap?"

I shook my head; not in response to his question, but in complete disbelief at what he was telling me. Lars nodded.

"It's true. Takes a while to get your head round it, doesn't it? Think of the whales, if that makes it easier. Come on," he said, slapping me good-humouredly on the thigh, as if that would make everything all right between us, "it's not me doing all these things, so you shouldn't be off with me. We're docking in Freistadt soon, our last stop in Africa. Let's have a good time." He stood up and straightened his uniform.

"It's not what you're doing, it's what you're not doing. How could you stand by and let all these people be murdered by the Nazis? What are you even doing wearing that uniform? You're not a German."

"Okay, I see why you're angry. But you have to understand the world isn't like it was when you left it thirty years ago. So much has changed."

"It's horrible."

Lars sat back down next to me. He pointed to the book and gestured for me to pass it to him. "Africa," he said quietly, absent-mindedly, running his hand over the front cover for several

172

seconds. I'm not sure what faraway, dreamy thoughts he was having, but they snapped back to our cabin and he looked at me as intently as I had gazed at him a few moments ago. "Marianna, my nickname, the one the captain calls me, it says it all, really. I'm known for getting out of... sticky situations. Well, the Germans have overrun pretty much all of Europe, and all the European colonies have fallen to them, too. In Africa, the Southern Ocean, everywhere. You can join them, or fight them."

"Why don't you fight, then?"

"They're unstoppable. Even here, this port we're heading to now, Freistadt. Not long ago it was called Libreville. Do you know what happened to it?"

"I guess the Nazis killed everyone in Libreville and renamed it Freistadt," I answered moodily.

"Well, yes and no. It was the only place in West Africa to resist the French when they controlled the area. As the French were fighting Germany in Europe, the local resistance in Libreville was inadvertently helping with the German war effort. The Nazis sent in their troops to help the locals, just a handful of them, and slaughtered all the French. Then they removed all the locals – resettled or killed, who knows? – and renamed the town Freistadt. That's the point. You can't resist them; they assimilate everything. The only way out of the... sticky situation, is to put on this uniform."

"So you gave up."

"So you adapt. You did the same, on Deception Island. You wore clothes that weren't yours, that didn't fit. You changed them, made them yours, didn't you? You did it to survive. We all wear what we need to survive."

"I think that's a bit different."

"Really? Not from where I'm standing. It doesn't change who you are on the inside, does it? Take that book. If you changed the dust cover, put a swastika on the planes for example, the Nazis would probably leave it alone. It doesn't change the story one bit. This uniform doesn't change me." Silence fell between us. I
173

understood his logic but felt appalled by it for reasons I could not even explain. He could see that I was struggling to respond. "Okay, put it like this. If we don't adapt to what's going on all around us, we fail. Just look at the climate. If we don't make the difficult decisions which, granted, will result in hardship for millions of people, then we're all doomed. You, me, everyone. Surely you can see that? Nature is the ultimate emperor, and we have to adjust to its whims. But on our scale, the human scale, we have our own emperors, our kings, rulers, and Führers. You must conform to their system, or similarly you will not survive."

"It's shit logic," I snapped, surprising myself with my crudeness.

"That's my point exactly."

After the hike to Mount Pond, I felt motivated to explore new coves and hills in the following weeks, but I had to stop when Hull hurt himself on a slippery slope. I didn't see what happened, alerted to his injury only by a high-pitched yelp. I was very concerned that he had broken his leg, because he was limping painfully. It nearly broke my heart to see him in so much agony. I carried him to the boat, and, once back at home, set the leg in a splinter as best as I could, but I didn't really know how to treat injuries and feared I might make it worse. I shouted at him a lot to lie down over the next couple of weeks, before he seemed able to walk without much discomfort again. I hope he understood I was just trying to help him.

For his sake, then, I was more confined to the base than usual, and during this time became increasingly bothered by the carcasses slowly rotting on my beach. The thousands of slaughtered whales were a daily reminder of the brutality committed by the people here before me, and, especially in light of my experience on Mount Pond, I considered myself duty-bound to remove the grotesque eyesore and restore the beach to its natural state. Quite apart from that, it looked awful and just gave me nightmares.

It would have been wasteful, almost disrespectful to the lives of these creatures, had I simply cut them up and cast them back into the sea. I thought they should have given their lives for something, at least, so endeavoured to make best use of the enormous resources contained in their bodies. I had seen men strip a whale before and had a very rudimentary understanding of what was required.

Using the tools I had found in the big shed, I began to chop away chunks of whale, piece by piece, storing the blubber in the huge vessels, sorting through the bones and piling them to the side, and throwing the rest into the bay. I am sure that through my ignorance I lost much of what the whales had to offer, but there was simply such a vast amount of it that it didn't really matter.

Just one whale would keep me occupied for weeks; this was a lifetime undertaking. However, in my little way, I felt I was making a difference, doing a good thing, and certainly the local birdlife benefitted, swooping down to collect scraps of flesh and carrying them off to feast in private on the beach or to take to hungry chicks, waiting open-mouthed somewhere on the cliffs.

It was bloody work, and even after immersing myself in the lagoon and rubbing my body vigorously I still could not scrub away all of the visceral slivers which pasted to my skin, pick out the shreds of entrails which clung to my hair, or rid myself of the stench of death and decay. I knew I had to do something about it when Hull showed greater enthusiastic pleasure in licking me, and even Mrs Chippy began to edge closer with avaricious eyes. That was when I recalled something Lars had told me about his grandparents.

"I wonder," I thought out aloud as I pushed Hull away from me one evening and got ready to throw a boot at the cat, "if I could make soap, like they used to."

I had seen some seaweed washed up on the beaches, so knew there must be forests of kelp somewhere beneath the surface. I waded into the bay, right up to my chin, and foraged up and down the coast, hoping to get my feet tangled in an underwater forest. The sharp chill of the water was almost heart-stopping, but nothing new to me; the lakes around Zürich were just as cold as this in the winter. But I found very little, just the occasional floating stalk or leaf.

By the end of the week, and after collecting every piece of stranded kelp from the beaches, I thought my disappointing haul might indeed be enough; my first soap experiment could begin. I cleaned one of the many kilns on the beach, put all of the seaweed in a big metal pot so that its ash wouldn't be contaminated by the coal or wood, lit the kiln, then stood back to watch.

My companions all observed the experiment with me: Hull, by my side; Carmen from the top of one of the huge storage tanks; Mrs Chippy took her place right next to the kiln, almost burning her nose when she inspected it; and Odysseus from where he always was, but he kept his eyes open for longer than usual.

When the fire had gone out, I opened the kiln door, fully expecting to see a pile of seaweed ash at the bottom of the pot. All I saw was dry seaweed. It hadn't burned at all. The experiment was a failure. However, I still had the kelp and could try again.

It took many attempts, and my companions soon got bored of the exercise, apart from Mrs Chippy, who never grew tired of

176

sleeping next to the kiln, but I finally devised a way in which I could get the seaweed to burn. The secret, I discovered, was to dry it in individual strands first; it seemed so obvious, but I hadn't done this before. Next, I pressed the dry strands into a briquet and let it stand for a few weeks; this squeezed out any remaining moisture and made it kiln-ready. Finally, I used a metal plate, and ditched the pot, so the flames could reach the kelp briquet; again, obvious to those who knew what they were doing. When I opened the door and saw a small mound of grey ash, I yelped for joy. I felt as if I had created a masterpiece. However, after so many failed experiments, my powdery pile was very meagre; indeed, I could fit it all on a spoon.

Nevertheless, I had a workable amount of ash. Now I had to mix it with some melted blubber. I knew I had only one shot at it. I thought a cupful might be about right. I boiled up the blubber in the kitchen – the thick black smoke and stench drove even Mrs Chippy away from the heat – then stirred in the ash, put it in a cup and allowed the product to set outside. I was very excited the next morning to see how it had turned out.

My excitement didn't last long. My 'soap' was a cup-shaped gelatinous mass, flecked with dirty grey spots. If I rubbed this on me, I thought, I would end up not only dirtier, but greasier too. However, I had sweated so much to get this far, I had to see the experiment through to the end. I walked to the lagoon, bar in hand. My companions followed me, even Odysseus. It was very unnerving, sitting in the lagoon with four sceptical pairs of animal eyes trained on me from the water's edge. I turned my back on them and scrubbed the back of one soot-blackened hand with the soap. The results were… satisfactory. The soap was a little slithery, it crumbled on contact, too, but it seemed to work, at least better than if I had simply scrubbed with water.

"See!" I shouted to my doubting audience. "You all thought that it wouldn't work! Well, have some of this!" I cheered, showing them the back of my hand.

Maybe they took the gesture as an insult, as Carmen flew away and Mrs Chippy slunk off; but Hull and Odysseus understood it as an invitation to join me, and both bounded into the lagoon.

"Oh no. Here we go again," I moaned, and exited as quickly as I could.

Summer was certainly coming to an end, now. Small, needle-like ice crystals, barely visible and forming in the shallows, pointed to the fact that autumn now had its grip on Deception Island. Soon, the water turned black with gelid slicks of thin ice, which then coalesced, merging to cover the entire expanse of Port Foster. I observed with fascination as this ice whitened, thickened, until, when winter had truly arrived, it was strong enough to support my weight and I could walk from one branch of the island to the other over the frozen harbour.

But with the change in temperature came a change in the volatility of the weather, too. Much of the time I was forced to shelter as winds more ferocious than I had ever experienced whipped around the inner ring, churning, surging, swirling with maniac unpredictability. Within the hut I was quite safe with Hull and Mrs Chippy, although the fear that a tempest would suddenly tear off the roof or send something crashing through a window never left me. Odysseus had long since departed, and I never saw Carmen once during this time. I prayed she would survive the storms.

I never gave up complete hope that the radio would work, but I reasoned that the chances of my signals being received were even lower during the storms. When I could, I busied myself with a further pastime, spending many hours in what I called the boat house, for I had decided to build a boat. Here a storm could be raging outside and I would barely notice it, so absorbed was I in the project. Apart from keeping my mind and body active, the boat would serve one of two purposes: I just hadn't yet decided which one.

I was convinced that if I were ever to leave Deception Island, it would be under my own steam, and my vague plan was to sail the boat all the way back to South Georgia. However, as I didn't really know how to handle a boat in those demanding conditions and had already seen how deadly the Southern Ocean could be, I wasn't too thrilled by this prospect. My alternative plan for the boat would be to cross the Bransfield Strait, the current of which I had been caught in, over to the main Antarctic continent. There, I rather wishfully envisaged, I would head to the South Pole and on my way intercept Shackleton's expedition.

Both ideas seemed fanciful, sure to end in failure, and failure meant death. Yet my extreme situation called for exceptional measures, and I proceeded with the project. The one thing I knew for certain, was that I could build a good boat, and I was building one bigger, stronger and more stable than the *Galicia*. This one I had decided to name after my new home; I decided to call it *Deception*.

We were approaching the archipelago

Cape Verde, which, I have been informed, was crucial in determining the outcome between the two European heavyweights, Germany and Britain. I had imagined two vast fleets coming head-to-head, slogging it out against one another, but Kapitän Ritscher told me I was very much mistaken.

"Not everything is about boats, Frau Dittrich. This clash was between the greatest minds of the lands, their Alan Turing against our Albert Einstein."

"What did Albert do to him?" I asked, instantly concerned for the British man I had never even heard of before.

"Ha ha, yes, you are right, Professor Einstein won, of course." Kapitän Ritscher then proceeded to tell me that these were important waters during the height of the war, as the British needed safe passage for their critical supply lines to Africa, and South and East Asia. So the Germans patrolled them in the hope of intercepting and destroying British ships. "Our submarines communicated via a coded machine called the Enigma. However, several years ago three German submarines were ambushed off this archipelago, leading us to conclude that the cipher had been cracked. Enter our friend Albert Einstein. He suggested keeping the Enigma operational, but now sending erroneous messages. To substitute it he created a further encryption device, called Gordius."

"So you tricked the British into believing they were gathering secret information?" I asked, only half-grasping what the captain was telling me.

"Yes! You should have seen the British!" laughed Kapitän Ritscher, "one day rubbing their hands with glee, then next running around like headless chickens! Headless chickens are already half-dead, and it was easy to finish them off!"

"So who was Alan Turing?"

"Ah, he was their best brain, the one who cracked the Enigma. But he was no match for Professor Einstein. A thousand of their Davids are no match for our Goliath! As you can see, look!"

I knew what I was about to see: a port, Nazi flags draped everywhere.

"It looks like all the other places you've captured."

"Yes. Wonderful, isn't it. We allow the Portuguese to administer Cape Verde, though. They didn't fight us in the war, and soon came over to our side when they saw we couldn't be beaten. To be honest, Frau Dittrich, they can have it. Some time ago, yes, maybe it was nice here, but now, nothing but hot mountains in the middle of the sea."

The ocean had not spared this archipelago from its incessant, rising incursion; it had already claimed the beaches, the captain told me, and would soon swallow up the low-lying ports, too.

"Can nothing stop this happening?" I asked him.

"Only Professor Einstein can."

I could take my time over *Deception*; with the harbour frozen over I certainly wasn't going anywhere soon. Boat design has always confounded me with one problem: how to increase speed while not increasing resistance or compromising on stability. I would have some distance to travel on the ocean and did not want to be floating around at slow speed, so I wanted the boat to glide swiftly through the water, but it also needed to be extremely stable; I could survive weeks on the open sea, but only minutes if I capsized. For considerable speed, a considerable sail or engine is essential, but both needed something large to hold it up or hold it in, and a tall mast or wide hull only increase the frictional surface; moreover, both required a strong hull to support them. All of this works against the extra power gained.

To try and resolve this conundrum, at least partly, I settled upon a flat-bottomed hull, which afforded the greatest resistance to rolling, but slightly rounded it to allow smoother displacement through the water. But I wasn't happy; the boat would still be too cumbersome. I had to make her faster, to get more of her keel out of the water. However, to be stable, she had to be wide. I spent many hours staring at my unfinished boat, wondering what I could do.

Deception put me quite literally between the hammer and the anvil, as I could not afford to compromise on either stability or speed, yet one had to give to the other. My frustrations were not helped by the ferocious winter weather. I had optimised the blubber-filled plate candles that Lars had shown me on Elephant Island, simply by putting the blubber in deeper pans and twisting some fabric ripped from rags into a usable wick. They could stay alight for days at a time without the need to refill them. Despite having many of these small fires burning around my workspace, it was almost impossible to warm the chilly boathouse, and my hands would sometimes be so numb with cold that I could barely hold the tools. When the raw elements attacked my senses so completely with their icy bite, I could do nothing else but retire to the main hut, which was kept pleasantly warm by the unfailing

182

generator, and while away the time reading or re-reading the many magazines and books, even those written in Norwegian.

Hull was an ever-present companion by my side, providing warmth of affection if not in actual heat. I could even just about bear to be in the same room as Mrs Chippy, so long as she stayed at the far end of whichever room we were in. I often relayed my boat dilemma to them. Hull answered by tilting his head, as if contemplating the problem with me; Mrs Chippy would just stare at me for as much as a minute, then look away, indicating that I should not bother her with such trifling matters. I found amusement in their reactions, but I did long for someone to talk back to me.

Only the radio offered any hope in that regard. But, however often I tried to engage with it, it would just crackle and hiss at me. Whatever vexations I had with the boat design, they were outdone by this persistent babble. Though I harboured some perhaps foolish notion that the boat issue would be resolved with a eureka moment of inspiration, the radio, this complicated instrument of indecipherability, would, I feared, continue to confound me. I would never understand its language; the Norwegian magazines made more sense to me.

The radio room was not a happy place for me. It had come to represent my utter detachment from normal society, a place of disabled connection, a world in which I could hear a thousand chattering voices, mingled and indistinct, fused in the whispering hum of white noise, while my single voice went unheard. I often cried in this room. Perhaps it was for this reason that Hull and Mrs Chippy did not dare to enter, remaining in the doorway, sleeping on the threshold between my lonely world of the radio room, and the cold, unlit recreation room.

One night I was fiddling around with the knobs and buttons, admittedly having drunk a little too much of the seeming endless supply of akvavit, while Hull and the cat were lying together side by side in the doorway. I was too tipsy to care about Mrs Chippy's proximity to me, and I think I had been building up a natural

183

tolerance to the animal, anyway; with each passing week I seemed to be sneezing less when she was around, and I hadn't suffered even the slightest rash for months. So long as I didn't actually touch her, she barely affected me at all.

"Hello? Anyone there? Deception Island calling the world...."

I knew it was futile, but it kept me occupied and, more importantly, justified staying up so that I could complete my self-imposed challenge of finishing the whole bottle.

"Ma...ri...an...na?"

Did I imagine that? Was that a murmur of my self-delusion, grasping a solid string of consonants out of the airy crackle?

"Mari...anna?" There it was again! Volume, tone, pitch, intensity – it *was* my name, spoken by someone familiar with it, someone searching for *me*. I grabbed the microphone, very nearly knocking over the bottle of akvavit, and spoke hurriedly.

"Hello? Hello? It's me! Marianna! I'm here! Who is that? Can you hear me?"

"Marianna? Is that really you? I can't believe I've found you!" I knew that man's voice. Even through the metallic drone of the loudspeakers, it sounded friendly, assured, intelligent. We said it at the same time: "It's Albert!"

We chatted for hours: I found out how he had discovered me; plotting my progress on a map once he had learned from some fishermen in Hull, probably Jack's 'friends', that I had left with Shackleton's crew; then, when he learned that I had set off on the *Sandefjord*, he researched the currents, tides, wind direction and calculated the possibility of survival until, finally, his pen rested on a small, remote horseshoe-shaped island off mainland Antarctica. Only Albert had the intellect, perseverance and attention to detail to accomplish such a remarkable feat of investigative work. The only person capable of finding me was Albert; the only person who wanted to find me was Albert.

Throughout the night and into the morning we talked, we shared, we laughed, we cried. Eventually, not even the excitement at speaking with Albert could keep me awake and my

184

heavy eyes, weighed down by lack of sleep and the drag of too much alcohol, closed for many hours.

When I awoke, I felt like a person reborn. The days now had an added purpose: I would bring some meat in to thaw, cut some snow blocks for the day's fresh water, exercise Hull, shovel snow off the roof or dig it away from the doors, repair the hut if an overnight storm had caused some damage, work on the boat, feed the dog and the cat, maybe walk on the ice or read in the warmth, and, best of all, towards midnight talk with Albert. He never grew tired of my stories. I could recount every minute of the day in detail, and he would still ask for more.

"Describe the snow for me. Are you not scared of falling through the ice and into the harbour? Where do you suppose Carmen and Odysseus have gone?" and many more questions besides.

Naturally, I asked him about his life, his wife, his children, his job, his interests. Carmen. He told me what I already knew: he didn't see too much of Mileva and the children; he was a very successful professor; he was still worried about the impact man was having on the environment; and he hadn't heard anything from Carmen.

I explained my dilemma about the boat to him and expected him to advise me to stay where I was, as help was on its way. I was somewhat taken aback by his response.

"You will find the answers around you. Keep your eyes open, your ears alert, for nature has a way of telling us what we must do."

"But, Albert, won't someone come for me?"

"Sure, eventually. But why wait for others? Help comes to those who act, not to those who sit idly by and expect some miracle. What is life but the constant choice between different rocky paths? Some are smoother than others, but all inevitably lead to some obstacle. You are at your obstacle now, and you must overcome it."

"So you're saying I should continue to build the boat and go to the South Pole?" I asked doubtfully.

185

"It would be a remarkable achievement," crackled his shrewd, tinny voice.

He had to go, then, and I sat back in the chair, contemplating his advice. It *would* be a remarkable achievement; he could have taken those words right out of my mouth. But, how was I to find the answers to my dilemma in this environment? All I had surrounding me was a near endless loop of frozen hills and a frozen harbour. It was not much to go on; no wonder my mind was frozen, too. I looked at Hull and Mrs Chippy, asleep together on the threshold, taking up all the space in the doorway, as always.

"Looks like it's down to you two to provide me with some inspiration," I said, then took myself off to bed.

The next day I was working on *Deception* and, unusually, both animals had braved the short but harsh trudge through snow and howling wind to the boathouse. I lit a plate of blubber, set it beside them, and told Hull not to put his nose in it. After lighting several more plates and placing them randomly around the workspace, not only to provide light during the sunless winter, but also in an attempt to take the edge of the biting chill, I sat at one end of the boathouse and gazed upon the structure of *Deception*.

The scene was reminiscent of some arcane fire ritual, small pyres burning in the close darkness of the boathouse around the skeletal frame of the boat, perhaps to pacify a sea deity, or mark a birth or death, the boat to aid their passage from one stage of life to the next. The crowded flames danced noiselessly on the rim of the plates, flashing in the eyes of my two companions. I wondered what they made of the spectacle.

"Don't worry, you two, I won't sacrifice you. But I have to sacrifice something. Speed or stability..." I rubbed my chin, mumbling those two words repeatedly while glancing from my companions to my boat.

"That's it!" I rejoiced and ran to Hull and Mrs Chippy, I wanted to hug them both, even the cat, but she darted away to a dark

186

corner, startled by my sudden charge. Hull sprang to his feet and wagged his tail hopefully as I flung my arms around his hairy neck. "Albert was right! You two lying there is just what I needed, taking up all that space with your slim bodies! I have to build a catamaran!"

The solution had quite literally been staring at me in the face all along. I knew that thousands of years ago people made these double-hulled boats to sail across the ocean and reach new islands, and this was almost exactly what I needed to do.

Of course, it would mean an almost complete overhaul of *Deception*: I needed to take a saw to her, split her in two, make one section longer than the other and cover it all with a deck. The more I thought about it, the more I realised it was the perfect design, for my catamaran also needed space for Hull and Mrs Chippy. Although at best my relationship with the cat could be described as mutual tolerance, I could not possibly leave her all alone on the island, but neither could she stay in the same space as me as we travelled across the ocean. The second hull would be smaller, and she could have it all to herself. I knew she wouldn't appreciate the extra effort I would have to make for her, but it gave me immense satisfaction to know I had the moral high ground, even as she glared at me disdainfully from the corner of the boathouse.

Albert thought the idea was wonderful and encouraged me to put all of my energies into the project. He even suggested there might be one further benefit to making the boat double-hulled: I could detach the smaller hull, use it as a sledge for a trek to the South Pole and pull off one of the greatest surprises in the history of Antarctic exploration.

"Just picture Shackleton's face!" exclaimed Albert. "What a photo that would make."

He was right, and I had an even stronger motivation: my father. I would never be able to tell him of this adventure, but I could take him in my heart and complete a journey that may not have been his personal aspiration, yet would certainly have made his

187

jaw drop with wonder and given him a tale to tell with enthusiastic pride in Aleksandra Inn. I would do it because he couldn't.

Looking at the charts, it seemed so perfectly simple: I could hug the coast of the continent, drifting anti-clockwise on the same current that had brought me to Deception Island, all the way to Hut Point. This was where an Australian group had planned to start laying supplies for Shackleton's crew. Their ship, the *Aurora*, should be anchored there now. If the ship and the supplies had gone by the time I arrived there, that meant Shackleton had already passed through. Yet even then I wouldn't abandon the plan, as I still determined to reach the South Pole. However, if the ship and supplies were still there, then Shackleton had not yet finished his expedition. I really hoped that would be the case, imagining his reaction as he saw me approach from the opposite direction.

Assuming Shackleton had not yet completed this part of his expedition, travelling from depot to depot to the South Pole would, I figured, take about a month, and another to return. Even if I added a further month, that would only be three months of travelling; I could easily take enough provisions in the catamaran-sledge to sustain me, as I didn't want to touch Shackleton's supplies; I could shelter in a tent and had already proven my ability to endure in the harsh climate. Once I had reached the very bottom of the world, I would return to Hut Point either with or without Shackleton. If I was on my own, I would reaffix the sledge and brave the open ocean to reach Australia, although I didn't much fancy that option; I really hoped I could travel on the *Aurora*. Even if it all went badly, and I had to abandon my sledge and my South Pole challenge somewhere on the ice, then I would still have a boat in which I could make the journey across the sea. Mrs Chippy would then of course have to travel with me; I hoped it would not come to that. Satisfied that I had thought of everything, I set to work.

After being at sea for many days since
Freistadt, I was very happy to have the chance to get my feet on dry land for a couple of days when we docked in the harbour of Praia, the capital of Cape Verde. I was not so happy, however, by the unrelenting heat, a discomfort exacerbated by the overwhelming number of people bustling past. I had only been on the island for a half of an hour by the time Lars led me to a busy tavern, but was already sweaty, irritable, and wishing we could be back on the ship.

It was no better inside the tavern, out of the glare of the sun, for the sweltering bodies of the rowdy patrons raised the temperature where the rays could not reach. Lars found a table in the corner, then ordered something I did not quite catch from a gruff, shaven-headed, burly man who would have looked more at home on a pirate ship; from the savage scowl he gave us from behind the bar, he seemed just about ready to run us through with a cutlass, too. Lars surveyed the scene about him.

"This is nice," he said with a smug smile.

"No it isn't."

"Don't mind him," said Lars, nodding towards the bar. "The people here don't like this uniform. But it helps to wear one; in getting this table, for instance."

"There are so many people here. Where've they all come from? I thought we were in the middle of nowhere in the Atlantic Ocean."

"Well, firstly, a lot of people have been displaced, because the sea has claimed or is threatening to claim their towns and villages on the coast. This city has built a lot of sea defences which, for the moment, is helping it to survive. Cape Verde has a lot of low-

189

lying land, so it's quite badly affected by the rising sea. Most of the people now live in the cities, where the coastal defences are better."

"I see."

"And secondly, this archipelago has become a useful stop-off point for those trading with South America. It's only the Yanks and some pockets of resistance in Europe who are still fighting the Germans in Europe, so now there's a flourishing trade between the continents on either side of the Atlantic. There's a lot of money to be made in Praia, before things reach their official destination."

"What do they trade?"

"Here's dinner," announced Lars, as the brawny innkeeper slung two plates on to our table.

It was a simple stew of meat and beans, but tasty enough. Lars explained that many of the forests which had been cleared for farming were now being allowed to rewild. As a consequence, beef, pork, lamb, chicken, goat – all of these meats and many others such as turkey, buffalo, goose, rabbit – no matter where you went and what the preferred local meat was, all of it was becoming a prized delicacy. I poked the scraps of meat around in my stew and remarked that this dish must be quite a treat, but Lars ignored my comment.

"Of course, you can still get meat, at a price. I have some whale meat with me, and in places like these you can do some great deals. A tavern is the best place to conduct this kind of business, away from the authorities' eyes." Lars clicked his fingers and the innkeeper came over with two drinks.

"You really do earn your nickname, don't you?" I smiled.

"Skål!" Lars raised his glass, and I did the same, and we toasted to his shady dealings. I took a gulp of the drink and my eyes nearly popped right out of my head in a sugar rush.

"What is this?" I gasped, blinking madly.

"Grogue. Sweet, isn't it?" he smirked.

190

It wasn't to my liking at all and I needed to counter the syrupy flavour quickly. "So what is this meat, then? Pork?"

"That," said Lars, "is what the Germans like to call green meat. There's a surplus of it, what with Einstein's final solution to save the world. It took me some time to get used to the idea, but you get your head around it, eventually."

"Green meat?" I studied the last scrap on my fork. "It looks normal. Some type of processed vegetable?" I popped it into my mouth.

Lars laughed. "Quite possibly, but definitely human."

The *Galicia*, an eight-metre-long whaler, had proven its credentials as an ocean-going vessel, albeit reliant on Lars's masterful seamanship. *Deception*, I decided, should therefore be at least as long. The outrigger, the shorter hull I needed both for stability and for the cat, was to be a third of that length. Rather whimsically I even named this second hull *Chip off the Old Block*, or *Cotob* for short. As it was going to transport Mrs Chippy and I made it from salvaged parts of the first half-finished construction, I thought it rather appropriate. Although I had to redesign everything, I was still determined to be finished by the end of September. Then I would begin my own expedition to the South Pole and, ultimately, towards freedom from Antarctica.

At times I thought I must be tired of life to even consider such a foolhardy adventure, but Albert insisted it was the right course of action. He plotted the route with me, assessing the prevailing currents and likely weather conditions. If I left when planned, I could reach Hut Point, about three thousand miles away, by the middle of November and then arrive at the South Pole about a month after that, in high summer. Three thousand miles! It seemed unfathomably far, yet, Albert assured me, if I stayed close to the coast, the current carrying me along apace and rowed with the wind, I could easily cover one hundred miles a day; all I really had to do was make sure the sail was pointing in the right direction. I had no illusions that the climate would be harsh, the winds ferocious, the temperatures freezing, but also knew that if it became particularly rough, I could find a cove and wait it out. The real challenge lay in crossing the icy landscape to the South Pole. However, I had every confidence in my ability to withstand anything the Antarctic might throw at me. Just as importantly, Albert did, too.

So it was with encouragement, excitement, anticipation and a little awe at my impending adventure that I set to building the new *Deception*. With an adze I crafted symmetrically bowed double-ended hulls, so that I could, if needed, sail just as easily in one direction or the other. I often pondered why all ships were not designed this way; it would preclude the need for the often laboriously slow rotation of the vessel when entering or leaving a harbour. For me, it meant I could quickly dash to the safety of the shore, no matter which way the boat was pointing. I attached a platform to the crossbeams with which I pegged and laced the two hulls together, then overlayed the main hull with lateral planks, under which I could store supplies, and where the husky
192

and I could shelter. I did the same for the outrigger, *Cotob*. Then I fixed the mast to the main hull and supported it with struts attached to *Cotob*.

There was some sail cloth in the boathouse and an abundance of sheets in the dormitory. While they would not be ideal, I cut and stitched a dozen of these sheets to shape; I could use them either for warmth or as emergency sails. Although I understood the basics of it, my scant competence in tacking and gybing when the wind was blowing from an undesirable direction compelled me to fashion the sail so that it could be moved forward to aft simply by swivelling the mast. I engineered an oarlock to hold a paddle as a rudder at either end of *Deception*, so that in a flash I could release it, spring to the opposite bow, and use the oar there to steer the vessel.

Whalebones, I discovered, were naturally shaped sledge-runners. If they could carry these huge animals, they could surely carry *Cotob*. So I bored holes in several pairs and used some more bones to complete the frame; it was a grisly carriage, fit for the Grim Reaper. Perfect to transport Mrs Chippy across the ice. When I reached Hut Point, I would simply have to detach the outrigger from the crossbeams and secure it to the skeleton structure. I disassembled the ghoulish frame and stored the bones in the main hull of *Deception*. Then I made another couple of skis for the main hull. I didn't intend to take the larger hull on my continental trek, but I would need to drag it away from the sea and place it somewhere safe while I journeyed to the South Pole, and the skis would certainly make this task easier.

During these months I practised pitching and striking the tent, sometimes even in atrocious weather for an extra challenge. If there had been a competition in tent-pitching, after all this training I would have stood a fair chance of bringing home a medal. No less important but certainly far less enjoyable, I assiduously slaughtered, skinned, salted and froze penguin and seal meat. I needed plenty of supplies for the several-month-long enterprise and had at least three mouths to feed. The kitchen still

193

contained more dried food than I could possibly eat, and I packed a few pans, cups and other utensils which might be useful for cooking. I even stashed several bottles of akvavit in the outrigger; its enlivening effects could not be underestimated.

The winter season passed with these preoccupations and as it gave way to spring the frozen harbour began to thaw and spots of greenery re-emerged on the rocky slopes. I overhauled *Galicia*, pushed her into the harbour and began to fish again, as much to vary my immediate daily diet as to stock up on the supplies for the trip.

The gradual return to life on the island breathed added heat into my excitement over the impending journey, which was only a few weeks away. As if the anticipation of what I had set out to do was not enough to make my heart skip a beat, when I looked out of the window one early spring morning, my heart nearly leapt into my mouth for joy: there, on the black, volcanic sand lay a huge, scar-faced seal, basking in the sun. On top of it, as still as a statue, stood a brown skua with white-tipped wings. Odysseus and Carmen had returned.

Hull recognised them instantly and bounded down the beach, jumping without plan around them. Odysseus opened one eye, then closed it again, but Carmen shuffled uneasily on the colossus's back, keeping the husky under careful observation. Mrs Chippy monitored everything from the safety of the hut.

I rejoiced at their arrival, and we celebrated that night with a bright bonfire on the beach, which neither Odysseus nor Carmen seemed to enjoy very much, both keeping their distance from the lashing ribbons of fire. However, they gobbled up the fish I caught for them, as did the other two, and I watched on with smug satisfaction as my strange, outlandish family feasted in the flickering light of the flames.

With *Deception* and *Cotob* nearly complete and the ice and snow disappearing from the beach, I devoted my time to building a slipway from the boathouse and into the harbour. I could have simply used the skis, but I liked to keep myself busy. Again, I found the whalebones were extremely propitious for this task. Cutting, shaping, polishing and joining the sections of the long slipway took hundreds of hours and thousands of bones, but when I finally slotted the last piece into place to complete two parallel rails into which the double-hulled boat could glide smoothly down into the harbour, I stood back to admire my creation. I shuddered at the sight: an ashen, cadaverous track sliding into the cold, sunless depths; the pathway to hell could not be any ghastlier.

By the beginning of September, I had caulked and tarred *Deception* and *Cotob* and was ready to go; I was in fact itching to go. I had been on the island for nearly a year, and although I had marked the many months with exploration, invention and industry, although the animals had kept me company, and although Albert had given me advice and encouragement from the moment he had located me, I was still desperate to escape my icy confinement, reach the South Pole and then return to normal society.

However, I knew that timing was essential; I knew that Antarctica did not offer any comforts, even when it was at its most temperate, and I had to ensure that I was only exposed to its formidable force during the less inhospitable summer period. If I left too early, I would miss this window and thereby decrease my chances of success. So, as much as I desired to get underway, I stuck to my plan, and Albert fully agreed with me.

In these final few weeks I laid out on the boathouse floor all of the equipment I would need: the ballast, sea anchor, compass, hemp rope, sextant, spare sails, skis, tools, matches, pans, water containers and so on, checking them off my list and adding items that I thought might be useful. I packed, unpacked, and repacked the boat to optimise balance, remembering to leave space for Hull and Mrs Chippy. As I still had time, I decided to add a splash of colour to my creation. The Norwegians seemed to have had a love of yellow paint, for it was the only colour in the boathouse; stacks of it piled high. Quite what they had planned to use it for, I could only guess. Perhaps to add a little sunshine in this bleak environment. But now it served a new purpose; yellow would be the colour of *Deception*, and *Cotob* I would leave unpainted. It was my personal snub to Mrs Chippy, as she snubbed me often enough. Then there was only one task left: my catamaran's shakedown cruise.

I removed most of the equipment and, using a winch, hauled her up a ramp and onto the skeletal slipway at the door of the boathouse. Mrs Chippy, who had long discovered her personal reindeer-fur-lined compartment, jumped into the outrigger and made herself comfortable.

"Not yet, Mrs Chi..."

The husky, rather more awkwardly than the cat's delicate spring, leapt with a clatter of claws into the larger hull. Carmen swooped down from the top of the boathouse and perched on the mast. I looked over towards Odysseus, who was eyeing us from a couple of hundred metres away on the beach.

"Okay, you big brute, you'd just as well come along, too," I shouted over. The animal shuffled ungainly along the black sand and disappeared into the harbour. I guess he would wait for us there. Then there was just me. I climbed in, released the hook holding the catamaran in place, and, slowly at first, the boat began to slide. She quickly gained speed; it was at least seventy metres to the water, and by the time we reached it we were travelling at full tilt. We plunged into the harbour with a jolt, throwing an arch of water forward, and all of the occupants were thrown forward, too: Hull tumbled ungracefully over; Mrs Chippy was flung from her bed; Carmen squawked and flew off; I grabbed hold of the mast to steady myself, then apologised to my animal friends, but giggled a little, too; Odysseus's large, scarred face, bobbing above the surface, remained impassive as he noted it all.

The bright yellow catamaran rode the waters like a dream. The light breeze which blew through the horseshoe island filled her sail and I cruised around the harbour, completing several circuits. Over the next few days I took her out for hours on end and, with my strange crew on board or swimming silently next to me, experimented with different ballasts and manoeuvres, zig-zagging and spiralling, thrusting and braking. The more I practised, the more I skipped from bow to bow, whirling the mast around as I flew past it and slipping the paddle into the oarlock, where I could steer the boat as with a rudder, then the more adept I became at mastering this double-hulled vessel, and soon she was skimming around the harbour as effortlessly as a dragonfly flits about a lake.

Albert was delighted at my progress and listened intently to my chronicles. He was still a keen yachtsman (although I assumed also still a clumsy one) and sailed as often as he could, so took added interest in these experiences with *Deception*. I was sailing high on my various accomplishments and told him that, weather permitting, I would leave the day after next. However, he brought me crashing back down to earth with his final comment of the day:

"To leave this island of yours, you have one last hurdle. You have to pass those bellows."

I refused to believe Lars; I was angry

at him for even joking about such a thing. I stormed out of the tavern and headed straight back to *MS Schwabenland*. I didn't like this hot, sweaty, busy harbour town anyway and didn't want to see any more of it.

Back in my cabin, I turned over in my head many of the glimmers of detail that had been flashed my way since being rescued from Deception Island. *Rescue*: I was beginning to wonder what I had actually been rescued into. Sure, I had noticed the rising seas and melting ice long before the German freighter had steamed into the harbour that had been my home for so many years, but there were so many aspects about the world that had since been revealed to me that seemed so completely alien: the preponderance of athleticism in South Georgia, or whatever that island was now called; Lars's cryptic comment about the overweight man at the market in Cape Town; the state-sanctioned poisoning of water wells in the mountains near Walfish Bay; the removal of the indigenous people in Libreville, now Freistadt; and now Lars's distasteful cannibalistic joke. What was this nightmarish world I had been pulled into? I decided to confront Kapitän Ritscher.

"Ah, Frau Dittrich, glad you have dropped by. I was meaning to pay you a visit soon," beamed the captain.

"Oh?" I had been ready to fire uncomfortable questions at him, and his familiar greeting had caught me off guard.

"Yes, let's go for a walk."

I didn't much fancy strolling anywhere in these sultry conditions, and, after we had walked in silence from the boat, told him I wished to sit in the shade. We found a spot under a large tree

198

with an expansive umbrella crown, supported by an intricate web of boughs and branches that spread from the thick trunk like veins in a wrist.

"Never seen a tree like this before," I commented, wiping the sweat from my brow.

To my surprise, Kapitän Ritscher pulled a sharp blade from his belt and cut into the bark. Thick blood oozed from the wound and I jumped away in horror. The captain laughed.

"Don't be alarmed; it's not real blood. Looks like it, though, doesn't it? They call it Dragon's Blood. They use it for medicine, I think. And polish. Remarkable what we can find when we cut things open."

"Actually, that's kind of what I wanted to talk to you about," I began.

"Really? Me too. You see, I've been chiselling into your story, into your past. There are a few... let's call them discrepancies, which I need you to explain."

"Huh? Like what?" I asked.

"Like I said just now, don't be alarmed. It's quite normal to delve into the history of strangers, especially when they claim to know Albert Einstein."

"What do you mean 'claim'? Of course I know him," I snapped.

The captain gestured for me to sit down. "I'm sure you can understand that someone of Professor Einstein's importance needs to be protected. There are many people who would like to see him dead; indeed, several assassination attempts have already been foiled. I have to make sure that this story you're telling is not some elaborate ruse to get to our distinguished professor."

"What!" I leapt again from the bench. "You think I'd hide out in the Antarctic for thirty years so I could get to Albert? That's insane! Anyway, he wasn't even famous, back then."

"Maybe you weren't there that long. Maybe you knew our plans to visit the island, and were placed there by an enemy agent. The idea of an assassination plot is no more insane, as you put it, than

199

actually being stranded in the Antarctic as a young girl and surviving for thirty years. I find *that* a little *insane*. Sit down."

His tone had definitely changed. The firmness of his voice told me this was no request. I sat next to him and returned the steeliness in his eyes with a frosty glare of my own. The Dragon's Blood began to congeal behind him.

"Just what is it you're saying?" I asked, trying to remain calm.

"Let's leave Professor Einstein out of it, for a minute. As I said, I've made some enquiries about you, and some of what you say does stack up. But I was rather surprised to learn from the authorities in the General Government in Krakow that you're a Jew."

"So?"

Kapitän Ritscher coughed, clearly taken aback by my response.

"Frau Dittrich, this is not good."

"Not that I see it makes any difference, but I'm not very religious anyway."

"It makes all the difference. And you can't decide not to be a Jew. It's in your blood."

I didn't really know how to react to that and was finding the whole conversation bewildering. Firstly, he threw this conspiracy to murder Albert at me, now he was talking about Jewish blood.

"I've no idea what you're going on about. I don't want to kill Albert Einstein; he's a very dear friend to me. And I don't know where you're heading with this Jewish thing and I don't know why it bothers you so much. Anyway, if you're so worried about it, then what about the fact that your precious Professor Einstein is also a Jew?"

Kapitän Ritscher not only coughed, he fell from the bench in apoplectic disbelief. He staggered to his feet, dusted himself down, and looked down at me. "Okay, Frau Dittrich. So be it. Now it's my turn. If *Albert* is such a dear friend to *you*, why does he deny having had any contact with you since you were a teenager?"

The sky was clear, the sea was calm, the time had come. I had given *Deception* and *Cotob* a rigorous shakedown cruise – it would better have been described as a shakedown bruise, so thoroughly did I put the vessel through its paces – so I inspected her meticulously for several hours before setting off. The mast was straight, the hulls aligned, no fraying or loosening of the rigging, no fractures or cracks, no sign of water ingress at all, no holes or tears in the sail or any sign of slackening where it was attached to the mast or rope. *Deception*, in short, looked as bright in her gleaming yellow paint as she did on the first day of sailing and plain *Cotob* looked just as plain.

Everything was packed: food, water, tent, equipment; I must have checked more than a dozen times before I committed myself to the open sea and, even then, I was sure I had forgotten something. Whatever it was, it wasn't Hull or Mrs Chippy, or for that matter Carmen or Odysseus, although I had little say about their presence.

When I finally clambered into the boat, positioned the sail to catch the gentle breeze and grasped the rudder to steer towards the exit that I had only once traversed, nearly a year ago, I looked back at the beach, the hills behind and the huts which had been my home for so long, and felt a sudden longing to stay.

Deception Island had appeared like a magical icy, rocky ring in the middle of a lethal sea; it had given me shelter, warmth, food, entertainment; it had even given me Albert. I had found responsibility, physical and mental challenges; I had discovered a purpose. Now I was given all this up for a possible suicide mission. My hand wavered on the rudder. I could still turn back.

"No!"

The command from the bow of the boat, from Carmen, jolted me out of my reverie.

"Did you just speak?" I knew how preposterous it was to pose the question, yet still I half-expected her head to turn towards me and hear a coherent exposition from my feathered friend as to why I should continue with the journey.

"Nay! Na! Gah!"

It had been nothing but the squawk of an excitable, mostly irritable bird. Perhaps I had heard my own inner voice, screaming at me to shake off my nostalgia. Although, I said to myself, Carmen might have been *trying* to say something. I shook my head and, heeding the instructions of the avian or inner voice, guided the catamaran to the exit.

No sooner had I reached the narrow gap when a strong gust took hold of the sail and, before I had time to react, whipped the boat around and blew her towards the interior of the island. Carmen flew off, taking up position on the rocky promontory I wanted to pass. I tried again, this time bracing myself for the sudden blast, one hand ready on the mast to swivel it around and tack at an angle into the wind. However, despite my preparations, I reacted too slowly, too feebly, and the boat was pushed back once more.

Another go, and the wind drove me around on the leeward side. Then again; this time I sheltered for as long as I could under the steep cliff face. But as soon as the sail inched out into the exposed

202

entrance to the island, the fabric bulged with a surge from the wild wind and almost threatened to flip my catamaran over. It seemed no matter what tactic I tried, I neither possessed the seamanship skills to guide my vessel through the narrow gap, nor the strength to resist the wind whistling through it. Just like on Elephant Island, it seemed that once the Antarctic had pulled you towards it's shores, it only very stubbornly gave you up again.

"Odysseus! That's it!" I cried. He had pushed me when the breaking waves were fulminating over the reef, I was sure of it. Now, faced with another insurmountable obstacle, I needed his help again. "Odysseus! Odysseus! Where are you?" I hailed repeatedly into the grey harbour; even Hull put his front paws on the gunwale and howled with me.

Whether he had heard his name, was intrigued by the wailing, or just by chance, the enormous, familiar, gnarled head punctured the surface just metres from *Deception*, then promptly disappeared again. That was confirmation enough for me; Odysseus would help us.

With fresh vigour in my arms and renewed determination in my mind and heart, I steered the boat towards the rift once more. I turned from the wind just as the icy blast filled the sail. The vessel hurtled forward, surely Odysseus's doing, towards the cliffs ahead on my left. I grasped the mast, strained every sinew in my arms and hands to maintain a firm grip, and swivelled the mast around. *Deception's* bow lurched through the wind and sailed onwards on a port tack. And so, with the aid of the colossus under the sea driving me forward, I summoned the skill and strength to tack the catamaran onward, battling through the bellows that would otherwise imprison me on this island fortress. For ten exhausting minutes or more I duelled with this prodigious squall, barely able to control my quaking arms, yet somehow reaching new reserves of energy to propel me past the two peninsulas and beyond that huge, stone sentry, still clutching his petrified victim.

When I had finally cleared the narrow gap and guided the boat to the relative calm of the open sea in the Bransfield Strait, I collapsed in a heap and my arms, now freed from their intense contest with the Antarctic gusts, trembled like the thin branches of a mountainside tree. It was as much as I could do to lift some nourishing biscuits to my mouth. Hull, of course, was happy to see the snacks and looked at me expectantly. Carmen returned to her mast-top perch but Odysseus was nowhere to be seen. Mrs Chippy, as far as I was aware, had slept through it all.

The quivering muscle spasms from overexertion were soon replaced with those of muscles shivering to stay warm, for sitting still in the boat, recovering my strength, filled me with a chill that reached every part of my body. I needed to get moving. I wanted to cover as much ground as possible; I hadn't forgotten Albert's calculation that one hundred miles a day would get me to Hut Point in a month.

I had brought many of the maps and charts with me that the Norwegians had left behind on Deception Island, so I could navigate my way through the strait and plot my progress with ease using the sextant. My first destination was Trinity Island, about fifty miles over the open water. This, I considered, was the most perilous part of my journey, as I was inexperienced, the boat was largely untested in these conditions, and I would be far from landfall should a storm descend down the straits. I pointed the bow in a southwesterly direction, picked up the slow current that brought me here, and positioned the sail so that the wind eased the catamaran along.

It went far more smoothly than I could ever have hoped. With just a light breeze pushing her, the boat flew across the water and within a few hours I could already see the snowy hills of Trinity Island. After five hours, I had brought my vessel to a stop in a cove, secured her on the beach and set Hull free to run around while I heated some blubber oil to defrost some penguin meat in a pan for me, him and Mrs Chippy, who refused to exit her cosy outrigger.

I hadn't lost sight of my target of one hundred kilometres a day, so turned myself to the next goal for the day, reaching the second largest island in this archipelago, Brabant Island, again about another fifty miles away. Going via Trinity Island had not been the most direct route from Deception Island to this new destination, but it had perhaps been the safest, for Trinity Island was the closest land to my starting point and now I would never be more than five miles or so from one coast or another. Now I was no longer crossing the Bransfield Strait, but travelling with it, exploiting the flow of the current and sailing past numerous icy islands with even greater celerity than before. Only occasionally I had to alter course to overtake loitering icebergs, wandering broken remnants of a once mighty ice shelf, now cleaved, broken up and, as these fragments, slowly melting in the cold sea. Some of them loomed high over the top of my mast, others barely peeked above my hull, yet even these miniature monoliths masked a greater mass under the grey swell and were still quite capable of crippling my vessel.

Brabant Island announced itself with mighty white peaks dominating sea and sky. I was well-used to seeing mountains in my childhood and had been exposed to the wild beauty of the Antarctic for nearly a year, but nothing could have prepared me for the staggering rawness of the icescape which soared before me. This island of snow-blanketed ridges, clefts and crags extended neither warmth nor familiarity, just bleak desolation and grim indifference. It seemed to be the work of some unsmiling creator and I felt no compulsion to linger, yet tiredness and coldness were hijacking my senses and I knew it was time to find shelter and rest.

I coasted around its edges, looking for somewhere to berth *Deception* and *Cotob* and eventually found a narrow entrance, just wide enough to allow the double-hulled boat to pass. It led to an icy cove almost completely screened from the outside world by sheer cliffs. After pitching the tent and feeding my land crew of two – I hadn't seen Carmen for several hours and Odysseus not once since leaving Deception Island – I studied the charts to analyse my progress and plan for the next day.

Travelling in the Antarctic had not proven as daunting as I had imagined: the wind was gentle, the sea calm, the temperature freezing but tolerable. If every day were to be as this one, then it would even be a pleasant experience. My satisfaction took a slight dent when I studied the charts; my progress was almost imperceptible, a tiny dash on a map which revealed so much more terrain to cover. I brushed aside that disappointment by reflecting upon how much ground I had covered in my lifetime, compared to which the journey ahead of me looked far more manageable. However, I was forced to face the harsh reality of my undertaking just a few hours later, when the furious barking of the husky and the cold bite of the sea rushing into my tent wrenched me from my sleep and threatened to bring my enterprise, and my life, to a very swift end.

After our altercation I half-expected

Kapitän Ritscher to abandon me on Cape Verde. He told me, however, that he was obligated to take me to Europe, even if I didn't deserve it after my grotesque allegations, as he called them, about Albert's Jewishness. It was just as well that he was kept busy as we steamed further north; I had no desire to speak to him about religion, Albert, or in fact any aspect of my past.

None of the questions I had wanted to pose to the captain had been answered. In fact, I only had more. His claim that Albert had denied having had any contact with me since I was a teenager was clearly a lie, but why would the captain say such a thing? And why this interest in my Jewish heritage? It had played such an insignificant part in my life that I had almost entirely forgotten about it. With each further degree north we were heading, it seemed, the further we were penetrating a world full of troubling unease.

I didn't know who I could turn to. I hadn't seen Lars since I had run from the inhospitable tavern in Praia harbour and vomited into the sea after his abominable joke. He had been the source of much of my disquiet, but I felt that even though I might not like his answers, they would at least be honest and not laden with recrimination or suspicion. I went in search for him on *MS Schwabenland*.

"Yes, I've heard about your conversation with the captain. Couldn't have been nice," responded Lars after I had relayed my anxieties. We were standing on the open deck, glittering blue sea sweeping in every direction.

"I just don't understand what he wants from me."

"I keep telling you, Marianna. Things are different now. Times have changed; people have changed; the world has changed. I'm not surprised it's all a bit overwhelming. This thing you said about Einstein: if there is any truth in it at all, then it has clearly been hidden for the greater good."

"Greater good? What does that even mean? Whose greater good? The captain said I might want to kill Albert Einstein. He thought I might be some kind of spy. He said that it was bad I was a Jew…"

"*You're* a Jew?" His eyes widened in shocked surprise.

"See, that's exactly what I mean!"

"Come with me."

Lars led me away from the two sailors nearby who were tending to a length of rope. We walked to the stern of the boat and traced the ship's churning wake, fanning ever wider and growing ever fainter as it stretched into the distance under the orchid sky.

"Just tell me the truth about what's going on, Lars."

Maybe the truth was too difficult to put into words, maybe the Norwegian had trouble understanding everything himself, but he began with a rather confusing allegory.

"You know what's in that direction?" he asked, pointing toward the east.

"Africa?"

"Exactly. The beginning of the Sahara Desert, to be precise. Do you know anything about it?"

"Not really."

"Well, it's enormous. The size of America. It is, or *was*, a great sand barrier, keeping the Europeans away from the sub-Saharan continent for thousands of years. Have you any idea how much gold the Africans were sitting on? But when the Europeans came, they took the gold and the Africans were exploited, enslaved, killed. That's just how things are."

"I've no idea what you're trying to tell me."

"It's the same with the Jews. They are the new Africans. They've been hoarding their gold for thousands of years and now the day of reckoning has come."

"Gold? What gold? What are you on about?"

"Look, I'm not claiming to know everything. But what I do know is this: the Jews have had it too good for too long; in fact, there are so many people who have been living at our expense, taking more than their share. But things are now being redistributed."

"Redistributed?" I asked.

"Well, perhaps I should say that there's been a *reorientation* of the world's resources."

"You're not being any clearer."

"I really have to spell it out to you, don't I?" sighed Lars. "There's such a surplus of people that some are being used for their *bodily* value. This has to happen, as there is no place, or even space, for individuals who want more than the world can give them. We have to get rid of those who are a drain on the earth's resources, so those who no longer fit in the system have to go the same way as the Africans did hundreds of years ago. That includes Jews, fat people, Jehovah's Witnesses, gay people; I don't have the full list, but when order is restored again, the world will be a much safer and fairer place."

"For whom?"

"For the rest of us." Lars looked furtively over his shoulder. "I wouldn't normally say this, but let me give you a word of advice. We've been through a lot together, you and me, and you don't deserve..." he trailed off.

"What?"

"Just don't go around shouting that you're a Jew. You don't look like one, and it won't do you any good if anybody else finds out. Just blend in, like me."

"Kapitän Ritscher knows. He's the one who told me. I probably would've forgotten otherwise."

"Shit. And I don't mean that in a good way."

"Shit!"

It is difficult to imagine a ruder awakening than a husky barking into your ear and just seconds later having to plunge into Antarctic waters. I couldn't strike the tent, even as the sea was threatening to claim it, for I had a far pressing matter to deal with: *Deception*, her yellow paint clearly visible under the midnight sun which was just resisting the pull of the horizon, was floating away, taking *Cotob* and Mrs Chippy with her. There was no time to lose; lives depended on my quick response.

No other option was available to me but to leap into the freezing sea and rescue my boat and cat. Within moments I had swum the ten metres or so to my boat; I clambered on board and began to row her back to the cove, now almost totally overwhelmed by the rising tide.

The tent stood under a foot of water, my belongings either submerged or floating away in erratic directions, as if each were fleeing frantically from me. I hauled Hull into *Deception*, checked Mrs Chippy was safe, then set about collecting what I could above and below the water, sometimes wading up to my waist while keeping a watchful eye on the boat. I was confident that I had

210

retrieved all my possessions, yet the price had been high: everything was sodden: the tent, my clothes, my blankets, Hull, me; it was imperative I found land and changed before the clothes froze onto my back.

The sun, permanently hugging the horizon, seemed almost too ashamed to shine a light on my floundering adventure, risking only a partial glimpse as I fought to maintain control over every shivering muscle in my body. I rowed as vigorously as I could to stave off the biting cold; anywhere remotely berthable would be fine.

Every second seemed prolonged, each one releasing a thousand quakes through my shuddering body; my hands, stiffened by a growing numbness, gripped an oar they could barely feel and arched with slackening speed under the power of arms slowed with leaden cold. Only my mind remained sharp, able to perceive the icy petrification of a body it was now struggling to control. I pressed on, heading towards a white slice of land which, although it seemed much like any other in this abominable landscape, hinted from a distance to be sloping towards the sea.

My hunch had been right; an icy shelf, angled favourably from the water and smoothed by tide and wave to glossy perfection, offered the perfect slipway for my vessel. I wasted no time in hauling the catamaran on to the land and securing her in case some unexpected event should try to sweep her away again. My tent had frozen stiff, so after lighting several blubber-fuelled fires, I beat the canvas until it became more pliable, pitched the tent and urged Hull inside. I had to carry Mrs Chippy from the outrigger, but whatever spore or hair the cat might throw at me could not penetrate the several protective layers of clothing, nor the coating of frost over my face, nor the icicle dangling from my nose. I put her in the tent, where she quickly ran to Hull.

An adjustable vent in the centre of the roof allowed most of the fumes to escape from the plates of fire which I brought inside, and the tent warmed quickly. I stripped and hung my clothes to dry, using the oars to prop them up. However, a cloud of black smoke began to accumulate and a thick, choking air of soot clung to my skin and attacked my eyes, nose and throat; I had to put all but one of the fires out. The temperature dropped significantly, but at least I now felt reasonably comfortable again, the animals were out of danger, and we could all get some much-needed sleep.

I had rather hoped Carmen would bring me a tasty fish in the morning, but she didn't make an appearance. I wasn't worried; I knew she would be around somewhere, observing from a distance with her shrewd eyes. Odysseus, too, would be watching from the grey depths. It was more than reassuring to know that two pairs of eyes were looking out for me.

The wind had picked up a little by the time I had tended to the morning duties of breakfast, feeding the animals, and stocking up on supplies of chinstrap penguins. It was not a task I relished, slaughtering these adorable little animals which had made a home here, nor did I find them particularly tasty, but their skin, meat and blubber were vital to my mission, and I could not afford to be sentimental about the issue. Once I had packed everything neatly into *Deception*, I could continue.

The conditions were once again favourable, with a bright sun casting long rays over a sea glittering and rippling to the measure of the breeze. Much like the previous day, the current swept me along a channel between many islands to my right and the long peninsula of Graham Land to my left. Occasionally an interested seal would poke its head out of the water or slip off a roaming ice floe and vanish under the surface, maybe spooked by the sail flapping vigorously in the rising wind.

I found myself being literally carried away in a white realm emptied of all concerns but the interplay of wind and sea; not even time had much relevance here, with the unsetting sun permanently shepherding me along, lighting up the vast peaks which gazed impassively down upon my vessel, a mere dot weaving through floes and bergs and past icy islands.

After many hours I entered an area known as the Southwind Passage. Almost immediately the strong breeze ratcheted up several orders of magnitude and I suddenly had a very grave problem. Ice floes, previously ambling along with the current, were now driven together, crashing and crunching, splitting and snapping in shocking collisions that, should I get caught up in them, would surely smash my vessel and consign us all to a calamitous end.

For a time I attempted to navigate this icy tinderbox, primed to blast *Deception*, *Cotob* and my life into unrecognisable fragments. However, my seamanship skills, while improving every day, were no match for the peril I found myself in. I had to head for land. Finding it was no problem – land was everywhere; getting to it was the issue. No sooner did a clear passage between two floes present itself, than in a thunderous cataclysm the icy masses pressed together, and the route closed just as quickly again. Danger lurked even away from the floes, with huge shards rearing up through the surface, as if they were spears shooting up from the depths; I was lucky enough to avoid them, though they still covered me in freezing spray.

The catamaran lurched this way and that as I fought to harness the wind, to keep the boat away from the bergs and shards and the death-bringing channels between the floes, and to drive her towards the peninsula, or an island, or whatever seemed in this ever-changing seascape to be the most attainable stretch of land.

Eventually I battled towards a steep cliff face of frozen ice, itself struggling to resist the battering from the wind as huge chunks crashed from it into the choppy waters. I made for a ledge, about one foot above the surface and just wide enough for me and the boat. I knew I would have to haul the boat up to safety to prevent it from being crushed by a migrant berg slamming into the cliff. I scrambled up easily enough, but dragging the boat up the sheer edge, even though it was just a foot high, was a different proposition.

I dug my shoes into the ground, but the wind swirled about me and waves crashed over the low ledge, making the going treacherously slippery. Once I lost my footing and tumbled into the icy water, banging my head painfully on the side of the boat. Hull barked and, it seemed, was about to jump in to rescue me, but I quickly heaved myself into *Deception* and the husky calmed down. This time, I unloaded as much as I could onto the ledge: the tent, the food, blankets, the tools; I even flung Mrs Chippy onto the small patch of frozen land, and I tried again.

All of my efforts had worn away the lip of the ledge, so that it was now sloping rather crudely, but helpfully, to the water. With the decreased weight, lifting the catamaran up provided no challenge, and I swiftly put everything back in place, including the cat. Here I was again, completely soaked, frozen to the skin, and in desperate need to get warm. I moved as far away from the edge as possible, lit some fires, changed my clothes and wondered what more my adventure had to throw at me. I didn't have to wonder for long.

Hull's barking alerted me to the danger. At first I thought he must have seen something, and these suspicions were confirmed when I turned around and saw Odysseus's scarred face staring at me over the ledge. It gave me quite a fright to see him there.

"Odysseus! I could've done with your help an hour ago!"

The elephant seal grunted in response, then inflated his large, bulbous nose, pointed the end into his open mouth and belched a strange rasping beat, like someone rapping on a hollow oil drum. I had heard him make the sound before, usually when he was warning off other seals.

"There's no-one else here, Odysseus. Hull, stop yapping!"

But the animals continued their discordant barking until a series of clamorous ear-splitting shrieks made them both hold their breath for a second. Carmen swooped down, again and again, screaming and squawking as she flew past my head. Even Mrs Chippy mewed, although I suspect she was, in her idiosyncratic way, demanding that the others stop the racket.

214

"What's got into all of you?" I shouted. In this largely silent world, my voice and their noise probably travelled miles over the sea. "There's nothing wrong!" I gestured into the grey, blue and white world, then saw what they had seen. The world was sliding by; not due to the drift of icebergs or floes, but the very mountains were marching past, as if being tugged on one planetary-sized chain. There was only one explanation: I was on an iceberg!

I had seen enough of icebergs, gazing from the hills on Deception Island, to know that these placid sea juggernauts belied an unpredictability which could upend them in a second, throwing any resting seal into the sea, at best disturbing its peaceful sleep, and even possibly crushing it to death.

What I had thought were chunks of melting ice falling from the cliff face were in fact pieces of the iceberg, degraded by the wind pummelling its side and the sea eating around the waterline. My sanctuary was a death-trap, and I had to get off.

A new problem presented itself to me: my ledge was flanked by sheer columns of ice; the only way off was the way I had scrambled onto it. Yet now innumerable slabs and chunks of ice, some several feet high, jostled and jarred in that very space, barring my exit. There was barely room between them for Odysseus to poke his head through, let alone to launch the catamaran. Until there was a watery clearing, I was destined to remain on the iceberg.

The creaks and strains of the iceberg filled me with dread; my heart lurched with every rise of the swell, every shift in direction, every slant and every shudder; every moment seemed to me to spell the end, the instant I would plunge into the sea, which would sap my energy until I expired. In my despair I screamed at the animals which had alerted me to my plight.

"Why did you warn me? I can't even do anything about it!" Hull came to me and whimpered apologetically. "It's not your fault," I said, stroking his thick fur. "There's nothing we can do. Let's eat and warm up as best we can. But if we have to leave all of a sudden, you leave the meat behind, okay?"

Mrs Chippy, attracted by the smell of cooked penguin flesh, nestled alongside Hull and licked her tasty slivers before gobbling them up. Despite her pretensions of elegance, she was not a delicate eater. I threw a few cuts to Carmen, who had landed next to us and was eyeing the meal greedily. I also considered throwing some scraps into the water, where Odysseus could snap them up, although what I had left would seem little more than crumbs to him.

I stood at the ledge looking for the seal, bloody flesh in hand, when a curious eddy began to form in the water just below my feet. An ever-increasing swirling, inky spiral of water, propelling the ice to its outer edges, was clearing a space before my eyes. Soon it was large enough for the catamaran, and still it grew.

"Odysseus? Is this your doing?" I called into the black murk.

I couldn't see him; could he be whirling somewhere in the depths to create this mysterious vortex? Were sea creatures even capable of such sophisticated manoeuvres? Was it simply some fluke interplay between the surface wind and the underwater currents swerving around the underside of the iceberg? Whatever it was, I had to seize my chance.

"Quick, quick!" Hull looked up from his meal. "In!" I ordered, pointing to the catamaran. His jaw dropped in disappointment, his head hung low, but he did as I commanded. Mrs Chippy completely ignored me, so I stomped over and flung her into the outrigger as unceremoniously as I had cast her out of it earlier. I threw their uneaten penguin flesh in after them, gathered up all the possessions, pushed the boat to the ledge, let her fall into the sea and leapt in. A channel was opening up from my pool, leading directly to a rocky outcrop. The rock wasn't much, maybe a few hundred metres in width and just as high, the smallest of islands imaginable, but if I could berth there, then I could wait out this rising storm and, just as importantly, get some rest.

I was in luck. Whether this ice-covered lump of rock protruding from the sea was an island, an islet, a reef, or simply the tip of an undersea mountain did not matter, for over the millennia the sea had gnawed away at its sides and carved a tiny cove, not even ten metres wide, at one end of the rock. This would provide me with a foothold, a respite, even if for just a few hours.

As I guided my vessel towards the shingled beach, a terrifying roar made me glance astern in fright. The berg I left had just moments before began to turn, and as it flipped it raised enormous volumes of water, which rained back into the sea as tremendous, fleeting waterfalls. Like an ice behemoth stirring in agitated sleep, the berg rolled this way then that, before settling down into a heaving sea. A huge wave shot outwards from the turbulence and smashed through the thick floes which lumbered through the water, flinging them, reeling them, driving them forward, and straight for me. I had to get around the other side of the rock, or I was doomed. I was only metres from shelter, but the wave was roaring towards me with lethal velocity. My boat was swift, but she was vastly outpaced by the hurtling wave. I braced myself for impact.

It came, as a nudge, even before the wave hit; although I couldn't see him, I knew instantly that Odysseus was under the catamaran. This powerful swimmer thrust me forward, swung me around the island and propelled me under the lee of the rocky cliff face, just as the wave pummelled the other side. The boat bounced and bobbed as the wave reverberated through and past the island, but she was undamaged. I had survived another of the Antarctic's assaults.

Once I had pulled *Deception* and *Cotob* onto the tiny shingle beach, I drew a canvas cover over both hulls, so that both Mrs Chippy in one, and Hull and I in the other, could rest in relative comfort. I was not going to be caught by the tide again, and staying in the boat was the only way to protect us from at least that hazard.

217

I knew it would provide me with no joy, yet, huddled under the canvas with only a slither of light penetrating our enclosed space, I could not help plotting our progress on the map. My last reading with the sextant had been on the berg, and when I translated the coordinates to the map in front of me, my expected disappointment was realised. The tiny dash I had marked before was only a slightly less tiny one now. Nevertheless, I told myself, I had travelled about two hundred and fifty miles in just a couple of days, I had survived everything the Antarctic had thrown at me, the boat was in good shape, I still had my four companions, and I was well on course to completing my mission.

I could easily write about each day of this adventure, of my three thousand miles hopping from one icy cove to the next, of how my boat climbed the undulating hills of water, its mast piercing the roof of heaven, and descended into the depths of briny valleys which even the never fading light could scarcely penetrate. I could write about how volatile currents and wayward winds would often drive in conflicting directions, raising slabs of water which crashed over the boat like blocks of concrete, compelling me to bail out water before the next pounding came to sink my vessel. I could write about the sheaths of ice which clung to the hull, mast, sail, to clothes and skin and fur, and how the very weight of this ice threatened to take us under, so that I had to brave cross seas and angry winds to chip off the accumulating ice and keep us afloat. I could write about how all the elements of the sea, land and air, the destructive waves and dangerous currents, the hazardous reefs and hard-to-reach coves, the shards of icy rain and squally winds, how all of these railed against *Deception*, against *Cotob*, to sink, smash or capsize my catamaran. I could write about the difficulty of sleeping, of rain dripping through the tent, of saltwater boils and of using ice to attend to my toiletry needs, though I'd rather not write about that one in particular.

I could write about the wonderful moments, too, such as when a pod of whales crashed through the sea ice, like great obsidian

218

shafts thrust upwards from volcanic depths, and exhaled booming blasts of vapour before vanishing once more into the sunken undersea bowels, and the ice crumpled back into place, its ruffled surface at dreamy, drifting peace again. Or when the sky cleared and the sun, rising ever higher in the sky, blazed down with little heat but glorious radiance, and the blue sea breathed, rising and falling so delicately I could only look upon this majestic Earth in silence for fear of waking her.

There were so many moments in that month of desperation and delight in which I loathed and loved the Antarctic in equal measure, but I will focus on one particular event near the end of my seaborne adventure.

For several days and hundreds of miles, I had been sailing past an impenetrable sheer wall of ice rising in places to over sixty metres above the sea. I knew from my charts that this must be the Great Barrier, a floating ice shelf larger than Germany. Occasionally I was able to find a snowy bank at the base of the vertical barrier on which I could rest, cook and eat. But with large hunks of snow, some as large as houses, fracturing from the wall and slamming with extraordinary destructiveness into the sea, it was not a place in which I felt inclined to linger.

In any case, I knew that Hut Point was at the western end of this barrier and I was keen to press on, so allowed myself only a few hours of respite at a time. It was a strange phase: as eager as I was to reach the end of the great ice front and continue the journey on foot, I was also already reminiscing about the life on the ocean that I had grown so accustomed to and had still not yet given up.

One day, while I was in this reflective mood and while the sun chased its own light around the flickering sea, a large, silhouetted bird swooped down and glided just metres above the mast. A curious albatross, its wingspan as wide as my catamaran, had come to inspect the strange double-bodied object floating in this remote region. With unmoving wings the creature cocked its head from side to side, its limited brain no doubt seeking to recall
219

similar such bizarre shapes as the one currently beneath it, and, probably finding none, glided away. I watched the albatross soar as high as the steep ice cliffs off to our left, then swoop with astonishing speed and skim across the surface of the sea. Again it ascended before rocketing down to the water again, where it grazed over the ocean furls, untroubled either by wind or wave.

Over and over the wandering albatross catapulted up and down and hurtled through the air, never once beating its wings, a marvel of nature at one with its environment. I set my sail to keep up with it and I raced across the sea at breakneck speed. Hull wanted to watch, too, and panted with excitement. Even Mrs Chippy peeked above the gunwales of the outrigger to enjoy the spectacle. Between the boat and the great barrier, I saw Odysseus fling himself out of the sea, repeatedly breaching the cold water in lusty loops. All the while the albatross, the sailor's symbol of navigation and exploration, of resilience, of freedom and hope, held us captive and drew us on. Until Carmen joined in.

Whether she was jealous, agitated, or as passionately enthralled as I was, it was impossible to say, but the skua plummeted from nowhere towards the albatross, screaming as she dived. The mighty bird evaded her with unnerving aeronautical mastery and, after hanging around for a few moments longer, resolved it could not tolerate this squawking intrusion and effortlessly sailed away.

Odysseus did not breach the sea again, Mrs Chippy returned to her bed, Hull put his head on my lap with a whimper, and I, following the disappearing bird back into the white sun, caught sight of something on the distant cliffs. A hut.

While Kapitän Ritscher undertook

some duties in the port of Lisbon, I was under strict orders to remain in my quarters. In fact, I was not to be allowed off the ship at all until we had safely arrived in Hamburg. I had already begun to feel like a persona non grata aboard *MS Schwabenland*, and this decree from the captain only compounded my isolation. Fortunately, the captain had overlooked a ban on visitors, or had not considered me dangerous enough to warrant this measure, and while we were docked in the Portuguese harbour Lars came to me bearing gifts.

"A local sandwich, called bifana. I've had three already. Delicious!" he beamed, passing me the paper-wrapped treat.

I took it from him warily and pulled the sandwich apart. There was just some greasy meat inside.

"What's this?" I asked suspiciously.

"Pork, I promise. Paid extra for it, given your... sensibilities. Besides, wearing this uniform gets you a good discount."

I had been feeling hungry but suddenly my appetite deserted me. I put the sandwich down and sighed.

"How did it all come to this?"

Lars only half-understood my question; I don't think even I fully knew what I was asking.

"If you mean, how did this uniform become so powerful, well we've got your friend Albert Einstein to thank for that."

I was getting bored of these conversations. "Yes, I know that. He's so wonderful. Everyone keeps saying he's saved the world. What exactly did he do, anyway?"

"You know those kamikaze pilots in Jap... no, of course, you wouldn't. There were pilots who flew their planes laden with explosives into American ships on purpose. They would die, but they would destroy all or large parts of the ship, and take out dozens or maybe even hundreds of American marines with them."

"And I guess that was all Albert's idea?" I scorned.

"No! Of course it wasn't. Einstein somehow managed to invent a way of guiding torpedoes with radio waves, so that they could be fired and steered into a ship. They almost always hit. No more need for pilots to die. They called it Detonating Independently Controlled Kamikaze. The sailors had a term for it: *throwing the DICE*. Brilliant, isn't it?"

I thought about it for a minute. "But it actually spells *DICK*."

"Yeah, well, they didn't go for that. Maybe the last word was *explosive*."

"Why did you tell me about the kamikaze thing, then?"

"Look, it doesn't matter. The important thing is, whoever controls the seas, controls the world."

"You once said you could never control the sea. The best you can hope for is to survive it."

"That was a long time ago. Anyway, what Einstein managed to invent for the sea, he also did for air warfare. Vast hordes of remotely controlled mini-aircraft would be released from a bomber plane and guided using radio waves. They could see exactly where the enemy was on the ground and target them precisely. They called them Aeronautical, Reconnaissance, Strike, Kam... Explosives," said Lars, quickly correcting himself.

I mouthed the four words silently, then gave him my reply. "*ARSE*."

"Look, do you want that sandwich or not?"

It was only a speck on a distant hill, perhaps two hundred metres above the sea, and it would have been easy to miss it. Yet the line of the albatross's flight guided my eye precisely to the spot as the sun glinted off what I presume was the hut's reflective roof. I was in no doubt that the sparkle of light was a beacon calling me in, and I steered my catamaran towards the shore, hoping to spot the *Aurora* in some protected cove.

As I approached the great cliff barrier, picking my way carefully through a labyrinth of shattered floes and scanning the land beyond either for the Australian ship or a berth for my catamaran, I became aware of innumerable, shifting specks, like twinkling black lights against a brilliantly white backdrop. Occasionally, a bright flash of yellow blazed from within this mass of dappled darkness, and then animated croaking reached my ears. I had stumbled across a rookery of emperor penguins, and a place to begin my inward journey.

I hauled the vessel out of the sea, took down the sail and mast, and dragged her several hundred metres inland before detaching

Cotob and fixing to it the skeleton skis. I planned to take the sledge to the hut, look from there for signs of Shackleton's relief party, then come back for *Deception* later.

The large penguins were as tall as Hull and completely unfazed by his growling as we strolled through the colony. I am not sure he felt brave enough to take on one of these birds, but certainly felt the need to at least be vocally dominant. However, when Odysseus crashed out of the sea and bounded towards us like a maniacal oversized grub, the penguins scattered in screeching hysteria, and soon we were all alone on the windswept ice. Quite where the penguins went, I could not say, and I was completely flummoxed by how thousands of tall black and yellow creatures could hide themselves in this all-white environment.

We pressed on, Odysseus apparently keen to accompany us to the hut. The large seal showed remarkable stamina, heaving his huge body away from the water and up a gravelly knoll of ice and volcanic rock, which stood in the shadow of an ominously named peak, Mount Terror. When we reached the hut, I could see more clearly what had caught my eye from the sea: strands from a torn canvas roof were flapping wildly in the strong breeze. The hut was in considerable disrepair, and if it were to provide me with shelter, I needed to get to work on it.

There were four fairly intact walls comprising large stones placed crudely on top of one another, with a small open gap on one side just high enough for me to duck through. With no wooden beams to support a roof, the only covering was the shredded sheet of canvas, which had once stretched from the thick, high weather wall on one side over the entire construction, but now hung loosely, pinned down by the various stones which prevented it from blowing away completely. If I was to stay here for any length of time, I would have to repair the walls and fix the roof.

Odysseus must have thought I had gone mad, for no sooner had I arrived at the hut and cursorily examined it, than I turned on my heels and set off back down the knoll again. If he considered following me, he soon gave up on the idea, for he slumped his heavy body just outside the battered hut and promptly went to sleep. Hull seemed pleased to be able to use his legs and skipped beside me as I returned to collect *Deception*.

Lugging the larger hull up the knoll was substantially more arduous than it had been with *Cotob*, and I was thankful for my foresight in making the skis exactly for this purpose. I pulled the boat past the sleeping seal and into the hut. It would be my bed while I stayed here. When everything was where it ought to be, I began to rebuild the hut.

There was no shortage of building material, as the ridge on which this hut stood had evidently been formed by a large and long since melted glacier depositing masses of rocks and sediment as it had slowly slid from the mountain which overlooked the area. Once I had squared off the walls, arranging the large stones so that they slotted more neatly into one another, I plugged the spaces in between with gravel and snow. Then I bolstered the walls with piles of lava rocks, granite, basalt, gravel and more snow, compacted it and smoothed it as much as I could so that, when I had finished, the hut resembled a giant igloo with sloping sides of ice, snow and gravel with a stone interior at the centre; it just lacked the top. I had plenty of covers from the beds in the dormitory on Deception Island, and a few spare sheets of canvas, so I made several layers of roof, locking each one into place with heavy stones, just in case a gale whipped one of them away. My stone igloo now had its protective membrane.

With the sun refusing to set, it was hard to know exactly what time of day it now was, or indeed how long I had even been labouring on my construction. My body, though, signalled that it was time to rest, and so, after a small meal and a drink of melted snow for me and my crew, I snuggled into my bed and fell into the most peaceful sleep that I had been able to enjoy for several weeks.

I could have been forgiven, when I exited the hut the following morning, for thinking that being so far away from the water had

225

somehow shrivelled Odysseus's bulk, for lying exactly where he had been sleeping the day before was a fleshy mass no larger than a fish. Then I realised that what I was looking at was indeed a fish, or rather several fish, placed there by Carmen, who was looking at me with her perennial scowl from the roof of the hut. Odysseus, it seemed, had taken his body back to the sea.

While I sat next to a small blubber fire and fried the tasty treats inside the hut, Hull and Mrs Chippy played the game they had so often played on our Deception Island beach. The rules, as far as I could understand them, involved Hull sneaking up on Mrs Chippy – who invariably kept at least one eye open and observed everything her canine opponent was up to – and then trying to nip her tail before the cat would leap at the dog and try to slice his nose off with a razor-sharp claw. Fortunately, both tail and nose remained intact, but amidst a screech and a yelp Hull was always chased away, until the game started a few minutes later all over again. It kept them busy.

This time, however, the yelp I heard was altogether different; this one was a cry of genuine pain. I raced outside, fully expecting to see a bloodied nose. But it was worse, much worse than that: Hull had injured his front leg, the same one he had hurt before, and by the terrible angle of the limb I was fairly sure he had broken it.

"You poor thing!" I cried. "What did you do?"

I could only guess that in characteristic overexuberance he had misjudged his step and landed awkwardly on the uneven, slippery ground. I wouldn't say Mrs Chippy looked pleased at this outcome, but there was certainly an air of haughty scorn about her as I gathered Hull up and carried him back to the hut. Despite having performed the procedure before, I felt no less doubtful about my abilities to help Hull; in fact, I was even more uncertain now, as evidently the leg had not healed well enough. Nevertheless, I could not leave the leg as it was; I had to put it back together, secure it with a splint, and hope that nature would take it from there. As the husky whimpered meekly in the light of the small fire, I chose one of the ski whalebones, cut a couple of long strips from one of the bed sheets and knelt beside him.

"Sorry, Hull, this is going to hurt a lot. I'm just going to tie this around your mouth, so you don't bite me," I explained as I muzzled him with a strip of cloth. He didn't protest; I think he understood. "Three, two, one..." I snapped the leg back into place. Hull howled under his makeshift muzzle, but made no attempt to flee, or scratch, or bite. He simply accepted my aid as I wrapped the cloth again and again around the whalebone and leg. I untied the muzzle and swathed the leg with this strip of cloth, too, so that when I was finished, the poor dog had a rigid, thick and very padded front leg which made any movement very difficult, and walking impossible.

"Here, these fish are for you." I said, breaking the flesh into pieces and feeding him every last morsel bit by bit, much to the chagrin of Mrs Chippy, who had come to the doorway, no doubt attracted by the scent.

Apart from making him comfortable, there was little else I could do for Hull, so I turned my attentions to my enterprise. It dawned on me that the entire purpose of coming here had been to intercept Shackleton's second party. However, apart from a small collection of items I had found in a corner of the hut while I had been making it habitable – a pickaxe and a three-metre sledge left propped against a wall next to a box of largely pointless supplies, including a rope, a sweater, a frozen penguin skin and a pile of rocks – there didn't seem to be any evidence that the party had passed through here at all. There was certainly no ship in the harbour, and I began to wonder if I had landed at the wrong Hut Point. This suspicion seemed to be confirmed when I noticed something tied to the handle of the pick: a match box, within which a note revealed that this hut had been built in July 1912, so three years earlier, and vacated just a few days later. This place had nothing to do with Shackleton.

I consulted my charts, but they were not very helpful. A circle had been placed around this fringe of the Antarctic continent and

227

marked *hyttepunkt*, which was too similar to the German for me to mistake as being anything other than Hut Point. But the area was large, encircling perhaps fifty miles of coastline and several high peaks. Shackleton's relief party could be anywhere in this region. It was a huge setback, but I told myself that I could not very well continue to the South Pole while Hull was out of action, so would use the time in which he recovered to explore and locate the missing party. In any case, although living and hiking on Deception Island for almost a year had given me some skills and experience of Antarctic exploration, the task ahead of me was in a different league altogether, so the forced opportunity to train and condition myself might in fact be a blessing in disguise.

Too worried about Hull to stray too far, I busied myself about the hut, shoring it up and even constructing an antechamber by the opening to try to reduce the draft which whistled with numbing eagerness past the sheet hanging across it. My efforts had some effect, mainly in keeping me warm while building it. I visited the penguins, who had returned after their scare, and raided their rookery for a few eggs. I knew I would have to slaughter some of the animals soon, but for now I had enough frozen meat to meet our needs. Finally, I put the abandoned sledge through its paces. It was in surprisingly serviceable repair, considering it had been half-exposed to the fierce Antarctic elements for three years. However, I made a few adjustments to it using the tools I had brought with me, and by the time I had finished the sledge's three metres had been reduced to two, but now it was very sturdy and all but unbreakable.

With each passing day I ventured further into the environment, sometimes going out for hours at a time. Occasionally I came back to find Odysseus slumped by the hut, or Carmen walking around inside it, sometimes squawking irascibly at Mrs Chippy, sometimes flinging small stones around with her beak. I had no idea why she would want to do this, but let her be. Hull, meanwhile, whimpered miserably, but I kept him warm, tried to exercise him at least a little, and generally maintained order in the remote hut while he recovered.

My first major expedition in those first weeks was to Mount Terror. Its peak was less than ten miles away, and I had already proven that I could trek over twenty miles in a day going to and from the hut, so concluded it was well within my range. Nevertheless, as always I took the tent, sledge and survival equipment; the Antarctic had a common habit of whipping up violent winds and snowstorms from the most benign of conditions, and I had to be prepared for any eventuality. To me, conquering Mount Terror took on the same significance as had scaling Mount Pond on Deception Island. If I could overcome a summit with a name as foreboding as Mount Terror, then whatever scares Antarctica had in store for me could be overcome, too.

I had made several sorties in this direction before, and in the first few hours made swift progress, gaining ever loftier views as I ascended. Another mountain, which I knew from my charts to be Mount Erebus, began to peek over Terror, like a big brother rising behind its younger sibling, complete with fuming cloud above its summit: it was considerably taller, more intimidating; challenging me to a fairer fight once I had triumphed over its smaller brother. Then, far beyond, innumerable peaks more immense than the two in my vicinity sawtoothed along the horizon, a gnarling, gnashing band which stretched far to the south. If I wanted to go to the South Pole, I would have to conquer them, too.

My excursion to Terror had, so far, been pleasant: a bright sun guided me up the mountain; the breeze, which was always chilly, was light and refreshingly cooling as I pulled along the heavily laden sledge; the snow gave way a little but did not completely crumple underneath me; and there were many stretches where I could almost hike on icy gravel while the sledge slid along smoothly behind me. The only concern were the huge crevasses, great rifts in the snow, many metres deep. Should I slip into one and survive the fall, I would most likely be unable to climb back

229

out again. However, they were easy to see, and I gave them a wide berth. I reached the peak far sooner and far more straightforwardly than I could ever have hoped.

The summit of Terror was flat and featureless, more like a plateau than the mountain tops I was used to in Zürich, but the wind was equal to any mountain I had been on, and much colder, too. I pulled my coat tighter around me and took in the vista. I realised that Terror, Erebus and another much smaller mountain just to the north actually formed an island, separate from mainland Antarctica, a fact disguised by a sweeping ice shelf, a permanently frozen land bridge joining these three mountains with the continent. Only the northern coast of the island, facing the open ocean, remained free from the grip of the shelf, although I suspected during the winter months the island would be entirely locked in ice.

The biting wind began to pick up. Within a few moments, I found myself being buffeted around, struggling to stand on one spot as the wind endeavoured to topple me over. Tears, stored somewhere behind my eyes, were driven out by the increasing ferocity, where they trickled for a moment down the surface of my face, before freezing almost instantly on my skin. I began to feel light-headed, too, and I recognised the sensation as a sign of altitude sickness. I had felt it a few times before, hiking in the mountains around Zürich. It was definitely time to leave.

I had barely begun my descent when the whole world became a blinding white void, a swirling mist of inscrutable snow churning amid appalling blasts from winds that seemed to rise up all sides of the mountain and unleash a merciless assault upon my body. I could not possibly progress further in this; I would have to unpack the tent and sit it out. However, my giddiness was disorientating, the blizzard was vengefully unrelenting, and I could not even begin to pitch the tent while irresistible gusts tore at the canvas and sheets which my water-strewn eyes could barely focus on. I bundled everything back together, secured it all with a rope and pressed on down the mountain as best I could.

230

Keeping the sledge under control added to my woes. It pulled, slid and meandered away from me so maddeningly that I almost gave up on it altogether and let it succumb to the fate of this demon squall. However, I only had the one tent; I had to keep hold of it. But the storm had other ideas, and with a malevolently strong blast knocked me from my feet. No longer under my control, the sledge hurtled past me, and for several terrifying moments I accelerated down the mountainside, clutching the rope and trying to dig my feet into the snow to bring our careering descent to a stop.

Eventually, more by the luck of rising mountain contours than by my own triumphant control, the sledge toppled over, and I came to a crunching halt. I was covered in snow: it was in my mouth, my eyes, my hair, in my boots and down my back; and I still had many miles to hike back to my hut. I pulled myself to my feet.

The wind was screaming ferociously now, as if furious at its failure to dislodge the sledge from my grasp. I was panting heavily from my exertions and the wind seized its opportunity, reaching its icy claw down my throat, clutching my breath, drawing it out and leaving me with ever tightening gasps.

"You've got to get off this mountain, or you'll die."

I don't know if I said those words out loud, or just thought them, but they rang through my consciousness with greater clarity than the raw blasts battering my ears. I righted the sledge, pointed it downhill, considered my actions for a further second or two, then sat on it and kicked myself off.

Within moments the sledge had picked up speed, charging down the mountainside, the wind shrieking past me. I could not see at all, visibility was down to just a few metres, snow whirled about me, tiny fragments of ice blew into my face, my eyes filled with water; it was all I could do to ensure we remained upright as the sledge continued its hurtling descent. *What if I plunge into a crevasse? What if I hit a boulder? What if I plummet off a ridge?*

All these questions had come a little too late; I could not stop myself now.

Further down I tore. Sometimes I felt as if the sledge had left the ground completely and was flying through the air, at others it drove through drifts of snow which checked its speed with a stomach-churning lurch and very nearly threw me from my seat.

For two, three, maybe four minutes my world whizzed by in a white blur, and I was besieged by both ceaseless screaming fear and a rush of adrenaline-pumping ecstasy. It was a curious mixture, giving rise to manic laughter. What would Albert make of this? How would his theory of relative time explain a moment of combined joy and horror, of this fleeting eternity?

However long it lasted, actually or relatively, it came to an abrupt end in a soft snowbank. Almost immediately the blizzard's onslaught abated, the skies cleared, and I could see, perched on the knoll perhaps just half a mile away, the dome-shaped shield of rock, gravel and ice which I called home. Terror. The mountain had indeed lived up to its name: terrifyingly violent and terrific fun at once. I felt fired up for the greater challenge of the big brother, Erebus.

Despite Hull's encouraging progress over the next few weeks – he could limp around the hut and take himself out for his toiletry needs, a fact which brought great cheer to both me and Mrs Chippy – he was still in no shape to attempt the journey to the South Pole, and of course I could not leave him alone for that length of time, either. Moreover, Terror had exposed my shortcomings both in being quite incapable of pitching the tent during a storm and of coping with altitude sickness. Either of these failures could be lethal once I set out for the South Pole. And so I determined to accept the more demanding mountain test of Erebus, which I calculated would require three days to complete, there and back. I spent the next few weeks trekking up and down the mountain closer to me, acclimatising to the altitude on Terror, pitching and striking the tent in all weathers, shoring up the hut to make it even more weather proof than it already was, and preparing food for Hull and Mrs Chippy, putting hers in a cavity on *Cotob* which I knew was accessible to her but Hull could not reach. I left his food in a corner and told him to ration himself.

"If you scoff it all on the first day, you'll just have to go hungry for a couple of days," I warned him.

Four weeks after my Terror adventure, I set off to conquer Erebus and it started with a huge surprise. The large brown heap of blubber and nose I called Odysseus was blocking my exit from the hut in the morning. I scrambled over the animal, causing him to grunt and turn his folded neck to see what the disturbance was. That wasn't really the surprise; this came in his reaction to my command.

"You're going to have to move, you big lump, I can't get the sledge out with you in the way."

Unexpectedly, a fleshy wave rippled from his neck to his tail and his bulky mass wriggled away from the antechamber. Perhaps he just wanted to find new ground after I had interrupted his sleep, but, all the same, the thought that he might have understood me made me smile. That wasn't the last of Odysseus's astonishing actions. I assembled everything I needed, checked several times that the food for Hull and Mrs Chippy was in place, lit a few blubber pans of fire, each of which should last for several days, and placed them in every corner of the hut to stave off the worst of the chill. The hut was like a bomb shelter by now and was well insulated. Then I was ready to leave. My plan was to walk around Mount Terror at the same altitude as the hut, then slowly work my way up once I reached Erebus. I began to pull the sledge away. After several metres, I heard the scrape of crunching gravel; Odysseus was dragging his long body after me.

"No, Odysseus. You stay here. You can't go where I'm going." He stopped and I smiled at him, then continued on my way. The scraping started again. "Odysseus, no!" This continued every few metres or so until, bored by the game and getting both cold and nowhere fast, I decided to ignore him and proceed undeterred. Odysseus clearly decided to do the same thing, for he followed me for perhaps two miles, when a wide crevasse prevented any further progress for either of us.

"Well, I didn't know this was here. I guess this is where you turn back, and I go up there," I said, pointing towards the peak of Terror. My change of plans meant I would have to climb the smaller mountain, at least in part, before continuing. Odysseus stared at me with his small, black eyes, and burped. "Fine," I responded and dragged the sledge uphill. Odysseus climbed with me. "You can't come up here! You're an elephant seal, for goodness sake! Get back to the sea!" However, my attempts to dissuade him from his foolhardy loyalty were as successful as my earlier ones. I resigned myself to his lumbering company; I also rejoiced in it.

I have no idea how Odysseus managed it, but he followed me all the way around Terror and up a diminutive mountain which I hadn't even noticed when I had reached Terror's summit a few weeks before. This peak, nestling between Terror and Erebus, would provide a good place to rest.

"How is it that a mountain can hide in plain sight?" I asked Odysseus, now quite used to conversing with him. His responses were normally to cold shoulder me completely, to grunt at me, or to stare at me for a few, long seconds, before continuing to squirm along the mountain. It was that last response I feared the most. It seemed so condescending. Anyone given a hard stare by a five-metre-long pinniped would understand how unnerving it can be. This was the reaction I received to my observations about the hidden mountain, so I gave up on talking to the seal, pitched the tent in silence, ate and went to sleep. Odysseus was still there when I woke. He did not respond to my cheerful greeting – perhaps he was simply eager to get on with the adventure – so, after packing everything back up, we pressed on in silence.

Erebus was a very accessible mountain, with a gentle gradient covered in crushed snow which made trekking up its slopes quite enjoyable. We made good progress, and considering I had an elephant seal in tow, that was no mean feat. The more we neared the summit, the more frequently we encountered strange ice towers that quite defied any explanation. They were frosted statues in bizarre shapes that resembled fossilised ghosts, some of them hissing steam as if the spirits inside were trying to escape their icy prison. At first I thought there must be rock formations underneath them, but they were made only of brittle ice under a thin layer of snow, and broke easily when I snapped a piece off, or shattered completely when Odysseus knocked them with his oversized frame.

This forest of ice spirits and the carpet of snow on which they rested gave way to a hard, gravelly and demandingly steep summit. It was impossible to drag the sledge up it and scrabbling up the slope was hard enough for me, let alone a four-ton animal with no grip on his blubbery belly. However, Odysseus doggedly persevered and lugged himself all the way to the top. I am sure he was as dumbstruck as I was at what we saw there. There was no flat peak, as with Terror, but a huge, gaping hole, a deep crater with bubbling lava, hissing steam and bombs of molten rock which peppered the inside walls of the crater rim.

"Have you ever seen anything like that?" I said incredulously to Odysseus. He burped again. "No, of course you haven't. You should be under the sea, not four thousand metres above it peering over the edge of a volcano. By the way, do creatures like you even get altitude sickness?"

Another hard stare, so I turned my attentions to the lava lake blistering hundreds of metres in the crater beneath us. It was a bewitching sight: every few minutes a jet of gas seethed with a piercing whistle from the lake; I could smell the noxious gases as they exited the volcanic vent to join the permanent cloud high above our heads. Occasionally the frothing lava would settle, just for a moment, then a burst of liquid rock would erupt and paint the inside of the caldera with streaks of brilliant orange, before oozing back into the lake or darkening as they cooled on the crater walls.

"Who would've thought this mountain was in fact a volcano?" I mused aloud. "Maybe we're the first to ever see it, Odysseus."

Just then a deafening explosion from within the crater knocked us both backwards. I tumbled away from the rim, sliding uncontrollably on the loose fragments of rock. I glimpsed the dark, rolling body of Odysseus spilling down the mountain, too, rolling and toppling with hideous torture. I soon came to a bloodied and bruised stop, but Odysseus kept on plummeting, crashing through many frozen pillars; I lost him in a haze of dust and snow. I had no time to think before molten missiles thrown from the crater exploded into the gravel next to me. Some were tiny pellets, others huge boulders, raining down in volcanic salvo, carpet-bombing the summit with fiery abandon. I raced away, my legs barely able to keep up with my speed, down the slope, following the path of crushed snow and smashed ice pillars, towards where Odysseus might be.

I expected to find a battered, crumpled, grisly sight of blood and torn flesh. What I found was Odysseus waiting by my sledge, his normally inscrutable eyes blazing with impatience. I flung my arms as far as I could around his huge neck.

"Odysseus! I thought I'd lost you! You've barely a scratch!" A lava bomb pounded into the ground, not two metres from the sledge. "Come on, let's get out of here!" I urged.

It wasn't long before we were out of range of the flaming stone cannonballs, and we could descend with more composure. I had lost my bearings during the rapid flight from the crater, so took a moment to assess our position from the sun. It was low on the horizon, indicating that we were in the middle of the Antarctic night.

"Time to rest, Odysseus," I announced. "Let's find somewhere to pitch the tent."

I noticed a dark spot, a little further down the slope, and headed there. A base of bare rock was infinitely more pleasant to sleep on than cold snow, which would inevitably seep a freezing chill into my body despite the strong canvas of the tent, the padded

236

reindeer hide mattress, and my warm clothes. However, what I had thought was a patch of rock turned out to be a hole, or rather an entrance, leading to an icy tunnel. I peeked inside. The tunnel dropped quite sharply, then continued at a gentler angle for several metres. I could just make out the beginnings of a cave. I had to explore this further.

"Wait here, Odysseus."

I slid down the entrance. The tunnel was at least a metre wide and twice as high. I trod carefully, mindful that the apparent stability of this icy tunnel might be deceptive, and it could come crashing down on me at any moment. After twenty metres or so it opened into a magnificent cavern. The bare, rocky floor was framed by rippled walls of ice, which for me instantly evoked images of the long white baleen hanging from the jaws of a whale's mouth. The walls were covered in glittering white ice crystals, and crowning it all, stretching above my head, was a brilliant blue dome, swirling with intricacy, an azure ocean roof chilled in icy suspension on the mountainside. The light filtering through this frozen sapphire sea cast a wondrous spectacle across the cavern, like dancing fairies flitting across the ice. I gaped, spellbound by the enchanted space, until a rude nasal blare trumpeting down the tunnel alerted me to my more immediate concerns.

"Okay, Odysseus, I'm coming!"

He took a bit of persuading, but eventually the elephant seal followed me into the cavern. I'd like to think he felt at home, looking up into the expanse above and imagining he was drifting under the ocean deep; at least he felt content enough to take no time in dozing off. I, too, was transported by my tiredness and the warm, soothing soil of this magical cavern into a long, submersive sleep from which I awoke feeling refreshed, reinvigorated, and ready to head back home.

Odysseus was still fast asleep, giving me time to check on the sledge outside the cavern, cook some meat and drink a cup of hot water. Still Odysseus slept. We couldn't very well spend another day here, so I decided to wake him. I felt slightly nervous about it; disturbing the sleep of such a monstrous animal was not a very wise thing to do. However, we had to get back, and I was left with little choice. I tapped him gently on the side.

"Odysseus, Odysseus, time to wake," I cooed.

No reaction. I tried again, with more force. Still nothing. I pushed his body, but barely made an impression on his thick hide; I would have to get more persuasive. I melted some snow, so that it was lukewarm, and stood next to his large head.

"Sorry about this, you big brute, but we have to get going." I threw the water over him and prepared myself to run away.

Nothing.

For the first time, I began to worry. With each new attempt to wake him, I grew more daring, more vehement, more panicked. I prodded him, pushed him, punched him. He would not wake, he could not wake; and when I lifted his heavy eyelids, I saw why. All life had left that once warm, deep, penetrating gaze, and they were as glazed as the icy walls which surrounded us.

"Odysseus! No! Wake up!" I yelled, even as I knew he could not. I hit him harder than before, grabbed his whiskers and pulled them roughly; I climbed onto him and pounded my fists into his blubbery body. "Odysseus, Odysseus!" I wailed. But the great beast did not flinch. Eventually, exhausted by my efforts, I lay down on his broad back and sobbed, whimpering his name every so often, as if, by some miracle, the salt from my tears and the spell of my words would bring the creature, my strong and reliable friend, my saviour of the sea, back to life.

At some point I knew I had to leave. I had to get back to Hull and Mrs Chippy; I had to leave Odysseus here in this blue, icy catacomb. I climbed down from him and did what I felt was right, piling a mound of rocks next to his body, and another just outside the tunnel. I don't why a pile of rocks meant so much; it was such a simple gesture. Perhaps that simplicity was the very point. Tough and lasting, the cairn would be an honourable tribute to my companion. At the same time, each rock carried the heaviness of my heart, and I could barely place one upon another without feeling utterly crushed. When I finally found the strength to complete the stone stack outside the tunnel, I returned to the cave, where I carved Odysseus's name deep into the glittering wall. I stared at him for a long time, placed my palm on his huge, scarred head, then turned and walked away, up the short tunnel and out into the eternal light of the Antarctic summer.

50°19' North, Prime Meridian

I gazed out of my cabin porthole into
the grey beyond, the dreary view obscured by trails of rain meandering across the glass, and I knew I was nearing what I had once called my home. I had been here before, on this arbitrary meridian line which wrapped around the earth, several weeks ago when we were approaching Cape Town. How different the world had seemed then, when I had been looking forward to returning to Europe and rediscovering a life long abandoned. The world had shown me how much it had changed in my absence, I was effectively imprisoned on this metal juggernaut and, now in a busy shipping channel sandwiched between the Nazi vassal states of England and France, I desired nothing more than to return to my icy isolation. But that life was gone, I knew I could not return to it, a dream melted into retreating streaks across the clear cold harshness of my new reality.

A knock on the door: Lars. His face was drawn, troubled, as if he had been struggling with some dreadful pain. Not like the time he had battled against the fury of the ocean and with broken arm and battered body arrived exhausted on Elephant Island. This time, something internal was afflicting him.

"Lars, come in. What's wrong?" I asked, concerned.

He remained in the doorway. "I… It's…," he stammered. I stood back and motioned for him to enter. Instead, Lars looked furtively down the ship's narrow corridor. "I can't come in. I can't come ever again." I hadn't expected that. His announcement left me speechless, and I shook my head in confusion. The clank of a heavy door, coming from somewhere within the belly of the ship, made him jump. "I'm sorry, Marianna. I have to go." He glanced

240

to his left and right, lunged forward to give me an awkward fleeting hug, and hurried away.

I stood in dumbfounded silence for a few moments, trying to make sense of the brief visit. His behaviour baffled me, but I was sure it had something to do with Kapitän Ritscher. I closed the door and sat at the window once more.

Another rap at the door. This time it was Kapitän Ritscher. His affability had completely deserted him now, at least when he was with me. He refused my invitation to enter, standing stern-faced at the doorway, a piece of paper in his hand.

"Frau Dittrich, I have an important message for you."

"Oh?"

"It seems that Professor Einstein has requested a personal meeting with you."

"See! I told you! I haven't been making anything up!" I was jubilant. Albert, my clumsy, amazing old friend, was coming to my rescue.

"There are no details. As far as I can tell, his interest in you might just as easily be that of a scientist probing an anomaly."

"You'll see! Are you sure you don't want to come in? I can tell you more about him, if you want." I was mocking him, and he knew it. He launched his counterattack.

"No. When we arrive in Hamburg, you will be driven by car to Berlin. You will remain under guard at all times."

Without any pleasantries, the captain turned and left. I didn't mind his parting words. They could do all they want; I had Albert on my side. I smiled and returned to the porthole, wiping away the condensation to gain a better view.

As bizarre as it had been to reach the summit of Mount Erebus accompanied by an elephant seal, it felt infinitely stranger to be undertaking the return journey without him. I felt drained by his loss, too physically and emotionally sapped by my heartbreak to even consider the long trudge back. However, I had others counting on me, their needs pulling me homeward. So after leaving Odysseus in his tomb, I drew on reserves that only the extreme intensity of despair could bestow and lugged the sledge for many kilometres through soft snow and across dangerously crevassed surfaces, taking the most direct route that the topography allowed me.

I was hoping, in fact half-expecting Hull to anticipate my arrival, either through his acute hearing or sharp sense of smell, and come bounding down the knoll to greet me. His leg, I reminded myself, would prevent this, yet I was still disappointed, and then concerned, that I couldn't even see him waiting at the doorway with wagging tail. I left the sledge and quickened my pace, hurrying up the barren knoll towards the stone hut.

I had already painted a dire picture in my mind before I even reached the hut: Carmen, ripped to shreds by Mrs Chippy's sharp claws; the cat, driven to desperation by hunger and now clinging to life with wheezing, shortened breaths; Hull, his movements fatefully restricted by injury, now frozen to death. It was another scene, however, which greeted me. All three of my companions were huddled together in one corner: Mrs Chippy, snug between the husky's front legs; Carmen, nestled on his furry back; all three staring at the dying flame of the final blubber candle still flickering in the gloom of the cold shelter. They seemed mesmerised by the wavering light and did not notice me at all.

What were they seeing in that flame? Fading hope? Or its opposite, the tenacity of life, flickering and trembling in the cold, yet still holding on? Or had they with their inscrutable instincts sensed Odysseus's passing, and this was their collected tribute to him? I would never know. Most likely the animals were simply bored and drawn to the only vaguely entertaining thing around. I smiled at my desire to read something into nothing, a self-deception probably born of the long lack of contact with other people.

Then Hull detected me. His ears pricked, his nose twitched, then, quite forgetting his impairment, he sprang to his feet, flinging Carmen into the air with an offended squawk, and bounded towards me. Either because he discerned my melancholy and was trying to cheer me up, or because he was blissfully unaware of it and driven only by unfettered excitement, the silly dog whined and whimpered and covered me with slobbery licks. I prised him away, gave him a big hug, and set about heating and cleaning the hut. It was in quite a stinking mess: the dog and the skua had littered the floor with excrement, which fortunately had frozen in situ and was easy to remove; at least Mrs Chippy had shown the decency to take herself off elsewhere when the need had arisen. The remains of half-eaten fish were strewn about, too. Evidently Carmen had taken over the role of provider in my absence.

It didn't take long to get the hut back into respectable order, or for me to collapse thereafter, weary and bleary-eyed, into my relatively soft bed. I didn't even bother to shoo Hull from me, so insistent was he on covering me with his hairy body as soon as I lay down, and I fell into a deep sleep plagued by images of a scarred Odysseus all alone in a cold cave on Mount Erebus.

Over the next few days it became increasingly clear to me that the chances of departing for the South Pole during the remaining summer months were exceedingly slim. Hull's leg would simply not be up to it. I would be away too long to leave him behind and I couldn't drag him all the way there on a sledge – my energy reserves were far too precious for that, and I would only end up killing us both. So I had no choice but to overwinter in the hut and wait for an improvement in both the weather and the husky's condition. It was a bitter setback, and the fact that I couldn't even tell Albert about it compounded the blow. I worried for my old friend, sitting in some book-filled office fretting over my journey. Now it would be a further year until he heard from me again.

I filled my days with extended tasks that I could have ordinarily performed much faster: checking on *Deception* and *Cotob* for signs of wear and tear, overhauling the sledge I had used on my excursions, slaughtering penguins to ensure I always had a plentiful supply in case a storm should keep me holed up for several days, and finally repairing weather damage to the hut, making it an almost impregnable, shell-like fortress that could withstand anything the Antarctic threw at it. Life in this icy environment was one of drawn-out tedium, occasionally punctuated with moments of terrific drama; a parallel, perhaps, of life in the world beyond these frozen borders. Under the enduring Antarctic sky nothing seemed to happen for weeks, and then weeks were compressed into an instant, and almost always with startling calamity.

244

It was Christmas Day 1916 when one such calamity visited my part of the world. I had marked the summer solstice a few days before by climbing Mount Terror. It was a balmy, windless day; the sun was beating down, raising the temperature to just above freezing point. I had taken Hull with me, both for the company and to build up his strength now that he was able to walk again. Then I heard it. An irregular and rapid crackling sequence of loud pops, whipping through the air behind me. My impulse was to flinch, instinctively ducking to avoid being struck by an unknown assailant. Hull, too, suspected danger and spun around to face the aggressor. There was no-one there, but, from my elevated position I could see that where before there had been nothing but the vast expanse of unbroken white ice shelf which I had sailed past a few months before, now there was a huge rift snaking through it, a black chasm stretching far as I could see; a massive chunk of the ice shelf had broken away. Just a few days later, on Christmas Day, the scale of this disaster was apparent.

I strolled with Hull down to the penguin rookery to fetch myself some choice game for Christmas dinner. There were plenty of chicks now and their flesh was far more palatable than that of the older birds. I had rationed my supply of dried food, too, not taking any for several weeks, and was looking forward to a warm stew of tender penguin meat and ground biscuits, sweetened by a couple of sugar cubes and all washed down with a cup of hot chocolate. As it turned out, my Christmas labours turned out to be quite different than cooking this festive dish.

The enormous iceberg that had broken away from the great ice cliff a few days before had travelled on the slow current circling the continent, floated down to the rookery and lodged itself there. Where this sixty-metre-high ice barrier had once frustrated attempts to access the continent, it now prevented anyone leaving it, blocking access to the open ocean. The penguins were squawking in confusion and disorientation, flapping their sleek wings, waddling aimlessly or falling over one another in an attempt to make sense of their new enclosed environment. With

245

no possibility of leaving the rookery and hunting for fish, the whole colony would soon perish. I could not take one of their number now; I had to try to save them.

"Sorry, Mrs Chippy, Christmas dinner has been cancelled this year," I announced as I returned to the hut empty-handed. She blinked and licked her paw. I found in the corner of the hut what I had come back for – the pickaxe – and after ensuring everyone had eaten well, returned to the rookery where a gargantuan task awaited me; I was going to hack out a tunnel through the berg and restore the penguins' liberty.

If I had known how long this would take me, I probably would never have even commenced the endeavour. It started off well enough. The ice fell away easily under my blows in chips or slices, accumulating quickly around me. It was a satisfying task, every half an hour or so, to gather up the icy shards and dump them in a pile away from the tunnel mouth. After half a day I had excavated several metres, so downed tools and returned to the hut for some refreshment. I had no idea how far I would have to dig, but I assumed that the berg would be at least as wide as it was high; it turned out to be much more than this. By day three, my wrists were hurting and I was getting frustrated with myself, frustrated with the ice, even with the penguins who came to investigate occasionally, often getting in my way as I cleared the chips and shards away. After one week, I considered abandoning the idea. I was so far into the berg that the light from the mouth did not reach me. Blubber candles lit my way, yet the smoke had nowhere to escape and it was a suffocating, stifling grind that seemed to have no end. The walls were blackened by the fumes and I was coughing, choking, and covered in soot. Then the chicks began to die.

When I found the first one, its mother clucking dolefully above its limp body, I felt a crippling sting of failure; my Christmas promise to save this little creature had ended in its death. Then I saw another one, both its parents leaning over the fluffy grey body which refused to move. Nor were they the only two deaths.

246

Those that had not died were close to it. Adult penguins had stopped battling to find an escape, the rookery now chilled into an eerie, deathly motionlessness, filled with the mournful sounds of a hungry, grieving, dying colony. Their elegy drifted over the ice and snow, drilled into my worthless tunnel and reverberated against its cold, black walls in reproachful lament. It was a time of despair, of anguish, of loss. I had failed them and I sensed how truly hopeless my cause was; they were not to leave their icy prison, and nor was I. Just as these unfortunate creatures, I would die here, in the silence of the snow. Then something wonderful happened.

Over the last week Carmen had been dropping the occasional fish at the tunnel mouth. Mostly a greedy penguin mouth would snap it up before I even got a good glimpse of it, and if I did reach it first, I would share it out as fairly as I could among heart-breakingly few of the countless snapping beaks. As my world now began to shatter around me, a distant cry from the sky pierced the sad penguin song; then there was another, and then discordant shrieks from a blanket of birds drowned out the dirge and a thousand flapping wings tore over the sheer face of the berg. Each bird dropped a life-giving parcel from its beak, and the skies rained with fish. The bravest penguin broke off his lament and waddled to the nearest offering which had fallen so unexpectedly from above. The others watched with interest. When he guzzled up the fish and moved on to the next one, the place was transformed into a seething carpet of black and white bodies sweeping over the rookery. I clasped my hands to my mouth and wept in delight, and when all the penguins were done, the rookery resembled the morning after a debauched party. I returned to the tunnel and redoubled my efforts.

It took me six months to complete the tunnel, three months of which I was shrouded not only in the gloom of the tunnel, but, when I had finished excavating for the day, also the darkness of the polar night, where the sun ceded the sky to the moon for half the year. During this same time of the year on Deception Island, I had savoured in the luxuries of a generator, light, warmth and many home comforts. Out here, there was only desolation: no power, no illumination save from the cold moon or the dismal flicker from a candle, no heat, and certainly no relief. It was hard not to sink into deep melancholy, yet the effort of digging the tunnel gave me a focus, a palpable demonstration that the darkness would, one day, yield.

I was keen to break through to the other side before the winter solstice, although I was in no hurry since the flying squadron had taken over the emergency penguin relief operation. After several weeks of that first extraordinary event, it didn't even surprise me when, every so often, dinner poured from the heavens. The arbitrary date I had set was more a signal to me than of relevance to the penguins' survival. The tunnel, the long, difficult path carved through ice and snow, had to be accomplished before the dark days began to shorten, to symbolise for me that even when a task seemed impossibly forbidding, with perseverance and tenacity the outlook would eventually begin to grow brighter. That I burrowed through the enormous berg and broke through to the Southern Ocean, some two kilometres from the mouth of the tunnel in the rookery, on exactly the 21st June 1917, the very day of the winter solstice, filled me with overwhelming hope and joy, and the heavens, brilliantly illuminated with curling streaks of neon light flashing across the midnight blue, rejoiced with me.

The penguins were pleased, too. To mark the occasion, I dressed myself as one of their kind, at least as best I could. All of my clothing was black or dirty brown, either because it was made that way or due to everything now being covered in soot and grime, so all I had to do was pull a hood far over my head and rub a circle of snow on my front, and I looked the part. Well, almost. Even Hull allowed himself to be disguised, although he was far less convincing as a penguin than I was. With a spitting hiss Mrs Chippy signalled that she would not be taking part in any fancy dress party. Getting the adult birds to follow me through the long tunnel was no easy task. They had become too reliant on their
248

free deliveries, too comfortable with their sedentary life, to bother. But, after seeing the younger birds excitedly chase me into the tunnel and, after having swum and fished for hours in the Southern Ocean, return to their rookery with full bellies and croaks of satisfaction, even the older birds abandoned the comfortable life, entered the tunnel and started to fish for themselves again. My long mission had been a success, and now I could look forward to the next challenge with unwavering eagerness and confidence. I had built the tunnel, the penguins were saved, my hands were hardened, my shoulders strengthened, my mind determined, and now I was ready to take on the South Pole.

I knew I could not leave for four more months: not only did the harsh winter weather preclude any possibility of an earlier departure, but I also needed to be able to use the sextant during the day; I had never mastered taking a reading by the stars. Furthermore, I was now much more familiar with the lie of the land than when I had arrived at my stone hut, and I realised that travelling over the snow and ice would take considerably longer than I had initially predicted. The continent of Antarctica was a very different beast to the comparatively tame Deception Island. I now estimated the journey to the South Pole and back, if I averaged about thirty kilometres a day, would take me one hundred days. It was an appealing number, giving me psychologically manageable ten-day segments to complete the arduous challenge.

For anyone who has not experienced Antarctic life, having to wait several months before departure in sub-zero temperatures must seem like interminable torture; for me, it flew by in an instant as I prepared for the expedition of my life, checking my equipment every day, practising skiing on the vast ice shelf, exploring the best route, at least for the initial stages of the journey, and laying down supplies along the way. Jack had told me that the *Endurance* crew had planned to make similar sorties into the continent for several months before embarking on their

249

expedition in earnest when they arrived in Antarctica, on the other side of the continent, so I knew that this would be crucial to my success.

In late August the sun first peeked over the Southern Ocean, and my heart leapt in expectation. With each passing day the weak orb climbed further from its dark winter retreat, gaining in strength, raising the temperature, and letting my anticipation levels soar. Eventually, on the morning of All Hallows' Eve, when the midnight sun had finally broken free from its winter shackles and was no longer pulled below the horizon, not even for a second, it was time to set off. I left a note in the hut, just in case I failed to make it back, and wrote another for Albert, which I sealed with congealed penguin blubber. I enjoyed picturing his screwed-up face as the gelatinous substance stuck to his fingers.

I pulled the fully laden, larger sledge and harnessed Hull to the smaller sledge *Cotob*. He would tug along some more supplies and the lazy cat. I was rather hoping Carmen would join us, or at the very least see us off, but there was no sign of her. Perhaps, I thought to myself, she was organising another rescue operation somewhere along the coast. So, with no further reason to delay, we made our way down the knoll, reached the ice shelf a short time later, I slipped on the skis, and we were off.

As I had already spent months probing deep into the area, scouting for crevasses and other obstacles, and had earmarked several locations where we would camp each night, the going was swift and trouble-free for the first week or so. The supplies I had lain over the last few months helped, too, and I was careful to leave some for the return journey. Every now and then Hull would stop, just to check on Mrs Chippy. Usually she was sleeping, but sometimes she peeked over the top, touching noses with the husky, and occasionally she even leapt out of *Cotob* to weave around Hull's feet or took herself off at a polite distance, her back facing us, to colour the snow. I think she thought that if she couldn't see us, we wouldn't know what she was doing. Afterwards she always scooted faster than I thought it was possible, darting into *Cotob*, where, I assume, she stuffed herself in blankets and went straight back to sleep.

I hugged the Transantarctic Mountains to my right; they were a natural, unmissable signpost, guiding me for hundreds of miles across the ice shelf. They were the strangest mountains I had ever seen, tangled stone structures standing quite apart from one another, more resembling long-abandoned palaces and castles, multi-turreted citadels in which ancient kings and queens might once have lived in luxury before some environmental catastrophe had covered the land in snow and driven all life away. These were, I believed, the peaks of colossal mountains, the rest buried under possibly thousands of metres of snow. What a queer continent this was. So much of it hidden, perhaps never to see the light of day, even when the light of day was never-ending. The only indication of what lay underneath were these majestic glimpses. I was indebted to these mountain tops, for within the fortifications of these curiously gnarled towers I was always able to find reasonable shelter from the whistling wind.

For many, many weeks I battled against the wind, sometimes blown off my feet by its ferocious strength. The chill it carried was more dangerous still, able to freeze the tears before they left my eyes. I was used to the cold, but I had not been prepared for the lethal wildness of this weather and sometimes had no choice but to bunker down for days on end until these baleful storms blew themselves out. Throughout it all Mrs Chippy seemed perfectly happy, but I was worried for Hull. I thought back to the *Endurance*, where he was one of dozens of dogs tasked to help with Shackleton's expedition. Here, he was on his own. For his sake as well as mine, I rested as much as I thought my supplies would allow.

Eventually I reached the point I had been aiming for: the end of the ice shelf and a break in the mountains which would allow me to pass through the range and onto the polar plateau. Hereon I would be heading directly south; the pole was a mere five hundred kilometres away. Before I forsook the relative sanctuary of the mountain range, as the departing kings and queens had done in some mystical time before me, I spent a long time reflecting upon whether I should risk this final stage of the journey. The most difficult part lay ahead of me, of that I was sure. No flat ice shelf across which I could ski, no protective mountains, no shelter, no break, just an unrelenting slog towards the pole. I studied my charts and plotted how far I had come. From Deception Island to my stone hut, from there across the ice to here: it was an immense distance, against which the final push seemed laughably short. I checked the sledges and saw that they were both undamaged, the supplies were still well-stocked, Hull and Mrs Chippy seemed in good shape. I would attempt it.

I grew obsessed by the wind. I thought it had been strong before, across the flat ice shelf, but that was a gentle breeze compared to the ruthless gales which blasted over the polar plateau. With nothing to impede or brake these gusts, they cannonaded across the continent for hundreds of kilometres, slamming into my body, pushing back the sledges and forestalling our progress. I felt at every new stage of my journey that the Antarctic was trying with all its might to drive me away: the storms at sea; the currents on Elephant Island and Deception Island; the great ice cliff; and now these winds. But where before I had Odysseus to power me on, now I was largely on my own; nothing but grit and obstinacy would get me through.

The air was getting thinner, too, as many millennia of falling snow had raised the plateau to thousands of metres above sea-level. I had considered myself well-trained for this. Throughout my childhood I had grown accustomed to coping with lower oxygen levels, but that was a long time ago, now. My recent ascents of Terror and Erebus had been of more help; but this was different, as it always was in Antarctica. The air was cruelly pinched by cold and altitude, and in the raging wind I had to gasp for any inhalable fragment. Even when I was in my tent, its sides rattling violently, I found it difficult to breathe with any comfort. Yet still, when the time for rest was over, I would press on.

252

Eventually, my determination tamed the weather, and the clouds, which often skirted the ground, obscuring all vision, cleared to allow the sun to shine unhindered, a smiling beacon guiding me to my destination. It is difficult to describe the sensations surging through me during those final few days, as I closed in on the goal which had once seemed impossibly distant, yet now was just an unknown but achievable number of steps away. Certainly elated and excited, yet also anxious, scared even. Quite what should make me apprehensive I did not know; perhaps it was a fear that the goal I had set myself would not, after all, be the decisive moment I hoped it would be, that I had falsely convinced myself that if I could complete this incredible journey, then all the burdens – what those burdens were exactly I was also not so sure – would be lifted.

My arrival was timed perfectly. Both by coincidence and, I suspect, some hidden direction on my part, delaying here, speeding up there, when I pointed the sextant to the sky and triangulated my position on the longest day of the year, the 21st December, 1917, it read 90°00' South, 0°00' East. I was standing above the southern axis of the earth. The world was quite literally spinning around my feet, and I felt giddy with unbidden emotions.

52°53' North, 13°38' East

As soon as we pulled into Berlin's

Anhalter Bahnhof I was blindfolded by one of the burly men guarding me. My smothered sight heightened my other senses while they marched me out of the station: I could smell the oil and metal of the steam trains; detect the essence of a lady's perfume as she passed by and hear her hushed curse when one of my guards bumped her with his shoulder; I breathed in the nutty fragrance of coffee to my left and picked up the chatter of a dozen customers, perhaps waiting for their departing train, or their arriving friend, or just enjoying the atmosphere of the bustling station. Everywhere the air was thick with the woody fumes of cigarettes. It seemed the whole world was smoking, almost choking, and I was thankful to get outside.

No sooner had I tasted the waft of the outside breeze when a sudden thunderous rumble coming from within the station made me and both of my guards instinctively duck.

"That's a bomb!" exclaimed one.

"These terrorists don't care who they hurt!" cursed the other. "Come on, we have to get this woman to the ministry. Let's get out of here!"

The men hurried me towards an idling engine, a car door clicked open, I was pushed inside. After ten minutes or so driving through the streets of Berlin, flashes of light occasionally permeating the dark fabric around my eyes, the car stopped.

The secrecy continued. I was quickly taken from the street and led into a large building. It spaciousness was evident from the echoing footsteps on the polished floor and the muted voices, reaching me from some distance away. Door after door was opened, some clanging heavily shut behind me. Short, hasty steps

254

revealed the presence of people coming the other way, pressing themselves to the side to allow me and my guards to march past, along the corridors, down some stairs, through more doors, until, finally, we arrived. I heard what might have been a gentle breeze, although I think it was a new set of doors being swung open, and I was ushered inside.

"Get that blindfold off her at once!" snapped a voice. A voice I recognised. *Albert!* "And don't you dare put it back on her. She is a lady and deserves to be treated as such."

The blindfold was quickly removed, and I shielded my eyes from the sudden influx of light. In front of me, forming through the luminance like a ship emerging through the haze, was the same ruffled hair and the same dancing eyes, twinkling in the brightness of the room, and the same generous nose, now sporting a pair of rounded spectacles.

Albert, sitting behind a desk in the centre of the room, smiled and bade me to sit. The guards took up position either side of the door. We were in some kind of large, windowless vault. The walls were stark and undecorated. Not even the all-pervasive Nazi flags were anywhere to be seen. Judging by the number of stairs we had descended, I figured we were deep underground. It looked like a place designed to house gold or weapons, not people.

"It's really you," I said, getting out of the chair to go to him.

"Sit!" snapped one of the guards, hand already on his gun.

Albert glared at him sharply, then motioned for me to return to my seat. "They don't let anyone get too close to me. I'd rather shoo them all away, but, well, I don't get to decide everything. One second, please." He collected some papers together, glanced at them, then carelessly cast them to the side. "The dolts," he muttered, "they'll never understand my motivations," he added, curiously. "Now, Marianna," he said, looking at me over the rim of his glasses, "I have been hearing all sorts of tales. Let's start at the beginning."

"What do you mean?"

"Well, I've read the report of how you came to be stranded on that island after the start of the Great War, but I don't know many of the details. Why don't you tell me how you managed to survive for so long."

"Eh? You know everything already."

Albert let his eyes wander over the room. They lingered on the guards, then returned to me. "Yes, the captain of your ship filed a report. He said you claimed we had been communicating by radio."

"Claimed? What are you talking about?" My voice was rising in frustration, even anger. Albert glanced over to the guards again. I turned to face them too and saw how they had fixed their gaze on me, their fingers almost twitching above their weapons. "Ah, I see," I said in sudden realisation. Leaning forward, careful not to leave my seat, I whispered towards Albert. "Kapitän Ritscher told me that Jews are not welcome here. You're just pretending."

Albert shook his head slightly, removed his glasses, which he folded and placed on the table. Then he, too, leant forward in his chair, and whispered. "Some things are kept hidden from the public. What we see, what we hear, is relative to the standpoint of the observer." Then he leant back and spoke audibly enough for everyone to hear. "There were several animals with you. A cat, a dog, a bird and..." he paused, "a whale."

"No! An elephant seal. Odysseus."

"Ah, yes, that's right. Sorry, I forgot."

"It's been a long time," I smiled, forgiving his lapse of memory.

"I'm sure it has. You know Marianna, your story would have been fascinating for an Austrian friend of mine, Sigmund Freud. Dreams, the unconscious, repression, the ego. This was just his kind of thing. Unfortunately, he died a few years ago. I feel I am slightly out of my depth in these matters."

I didn't really know how to respond to that. "How's your wife? I asked. "What about your sons? You never really talked about them. I guess they'll be grown men by now."

The question changed Albert's cheerful demeanour at once. "I never talked about them because we never talked," he snapped. He drew in a deep breath, composed himself and put his glasses back on. "Many things have changed in the thirty years since you've been away. I'm sure you have heard about some of them on your way here."

"Yes. Heard and seen." I was wary of what I should say. So long as the guards were present, Albert was going to keep up the pretence of not having spoken to me during my absence. I would keep my answers short, until I could speak with him more privately.

"You might recall that back in Zürich I was troubled by my observations, by what man was inflicting upon his environment." I nodded. "I felt despair at my inability to do anything about it," he continued, "and turned much of my attentions away from the problems here, to the problems above us, to questions of the stars and universe."

"The sextant!" I blurted, in much the same manner I had done when I was a young girl sitting at his side.

"Yes, but not just that. Other things too, such as how everything came to be, and how everything ends. How time ends."

"How time ends?" I said, not having any idea at what even my question meant.

"I have seen things here on earth and observed things in the universe that have had a profound effect on me. One of my dearest friends, a brilliant scientist called Karl Schwarzschild, was working on this with me when he died a horrible and painful death in the trenches in the Great War."

"I'm sorry to hear that, Albert."

"Well," Albert continued, "I vowed that I could not allow our greatest minds and the secrets that they might have uncovered to be lost like this. For the next ten years or so I observed with increasing horror how the earth was being ravaged by industrial processes, and that, too, became something I needed to stop, for the sake of all mankind. When the National Socialists came to

257

power, they had the means, the momentum and the might to do something about it. You could say, we had a common purpose. I turned my attentions to rockets and, well, the rest is almost history."

"They murder people."

Albert put a finger to his lips. "I would use a different term. So do they, for that matter. They call it the 'Final Solution'. We have, granted, quite different motivations, but the result is the same. Let's just say, together we have found a solution which answers our different problems. And *my* motivation, Marianna, is that if we don't find a drastic solution, we all die."

I turned in my seat to look at the guards once more. They seemed to have relaxed and were staring mechanically ahead, apparently disinterested in our words and activated only by any sudden movement I might make.

"You kill people who are overweight; you kill people who are black; you kill people for meat. Nothing could possibly justify all these terrible things. It's... it's just horrible."

"I was wondering when we'd get on to this. You deserve an explanation. I've given it some thought, you know, how to explain it all to you. You did save my life once, remember? You could even argue, without you, none of this would have even been possible. Our backgrounds are important, Marianna. Maybe I can now return the favour." When I didn't say anything, Albert raked through some papers on his desk. "Ah! Here we are. Chinstrap penguins are what we need."

"What?"

"You've been in Antarctica for a very long time. You must have noticed a change in the penguin population."

After what I had just said to Albert, I certainly did not expect him to talk about penguins. Perhaps he wanted to reset the conversation.

"Yes, I did, actually. The colonies of chinstrap penguins on Deception Island were getting smaller, and fewer. Why is that important?"

258

Albert chuckled good-humouredly. "It's *all* important, Marianna. It's *all* related. And, at the same time, the gentoo penguins are flourishing."

"Not that I noticed."

"Well, they are. Maybe not where you were, but there have been several studies on it already. That's something I've insisted on – greater scrutiny of what's taking place around the world. Marianna, it's all about adaptability. The world has shifted, perhaps irreversibly so, and those species which fail to adjust will decline, just like the chinstrap penguins have declined. You see, all penguins eat fish, but the chinstraps' fish of choice eat krill, and unfortunately there are not as many of those little crustaceans as there used to be. Krill do not fair well in the warmer seas which now lap our shores. The seas have been warmed by those industrial processes I mentioned a minute ago. Anyway, fewer krill, fewer fish that eat them, and then fewer penguins that eat those fish. The fish which the gentoos eat, however, do not feast on krill."

I had no idea where all of this was leading and sighed heavily. This was not the reunion I had imagined. There were signs that the Albert I knew was in there, still. He had always had an obsessive streak – sometimes boating, sometimes music, sometimes something I could not possibly understand. But this was different. His eyes were wild with intensity as he spoke, sparkling not with the glint of cheekiness, but with fanatical fire. He had changed, fundamentally.

"So you are doing this to save the penguins?"

Albert roared with laughter, flinging his papers in the air. I think I even heard the guards snigger. "Priceless! No, my dear. I am doing this to save us. Let me help you to understand. When we have bugs on a plant, what do we do?"

"Don't know. Nothing?"

"Well, yes, that's precisely what we have been doing. But now we can spray them, with pesticides. Those that are fortunate enough to survive leave the plant and hop on to another one."

259

"Okay."

"But we, we humans, we don't *have* another plant to hop on to. All of the harmful bugs must die."

"Are you saying humans are bugs?"

Albert steepled his fingers, touched his chin with the tip of them and nodded slowly. "That's exactly what I'm saying. Humans are bugs, and this earth is our only plant. If we're careful, both the bugs and the plant can flourish. But we are too many and take too much. The plant is dying. The plant, the planet, our earth, is shrivelling under rising temperatures, the seas are rising, the storms are intensifying, the air is growing toxic. All of this is killing our one and only plant. If that happens, we all die. The solution is to remove the bugs that cause the most damage."

"How can you talk like this? You used to see the good in everyone."

His eyes dropped. He combed his unkempt hair with his fingers. There he was! "There is no room for sentiment, Marianna. I'm sorry," he murmured.

I felt I nearly had him, the old Albert, and pressed my advantage home. "Think about the wind in the sails on your boat, the glassy lake, the clouds brushing past the mountains. That's what life is all about. You don't need this."

His head sprang up, I had stirred something within him.

"Exactly, Marianna. That's exactly it. The wind, the lake, the clouds, the mountains. To preserve all that requires dispassionate action now. Have you ever heard of pathetic fallacy?"

I had lost him again. I knew he was about to delve into a world of words and ideas which I would barely recognise.

"No."

"It is the belief that the operations of nature reflect man's actions. That the lightning storm symbolises man's anger; that the wind represents man's fury; that the bright sun reflects his cheerful disposition. You see this device everywhere in literature. Scientists have, typically, dismissed it as the foolish stuff of imagination. Well, Marianna, the only pathetic fallacy about this is

260

the belief that it is indeed a whimsical quirk of man's invention. *Of course* nature responds to the movements of man. Our ultimate deception has been the belief that we could recognise our own artifice. In the face of screaming evidence around us, indeed even within our own creative works, we have turned a blind eye and deceived ourselves."

Albert's words baffled me. I imagined a group of students listening to Albert lecture, watching him skilfully lay a mosaic of concepts and walking his bemused audience across it. In his element he was as a magnificent galleon, the king of the seas, gliding across the ocean with undeniable complexity and stature. For the students it might have been an exquisite experience. But for me it was an alienating one. Whereas I could more or less understand the intricacy of multi-layered galleons, when Albert had the wind in his sails, I was stranded, unable to grasp the breath of genius which drove his mighty intellect. I had lost him again, and he had lost me.

"I'm sorry, Albert. I don't really understand. All this talk of bugs and nature and deception. It doesn't make any sense to me. All I can see is a horrible world."

Albert pointed at me. "That's because you *can't* see. I've said before that the observable is relative to the observer. It's all bound up with a general theory of relativity, the implications of which," Albert chuckled, "I've barely begun to examine. I don't expect you to understand, but things can both exist and not exist at the same time, depending on where you're looking from. You've been away too long, shielded from a very different reality. Take your companions in the Antarctic. The cat, the dog, the bird and the seal. Think about it, Marianna. These things were not real, at least from most perspectives. How could they have been? They were necessary constructs of your imagination to cope with a life of utter isolation."

"That's not true!" I flared. I stammered to explain how I had found Hull and Mrs Chippy after leaving South Georgia, how Albert could check with the survivors of *Endurance* that there had

261

been a missing dog. He could even check with Lars Anton Anderson about the husky, and he might even be to recall the skua. I stumbled over my own words, compelling him to explain how so many of my experiences could have been invented, that I had written all of it down, and it was all as true as the pathetic fallacy, or whatever it was called, that he had just outlined to me. He dismissed my outburst.

"Like I said, I don't profess to understand the workings of a castaway mind, but it is not a great leap to suggest you craved companionship, friendship, love, that you found an inner strength to cope with the tribulations of your existence and all of this manifested itself in these imagined projections. The names… the names, Marianna! Hull, Mrs Chippy, Odysseus, Carmen… this boat *Deception*. Somehow all of your life was bound up in these terms: the mother you never met, your father, John Vincent, Perce Blackborow, his friends and the rest of the *Endurance* crew, Lars Anderson, the Jacobsen family, even me. Your animal companions were a constructed *fabrication*, just like your boat. I simply…"

"I know why you're doing this!" I interjected, "You're just trying to discredit me, to save your own skin. You're just like Lars. You don't even need to ask him about the animals. I know what he'll say. You're all the same!"

"Mari, come on now…"

"Don't call me that!" I cried, springing from my chair. I didn't care about the guards anymore. Albert also stood, but if he intended to hug me, to apologise, to tell me that he had got it all wrong, then he was stopped in his tracks by the guards. They were at my side in an instant, each one grabbing an arm. "Let go of me!" I resisted, trying to yank my arms free. "I just want to leave. I just want to go home!"

The guards looked to Albert. He dropped his head. "Do as she says," he mumbled. "Take her home."

Sextant in hand, I stood on the South Pole. Nothing I had ever experienced before seemed important now, yet, simultaneously, everything converged on this very spot and gained in significance. Time had no meaning, for it was always day or always night, a contrast of extremes which served to underscore each living moment; location was pointless, for there was nowhere to go but north, yet this was the very pivot around which the whole earth turned; perspective was meaningless, as everything faced the same direction, yet, at the same time, the range of this was limitless. Even intricate human thought was reduced here to reflect on its own inconsequence when surrounded by such vast desolation, yet this singular encompassed such a bewildering array of emotions as I had never felt. At the South Pole nothing and everything existed in one place and for eternity.

I tracked the motions of the sun, migrating high around me, as if trying to get a better view of my position. It blazed with brilliance upon the icy world beneath, at which I was now centre stage.

Nowhere was spared its gaze, neither me, nor Hull, nor Mrs Chippy, who was basking in the cold sunshine. Neither could a single one of the infinite ice crystals, sparkling on the ground, escape this all-encompassing radiance. The penetrating rays chased away the shadows, which scampered across the ground in constant flight from the circling sun's determined glare. *Let there be light*, it seemed to declare, *and I will separate it from the darkness*.

Then, from out of the blue ether above me, two flaming orbs appeared, each on either flank of the sun, like a couple of shining companions escorting the great star.

"It's you two," I whispered, addressing Hull and Mrs Chippy, although so quietly there was no possibility that they could have heard me. "And these are for you, Mama and Papa," I said, retrieving the stones I had carried with me from Deception Island. I placed them on the apex of the earth; nothing in the entire world would ever spin more gently than these two silent objects before me. "Now you are truly together again."

I looked back up to the sky and perceived two thin streaks of light leaking slowly from the top and bottom of the smaller glowing spots. They reached towards each other, arching over and under the sun, until their tips touched to form a large, delicate halo, a sliver of fire encircling a misty interior, in the very centre of which the enduring sun burned unabated.

"What an amazing thing!" I marvelled; but the Antarctic had yet more to offer. From one of the infinite norths I spotted a wraithlike form tumbling towards me. It was barely visible, an amorphous, faint cloud spilling slowly across the ice, glinting occasionally in the sunlight. With little landscape it was difficult to judge its dimensions; only as the twinkling haze drifted closer could I see it stretched for thirty metres across, and within its indistinct boundaries shimmered a myriad of tiny glittering diamonds. Then it was upon me, and I was engulfed in a cloud of jewels, so microscopic that many dozens flashed in front of my eyes for a mere instant before being replaced by countless more dazzling brilliants. "Sun dust!" I exclaimed, trying to scoop some into my hand. But the airy sparkles refused to be captured, dissolving even as I touched them. Within moments, the magical cloud had passed and rolled on across the polar plateau. Then I saw another cloud hurtling towards me. This one filled me with quite another emotion: dread.

It was a huge, wedge-shaped monster, tearing in across the full expanse of the horizon, and so low-hanging that it scudded across the surface of the ice, whipping up a wall of whirling snow and ice as it advanced. I could already feel the headwinds panicking past me, fleeing from this leviathan. There was no time to run; there was no time to pitch a tent; we were going to have brace ourselves.

"Quick, Mrs Chippy, get back in there," I cried, urging her back into *Cotob*. "Hull, come here."

I positioned the larger sledge in front of us, to take some of the force of the gusts which I knew would be upon us in just a few moments, and, facing away from the approaching storm, we crouched between both sledges. The roar of the squall grew terrifyingly intense; and then it engulfed us.

Within an instant there was only this, the grim Antarctic onslaught, a dense nebulous beast materialised from the elements to assault me. It took over every sense: it screamed into my ears; the billowing ice and snow threw a swirling curtain around my eyes; I could smell and taste only the bitter, sharp bite of cold; the sudden chill numbed my fingers, the ice stung my face, and the gusts battered my body with pummelling relentlessness.

I couldn't maintain even my crouched position and held on to the side of *Cotob*, for fear that it, or I, would be carried away with the storm. I slid and veered over the snow, trying hard to keep Hull with me but, at some point, I lost sight of him. He might have been only a few metres from me, but the storm had hurled an impenetrable seething, swirling barricade all around me and blew with such ferocity that even opening my mouth to call to him

265

would have required a mighty effort, let alone being able make myself heard.

Then I heard a yelp that pierced through all the loud disorder and right into my heart. It was a fearful, harrowing howl of pain; Hull had been hurt. Not even the cruel might of this continent could keep me pinned down now, nor prevent my ears from zeroing in on my distressed companion. I struggled to my feet and fought through raw wind and stabbing ice towards the sound of the husky's yelps, dragging *Cotob* with me. I found him, lying next to the large, upturned sledge. It was clear he had been struck by it, but only when I went to him could I see to my horror how badly. His front leg, the one he had already injured twice before, was terribly disfigured; bone had broken through the skin and jutted at a torturous angle; blood spilled from the wound, pooling in dark spots on the ground just as quickly as the constant turbulence whitewashed it all away. Poor Hull lay with his head on the ground, whining, whimpering, sporadically howling, gradually being buried by drifts blown up against his body and flurries of falling snow and ice blanketing him.

I brushed the snow away, took off my coat and covered him. I placed my hand near his wound, then withdrew it. I didn't know what to do. I couldn't treat this, and certainly not here, not under this bombardment. I had to find shelter, and even though I knew it would take too long, I had to race back to the hut where Hull could rest and heal more effectively than out here on the polar plateau. But as long as the tempest raged, we could go nowhere. Without my coat, a shivering coldness began to take hold of me. Moving as swiftly as I could, I hauled the sledge back on to its runners and removed the tent from the bags. I knew it would be a futile endeavour to pitch it in these conditions, so I unfurled it and used the weight of the sledges to pin it down and form a makeshift shelter. The canvas thrashed and flailed; I was sure it would take off with the wind and be lost forever, so I held on to it for dear life – our lives truly did depend on it. I threaded some rope through several eyelets and bound it to the sledges and,

266

finally, coiled the rope around myself as an extra precaution. I retrieved as many blankets as I could find and threw them under the canvas. My body was trembling quite uncontrollably, through cold and anxious desperation, but my concern was focused on Hull. I needed to get him off the frozen ground, so pulled him as carefully as I could onto a blanket. His high-pitched howls at every dragged centimetre were as daggers stabbing further into my sorrow; I could only guess at the actual pain it was causing him. His leg was a mess; I could barely look at it without feeling sick to my core; but I had to overcome my nausea and at least try to prevent the bleeding. I took a piece of whalebone that I determined *Cotob* could manage without, and with it made a splint. I snapped his leg back into place. The operation almost made me gag, but Hull showed remarkable tolerance for all my clumsiness; he probably knew I was trying to help – we had been here twice before already after all. Then I made a tourniquet with some fabric torn from a sheet which had formed part of Mrs Chippy's bed; I had never done this before and could only pray it would have some effect. The leg, I guessed, could not be saved, but that was a thought for another day. For now, Hull was as comfortable as I could make him, so I lay down next to his body, stretched my arm over him and covered both of us with several blankets. Then Mrs Chippy emerged, jumped onto the top blanket and pawed at the edges to get underneath. I let her, blocking out my allergy, and under the covers she found a place close to Hull's belly. I pulled the blankets tight over us all and prayed that the shelter would hold. I closed my eyes and wondered if I would ever open them again.

Immediately upon wakening I checked on Hull. His eyes were shut, but he was alive. The canvas was not rattling at all; the storm had rampaged past. The stillness was eerie. I strained my ears and could hear only Hull's uneasy breathing. Where before there had been a violent assault on all my senses, now there was an unnerving nothingness, as if perception itself had been ripped away. I peeked out. The air was gloomy grey, an opaque mist had
267

descended across the plateau. It would be difficult to navigate in this, but I had no choice; it was time to get going.

I was surprised, but pleased, that Hull still seemed willing to eat. He was still a dog, no matter how injured, and would never turn his nose up at the chance of a tasty morsel. Rearranging the supplies so that Hull could comfortably lie on the sledge was not easy, as I could not afford to leave anything behind. But I just about managed it, fastening him to a bed of blankets and overloading *Cotob* with whatever could no longer fit on the larger sledge. It would be a hellish journey for him, with each jolt shooting terrible pains through his body, yet it was Mrs Chippy who seemed most put out, her comfortable bed having disappeared and reduced to just a minimal slot alongside boxes of biscuits.

We set off. It was slow, exhausting work. Not only was I now pulling both sledges, with the additional weight of the dog, but I had to stop often, too, to gain my bearings in the thick haze which obscured the clear sight I had enjoyed on the approach to the South Pole. For three days and nights I toiled, the sun failing to disperse the mist, the sledges seeming to become heavier with each kilometre, the blisters on my hands and the sores on my shoulders growing more painful with every step. Yet I kept on going, kept Hull alive, even stroked the cat through protective gloves every now and then. It might take me an extra month to return, I told myself, but I would do it. And Hull would live.

On the fourth day my world came crashing down. I untethered Hull for his regular toilet break, then set about preparing the food and pitching the tent. The mist still hung in the air, now filled with the faintest fall of snow. We were still a long way from the foothills of the Transantarctic Mountains and the pass that would take us onto the ice shelf, but I had decided after four bleak days we needed cheering up. A warm, meaty stew would give us all a welcome lift. I poured a generous portion into Hull's bowl and took it to him. He was not where I had left him, a few metres away from the sledge.

268

"Hull!" I called. No response. "Hull! Where are you?" I shouted into the gloom. Nothing. I tapped the bowl, hoping to encourage him back. "Food!"

I knew he could not come running to me; perhaps he had limped off a little and was now unable to struggle back. I checked the ground for pawprints. I could see where he had been sitting, but the snow here was almost as hard as ice, with much of the top layer most likely having been blown away by the previous storm. I followed a weak track, shouting Hull's name all the while, until the trail vanished under the delicate flakes falling to the ground.

"Hull! Hull!" I yelled, again and again. Then I saw him. A shadowy form, sitting some way off. It seemed like he was watching me. I ran to him, but by the time I had reached the spot where I thought Hull had been, the flimsy silhouette had melted into the surrounding gloom. "Hull! Stop playing stupid games!"

Over and over I rushed from one place to the next. Sometimes I scrambled toward an indistinct shape in the distance, but most of the time I dashed in any direction my despair took me. Whether it was for one hour or several, both Hull and my hope proved elusive, until the mist began to clear. And then I really did see him, lying on the ground. I raced over, but I knew before I got there; I knew just from the way his body was positioned; I knew Hull was gone. His ears did not prick when I called his name; his tail did not wag when I grasped his head and hugged him tight, his sky-blue eyes did not turn to me when I begged him to come back; his cold body did not respond at all to my warm and streaming tears. I knew my loyal friend had sacrificed himself for me; I knew he had taken himself away to spare my grief; I knew he had left the adventure to give me a chance of completing mine; I knew I would never share another happy moment with him again.

52°48′ North, 13°26′ East

Platform 17, Grünewald station. It is as bleak a place as I have ever seen. Low, grey buildings of concrete and steel stretched in both directions along the track. Between them and the black carriages which waited with open doors on the track were hundreds, maybe thousands of people: men, women, children, from new-born to the very old. Each carried a suitcase, or bag, or doll, or some other tragic relic from a previous life in their hands, and a world of worry on their faces. They spoke a multitude of languages, many of which I could not identify. I had seen and heard enough about Nazi Germany to know that this did not bode well.

"What are all these people doing here?" I asked the guard who had brought me to the station. He looked smart in his black uniform, with a trim moustache and purposeful eyes staring out ahead under his peaked cap. Smart, but not very friendly. He didn't answer.

I turned from him and approached a man who seemed in some distress. However, before I could get to him, my guard grabbed me by the arm and pulled me back.

"You stay next to me!" he barked.

"Get off me!" I snapped back with such indignation that he seemed to be taken by surprise.

Within a moment he had regained his mean, authoritative composure and was perhaps within seconds of unleashing some heated response on me, when a voice from behind stopped him.

"Wait! Wait!" cried the voice. Another similarly uniformed man, puffing from his excesses, ran up to us. "I have a letter here from the *Reichssicherheitshauptamt*."

I almost laughed at the word. "I've heard of all sorts of *Amts*. What does that one do?"

Both men glared at me.

"*We* are officers who fight all enemies of the Reich. *This* letter has been written at the behest of Professor Einstein! You should watch your tone," snarled the newcomer.

I moved to take the letter, but my guard intercepted it. He read its contents without any expression. "Hmm," he said cryptically once he had finished.

I waited for more. My guard simply folded the letter, pocketed it and looked at me while stroking his moustache.

"What?" I pressed.

"I am to ask you if you really do want to go home."

"Of course I do!" I exclaimed.

"Home as in Antarctica, Zürich, Hull, or …"

"You've clearly never been to Hull," I interrupted, "or you wouldn't even ask!" Even the implacable guard couldn't stop his moustache from twitching in mirth at my comment. "Take me to Oświęcim. It's where my mother was from. It's where my life started. It's where I belong. I want to start over again."

"Oświęcim?"

"In Galicia. Have you never heard of it?" I asked.

The newcomer leant in and whispered something into my guard's ear. He raised his eyebrows in response.

"Yes, yes. I know the place. But it's now called something else."

"Oh no. Not again. Go on then, tell me. I hope it's not some kind of joke name like the others."

The guard looked affronted, again. "It's called Auschwitz. And I can assure you, it is *not* a joke name."

"Auschwitz," I said, practising the word several times. "Okay, not too dissimilar. I can live with that."

"Professor Einstein has insisted that you are not to be taken to Auschwitz."

I was surprised, angered even, by Albert's intervention. He had no right to dictate where I went, and I was certainly not going to be deterred from going home after having come so far.

"You *will* take me to Oświęcim." I asserted.

The two guards looked at each other. "Look, you don't want to go there," said my guard. "All of those people over there. Look at them. They're going to Auschwitz. Are you sure you want to join them? It's not a nice place."

"Really? It's just a small town on the river. What are they all going there for?"

The guard shifted on his feet. "It's changed. It's a... processing centre for people from all over Europe. You could say that your home town is the hub of a resettlement programme."

I nodded. It made sense. I briefly told the guard the story about my father after HAPAG had opened a branch in Oświęcim. Maybe its geography in the centre of Europe made it a good location for such things.

"Maybe," said the guard. "Look, this letter is a lifeline. You should take it."

I sighed in frustration. "Give me that letter. I will sign it and say I insist on being taken to Oświęcim, or Auschwitz as you call it. It's where my life began, and I can't start with my new one until I go home. I don't expect you to understand."

My guard retrieved the note from his pocket, wrote something on it gave it to me to sign, then handed it back to the newcomer, who had by now just about regained his breath.

"You are the witness to that. It's her choice."

The man nodded, took the letter, and left.

I carried his body back to my temporary base, somewhere between the South Pole and the Transantarctic Mountains, so that I could give him a proper burial. I had the pickaxe and shovel to excavate a shallow grave for Hull, but heartbreak was sapping my energy and weakening my arms, so I struggled to make any impact on the ground. Grief was further making my shoulders tremble and piles of snow kept tumbling from the shovel back into the hollow. Even when I had managed to dig deep enough, I fell to my knees in despair, for the grave was an icy symbol of the emptiness and depression which was gripping me. Pulling Hull into the grave required far more mental than physical effort, but once I had done so and covered him, I found some form of relief, and it comforted me to think that his body would be preserved in ice for millennia, each year piling another protective layer upon his final resting place.

If Hull's sacrifice were to have any meaning, I had to get moving; my hut was still over a thousand kilometres away. Before burying Hull, I had removed the whalebone splint, which I now returned to *Cotob*. This helped it slide more smoothly across the snow, and now that the large sledge was free of Hull's weight, I could distribute the equipment more evenly. It made the going a little easier. Yet it still took a few weeks to arrive at the mountain pass. During this time the polar plateau plagued me with winds and plunging temperatures, but nothing it could throw at me was as painful as the loss of Hull, and I resisted the wild onslaughts with a mind closed to physical duress. I pitched and struck my tent, I cooked and ate, I fed Mrs Chippy, I pulled the sledges through storms, sunshine, furious gusts and foggy gloom, I trudged on as an automaton focused solely on its own mechanical propulsion to arrive at the pass and cross the ice shelf. Everything else was of no consequence.

That was until I actually navigated the pass I had been so doggedly striving for. Soon after, once I was well underway on the huge expanse of ice, something reached out to me. It approached almost imperceptibly at first, as a murmur purring from somewhere far off in the vast stretch before me. It caught my attention, but only for an instant, and then my mind returned to its single-minded purpose of getting home. But the muttering, humming whisper would not be shut out; it rose in intensity, its pitch mounting to a random, rumbling hum. It could not be ignored. At first I thought it must be the wind, whistling through the mountains to my left, bouncing off the jagged, hard stone surfaces and somehow echoing down to this flat ice shelf. But the sound was not just coming from that direction; it was coming from everywhere.

A sudden, disturbing thought struck me. What if the sound were somehow coming from the penguins? What if the huge iceberg had drifted again and blocked their access to the ocean? What if in desperation they were wandering inland in the hopeless search for a way out, and their distressed calls were travelling across the ice to me? I became convinced of the fact, and although I was still many hundreds of kilometres from home, I quickened my step, determined to intercept the wretched colony and lead it back to salvation.

The mournful drone pulsed with irregularity: at times a higher timbre trembled through the thin shroud of mist overlaying the entire ice shelf; at others a deep reverberation shook the sprinkling of snow at my feet; sometimes it stopped altogether, and then picked up again with an aching quiver. It was impossible to pinpoint its origin; it was simply omnipresent and yet, at the same time, nowhere. I pressed on and, days after the mysterious lament had begun, it just as inexplicably stopped. I didn't hear it again, not once more in the weeks and weeks it took to complete my return journey; nor did I encounter any penguins. In fact they were just as content in their rookery as they had been when I had left them many months before, diligently waddling through their tunnel in orderly fashion to keep the colony fed.

Returning to the hut did not fill me with the relief I had expected. It just didn't seem like a home without Hull. Not even Carmen was there to welcome me. I suppose she had grown so used to the place being uninhabited that she had stopped coming altogether. It pained me greatly to think that I might never see her again; in some respects, in was even harder to cope with her unexplained disappearance than it was with Hull's death. Although it was still incredibly raw, the weeks that had passed since losing Hull and the many lonely, cold nights I had spent reflecting upon his life had allowed me to find a method of carrying the burden of grief. But with Carmen, I did not know if I should grieve, or search, or call out for her, and this uncertainty weighed like dense, dark matter, pressing ceaselessly upon my mind.

Without her, without Hull, my home had now become a cold husk, bereft of meaning. Of course, there was Mrs Chippy but, well, our relationship still had issues, and I could not see past the void that the husky and Carmen had once filled. There was now only emptiness where he had slept or she had flown, where he had eaten or she had landed with a fish in her mouth, where he had scampered around in mindless circles or she had scattered stones. I touched all these places, trying to draw some comfort;

but I merely felt their absence and saw no reason to delay my departure from this lifeless shell.

Time, however, was against me. My South Pole expedition had taken far longer than I had planned, and it would not be long before winter descended again and the weather would acquire an even fiercer and frostier temperament. But I could not face remaining on this continent any longer; just the thought of it was more chilling than even the vicious bite of winter. I would trust in my abilities and take my chances with the high seas.

A week is all it took: a week to overhaul *Deception* and *Cotob*; to mend any rips or tears in the sheets caused by age or Mrs Chippy's claws; to restock on supplies; and to plan the route to New Zealand. I noticed there were several irregular markings on my charts between Antarctica and my destination. My hunch was that they were islands, and that if needed I could land on any one of these, island hopping until I reached civilisation. I estimated the distance to be five thousand kilometres, a total which, when I wrote it down, stared back at me with taunting impossibility. Yet, just as I had done so before, I recalled how far I had come and reminded myself that I had just walked about half as far to the South Pole and back, pulling an old, large sledge and another one barely fit for purpose. This time I would be sitting down in a boat which I had crafted myself, flying across the sea at speed. I circled the number with confidence and packed the charts away.

Dragging the boat to the shoreline was a chore. I intended to tie *Cotob* behind *Deception* and, in convoy fashion, pull both through the tunnel. However, the smaller outrigger frequently snared on the side walls, so in the end I unfastened it, left it standing, and continued with the larger hull. When I returned to *Cotob* in the dim candle-lit tunnel, I found it had been commandeered by a dozen penguins, and Mrs Chippy was hissing at them all. If the birds perceived this as a warning, they didn't show it. In fact, they seemed to be laughing at the cantankerous cat, which only made her hiss more.

By mid-morning I was ready. It was more than a little daunting, staring out at the open ocean, the nose of my now reassembled catamaran pointing expectantly towards the horizon. Breath vapour exhaled from my mouth and nostrils, as if fuelling the thin mist which hung in the air, throwing a hazy contour around the sun and hampering precise measurement with the sextant. However, at this stage, an approximate reading would suffice, and once I had established the direction, perpendicular to Antarctica, I sailed away from the icy continent.

Far sooner than I would have imagined, I lost sight of the great cliff barrier. Not that I had much time to gaze nostalgically behind me, as soon all around my passage was filled with bergs emerging from the fog. I knew it could not be true, yet it seemed as if they were deliberately aiming for me, like confused bulls which, upon seeing me, clumsily angled for my boat to upend it. There was an inordinate number, more than I had ever seen during all my time on the sea or staring out from the safety of some frozen peak: some were cuboid, like huge floating building blocks; others, wedge-shaped, carved through the waves; some were domed, resembling tiny desert islands, only made of ice; more still were pinnacled, as if a mountain had become detached from its range and was condemned to wander alone across this watery wasteland; and some were split in two, like giant frozen models of my own catamaran. With these ones I was sometimes forced to pass between each looming column to avoid being crushed. There were white ones, blue ones, black ones and dirty ones; it seemed as if some awful catastrophe had cast them all at once into the ocean, where they would now slowly melt in this misty graveyard of lost icebergs.

Eventually, they dispersed, and so did the hanging fog as the wind increased. Although I was pleased that the way was clear, I began to grow concerned at the swelling heaviness of the sea. Waves began to topple over the gunwales, and I spent as much time bailing out the water as I did contending with the sail. Reaching Mrs Chippy's outrigger in these choppy conditions was problematic, yet both to protect her and to stop the boat from listing to that side I had to scramble over and bail the water out there, too. After many hours of battling to keep the boat afloat, a new problem presented itself: the build-up of ice which was now weighing down both *Deception* and *Cotob*, allowing more of the sea to spill into the hulls. The forceful winds, the rough ocean, the water in the hulls and now the burden of ice – it was all becoming too much, but now, unlike my long journey around the Antarctic coastline, there was no haven within easy reach, no shore I could race to within a few minutes. The sea was pouring in, the ice was building up, the wind was blowing itself into a gale and I was out in the open ocean; I was in trouble. I was out of my depth. I had to turn back.

I had to run the gauntlet of the bergs again, but my handicapped boat and the rising sea now made it even more difficult to avoid them. A huge building-size chunk could be thirty metres away, then with a fatal lunge it would be on top of me in an instant. At any moment my boat could be shattered into fragments; at any moment Mrs Chippy and I could be lost. However, with adequate seamanship, with the accomplished design of my catamaran, but most of all with luck, we made it through to the other side; then the white ice cliffs and black mountains of Antarctica loomed into view. It was depressing to see them. Within a day my hopes of leaving the continent had been crushed, the ocean was a barrier I could never surmount, and I seemed destined to perish in this abandoned, friendless realm.

Why was Antarctica doing this to me? Whether I was trying to get on or off the continent, whether I was out on the sea, or in on the land, I was beset by such furious obstacles which both hindered my departure and my arrival, as if the very environment was struggling with some internal dilemma and ranged its frustrations specifically against me.

For now, though, I had to reset and reassess my situation. Mount Erebus was clearly visible now, so I steered the catamaran

278

towards it. At the very least, I thought, I would have to overwinter on Antarctica. Perhaps I could try again to leave at the first flush of light next summer; or maybe, just maybe, Shackleton or someone like him would stumble across me and lead me to safety. The best thing to do now was to return to my hut, where I knew I could survive whatever cruel contrivance the continent devised. As these thoughts whirled around within me, stirring up a modicum of optimism in a desperately discouraging situation, I spotted a hint of red, glinting among the surrounding black and white landscape, many miles west of Erebus. Could this be a roof? Or even a settlement? Could it be fire? Could I have chanced upon the true location of Hut Point? With renewed excitement, I headed towards this flaming beacon.

Drawing nearer I could see no signs of life, neither huts nor smoke, nor anything that might indicate the presence of people, yet the reddish hue intensified. In a world devoid of all colour, this scarlet anomaly had to be of human origin, I convinced myself. My view of it was obscured when I made landfall, so I pulled the catamaran out of the water and trekked towards the spot, which I estimated to be about a further five hundred metres inland. I wish to this day I had never made that short journey.

I scrambled over a large rock to reach it, and before me was a sight of sheer horror. A fountain of blood was oozing from a huge scar sliced into the tongue of a long glacier and was slithering down the slope towards me. It was syrupy, viscous, barely moving, and by the time it had fanned out some one hundred metres from the gaping wound, it had frozen solid. I dreaded to think what nightmarish scenes were unfolding, unseen, under all of that ice, what ruthless industry had carved a factory of death deep within the glacier. I imagined a slaughterhouse of measureless numbers of whales, for my tormented mind could picture nothing else that might produce such hideous quantities of gore. The thick liquid slid over the black rock and flowed down the grisly slipway until it froze at my feet. I retched and turned my back on the carnage. This was no place for me; this was no place
279

for anyone. If Antarctica was sending me a message, exposing with merciless honesty its inner cruelty, then I understood it unmistakably. I did not intend to spend another day on this continent.

I hurried back to my vessel and prepared her again for the open water. I bailed out every last drop of water, chipped away any residual ice, fried some penguin meat, and told Mrs Chippy our plan.

"We're going back to Deception Island," I said. She didn't seem to mind. I laid out the charts on the icy ground and traced the distance we would need to cover. "Well, I don't even want to work out how far it is," I admitted, "but if we stay in the current that brought us here, hugging the coast westwards all the way round, then eventually we'll get there." Mrs Chippy finished her meal, licked her lips and blinked at me. "Oh, I'm sure we'll find more food on the way. Let's see if we can do it in less than one hundred days. Then I'll tell Albert to come and get us. I probably should have done that at the outset," I smiled and stroked the top of Mrs Chippy's head.

It did indeed take almost exactly one hundred days: one hundred days of struggling against adverse winds and battling through snowstorms and icy bullets of spray; one hundred days of waiting out tempests in the shadow of melting glaciers or straining my eyes through milky mist, scanning the sea for lethal brash ice or deadly growlers, both of which were capable of destroying my vessel, yet far harder to spot than monstrous icebergs; one hundred days of shocking discoveries, such as a lake by which I camped for several days, its banks littered with the corpses of penguins which had been tempted into its deceptively enticing waters, only to discover that it was lethally colder than the ice itself. How it was possible that this lake did not freeze I would never know; so much of this continent contained secrets which would forever be sealed in chilling mystery. But after one hundred days, just as the polar night was beginning to spread its darkening blanket to cover the sky and the Southern Lights flashed a dazzling display of emerald streaks across the firmament, I arrived back on Deception Island.

My seamanship skills were so proficient by now that I did not need the might of Odysseus to power me through the bellows. I steered my boat through, hauled it onto the beach, walked around to see if anything had changed, then after a warm drink climbed into one of the bunk beds and slept so soundly I would not be surprised if several days passed before I woke again.

I spoke to Alfred every Friday night; it became our ritual. I asked him if anyone else had ever circumnavigated Antarctica; to his mind, I had been the first. It was, he commended, as great an accolade as reaching the South Pole itself, if not greater. Mrs Chippy survived a few more years. When she died I mourned for her as much as I had for my father, for Odysseus, for Hull, for Carmen. I buried her at the peak of Mount Pond, the highest elevation on the island, next to a vent. I thought the cat would like the view, and she would certainly like the warmth. I went up there often to speak with her.

I was not completely alone when she went; I had already started training another skua, which I had raised from a chick stolen from a nest. She was no Carmen, but the task kept me occupied. Every few years I repeated the process, when my feathered companion died, or failed to return one day. My attempts to train a seal, however, failed completely. The closest I ever came to success was with a seal pup I had found abandoned on a shingle beach on the far side of the island. I fed it well and the first few months seemed promising, but one day it followed me into the water, and I never saw it again. It was a painful loss and, after a few more unsuccessful attempts, I gave up.

I noticed with growing consternation how the shoreline was creeping further up the beach each year, and how the snow and ice on the mountains was in some places disappearing completely, but when I spoke to Albert about it he simply told me that these were natural cycles and I should enjoy the warmer climate. He was right, but the rise in temperature had its
281

drawbacks, too. The penguins didn't seem too keen on the change, and their colony numbers began to shrink rapidly. Violent storms were more frequent, too. During one particularly warm summer, a small avalanche crashed through my hut; fortunately I was fishing in the bay at the time. It spared the most important parts of the building, namely the radio room, the kitchen and the small space housing the generator, but destroyed the dormitory. I slept in the kitchen on a mattress while I rebuilt the hut.

Apart from reacting to events like these, nothing much happened on Deception Island. Slaughtering penguins or the occasional seal, collecting seaweed to eat or for making soap, simply surviving – these were my chief pastimes. Until one day everything changed, when an eight-thousand-ton, four-stroke-diesel engine German freighter discovered the entrance to my island.

The surprise of *MS Schwabenland's* arrival was matched only by the surprise of her departure, for while passing back through the bellows, this time with me on board, the huge vessel scraped a stone column hiding a couple of metres below the waterline, tearing a huge scar in the ship's hull. We had to return to the safety of the natural horseshoe harbour for some fairly urgent repairs. I had known nothing of this stone column's existence all these years and even in this setback had to smile at the secrets Antarctica begrudgingly revealed, and at the others it no doubt still withheld. Once the ship was seaworthy again, we steamed carefully out of the harbour, and the then friendly captain promised to take me home.

49°97′ North, 19°14′ East

How fitting it is that I should return

to these coordinates, for I am exactly forty-nine years and ninety-seven days old today, and 1914 was the year I left Europe with the continent plunging into war. I have arrived at Auschwitz and am writing this by the side of the train while the guards begin their task of processing us.

The conditions on the train that brought us here were terrible. Nearly one hundred of us were all herded into a black wagon, more suitable for transporting cattle than people. It was hot and stuffy inside, with barely any room to sit. I complained to a guard and threatened to inform Professor Einstein if we were not given more comfortable transport. He simply laughed and said that they were economising on fuel, and Professor Einstein would see the relative value in that. One of the young girls raised her hand, saying that she needed the toilet. The guard pointed to a bucket in the corner, then slammed the wagon doors shut and locked them. Thin slivers of light peeked through the wooden slats; it was dark, and we could not get out.

After a moment's silence, wailing began to fill the darkened space. It began as a faint murmur, like the hum of a distant wave, but within no time it engulfed the entire wagon with a grim crescendo. An old man next to me whimpered and said we were all going to die in here.

"It's all right," I reassured him. "I know it's unpleasant, but I've been through worse. A good friend told me about the problems everyone's having with fuel and living space. I guess it's the best they can do for us right now. Just grit your teeth and bear it. Once we get to Auschwitz, everything will be all right." I held his hand, and he calmed down.

283

But his words stayed with me. I began to ask myself, as the train jolted painfully along the track and the sky was hidden from us, if in fact there might be some substance to the man's fears. I recalled all of the horrors that I had learned about on my way here: in Cape Town, in Freistadt, in Cape Verde; every stop had peeled back more flesh to reveal the visceral reality of human society. The more these thoughts gripped me, the more I yearned for the bleak isolation of Deception Island. I hadn't realised it then, but life away from everyone and everything, where the demands of food, water and warmth dominated every waking minute, was far more hospitable than the chilling nature of the world that had been crafted in my absence.

I began to panic in the oppressive, cramped conditions of the train. I began to long for the cold, open brightness of the eternal day and the wondrously illuminated skies of the polar nights. What freedom there had been in that simple, harsh existence. I had lived for a generation in bliss, perhaps the last person on earth to have done so. Why did I only see this now? I didn't even realise that quiet, half-swallowed sobs were accompanying every one of my thoughts.

"It's okay, dear," said the old man next to me, now taking my hand in his. "I'm sure you're right. Once we get off this train things won't be so bad."

Now I am here at Auschwitz, I am certain that everything will be bad. I can see a sign above a factory gate reading *Arbeit macht frei*. People from our train are filing through it, while others, mostly women, children and the infirm, are being removed from the line and forming another group of their own. I know that this sign is a deception, that the people passing through that gate will never be free, no matter how hard they work at it. Everyone is having their possessions ripped from them: the suitcases, bags, dolls; the guards are tossing it all carelessly onto heaped piles before pushing the distraught owner along. I have no doubt that my book and I are going to go the same way. I only have a few minutes left. I have decided to complete my story and hide the

284

book in a niche under the train. I'll leave a note inside, instructing the finder to post it to Professor Albert Einstein. He'll keep it safe for me. But for now, as bombs rain down all over the earth and the sea is engulfing it, I can only stare at the factory in front of me, wondering where it has all gone wrong.

Dear Reader,

Should you discover this book, please look through it, devour it, enjoy it, learn from it, ignore it, whatever you desire. But please ensure it finds it way to Professor Albert Einstein. If this is not possible, then I would urge you to pass it on to anyone who you feel might benefit from its message.

I sincerely hope you find the world in a better shape than it appears to be in right now, for then there is truly hope. Maybe it is not so bad, maybe things will be all right, but if my assumptions are correct, and you read this note without much having changed at all, then I fear it is only a matter of time before you, dear reader, will succumb to one of the many fates that I have outlined in this book. Let's pray that does not happen.

MD

Note from the author

Thank you very much for reading Deception. I feel the need to mention that any similarity to persons, living or dead, is not entirely coincidental.

There are the more famous personalities, such as Einstein and Shackleton, and then the perhaps less well-known figures, such as Jack Vincent, Kapitän Ritscher and even Mrs Chippy. Other characters are wholly invented, such as Odysseus, although I am sure a scar-faced elephant seal is roaming the oceans somewhere out there.

But what of those wholly invented characters? Do some of them exist at all, even within the confines of these pages? This is something I wish to allow reader to decide for himself or herself, suffice it to say that in every one of these characterisations, in the invented and the stolen, my guiding principle was to portray a world which, with a little imagination and a touch of horror, might not be so very far away. In this sense, authenticity (such as Einstein working for the Nazis or an elephant seal scaling a mountain) must give way to creative possibility.

We are living in dangerous times, in times where it is often difficult to know who or what to believe. This is not only true in terms of the conflicts brewing or tearing through parts of the world, but also in those of the damage every one of us is doing to our planet. Even you.

With such overwhelming political and environmental forces railed against all of us, what is there to do? Anybody can be forgiven for feeling frustrated and disempowered. Perhaps the true Einstein would have really been able to figure it all out. I certainly do not have the answers. However, maybe we should start by turning the eye inward, focusing on our individual actions.

This is not a remarkable insight; it is in fact really a very simple observation. Sometimes the solutions to the most urgent and seemingly complex problems boil down to a few plain truths. When we all start recognising these truths, we can recognise the power of the individual.

As a self-publisher, I reliant on reviews and word-of-mouth to promote my work. Therefore, I would be extremely grateful if you could post a review on

Amazon or Goodreads, and perhaps recommend this tale to your friends and family. Thank you very much and enjoy the rest of the year.

Other books by the author

Mo
Exit Velocity
Alone
The Spotlight Tales
Devushka
Where Rivers Divide
Mansa Musa

 Simon Pearce was born in England. His post as Coordinator for International Affairs brings him into close contact with people from all over the world. He is interested in dictatorships and researched the East German regime for his doctorate from the University of Nottingham.